P9-CEN-836

5.50

# Basil Street Blues

*By the same author*

**Non-fiction**

HUGH KINGSMILL

UNRECEIVED OPINIONS

LYTTON STRACHEY

AUGUSTUS JOHN

BERNARD SHAW

**Fiction**

A DOG'S LIFE

**Editor**

THE BEST OF HUGH KINGSMILL

LYTTON STRACHEY BY HIMSELF

THE ART OF AUGUSTUS JOHN
with Malcolm Easton

THE GENIUS OF SHAW

THE SHORTER STRACHEY
with Paul Levy

William Gerhardie's GOD'S FIFTH COLUMN
with Robert Skidelsky

ESSAYS BY DIVERS HANDS
New Series: Volume XLII

# MICHAEL
# HOLROYD

## *Basil Street Blues*

**W. W. NORTON & COMPANY**
New York • London

For information about permission to reproduce selections from this
book, write to Permissions, W. W. Norton & Company, Inc.,
New York, NY 10110

Manufactured by Quebecor Printing Book Group

Library of Congress Cataloging-in-Publication Data

Holroyd, Michael.
Basil Street blues / Michael Holroyd.—1st American ed.
p. cm.
ISBN 0-393-04850-0
1. Holroyd, Michael—Childhood and youth. 2. Authors, English—20th
century—Biography. 3. Maidenhead (England)—Social life and customs.
4. Biographers—Great Britain—Biography. 5. Family—England—
Maidenhead. 6. Holroyd, Michael—Family. I. Title.
PR6058.O47 Z464 2000
920—dc21
[B]
                                                            99-056057

W. W. Norton & Company, Inc.
500 Fifth Avenue, New York, N.Y. 10110
www.wwnorton.com

W. W. Norton & Company Ltd.
10 Coptic Street, London WC1A 1PU

1 2 3 4 5 6 7 8 9 0

'The past puts a fine edge on our own days. It tells us more of the present than the present can tell us.'

William Gerhardie, 'An Historical Credo'
*The Romanovs. An Evocation of the Past as a Mirror for the Present.*

# Contents

# *Acknowledgements*

I am indebted to many individuals and organisations in the preparation of this book. Among the former are: Margit Andréen, I.V. and A-M. Atwell, David Benedictus, Jeffery Bowman, Christopher Capron, Anne Chisholm, Anders Clason, Keith Clements, G.C. Frowde, Viola Germain, Hilda Gledhill, Winston Graham, Vicky Hall, Leslie Hodgson, Jennifer Holden, John Holroyd, Sessie Hylander, Jeremy Isaacs, Robert Lescher, Maureen Levenson, Richard Magor, John Mein, Niall McMonagle, Michael Ockenden, Anders Öfverström, Roger Packham, Griffy Philipps, Merle Rafferty, Michael and Moussie Sayers, Michael Seifert, Michael Sevenoaks, Ronald Stent, Lena Svanberg, Richard Vickers, Mary Young.

I am also grateful to: Head of Administration, the General Council of the Bar; Mary Stewart, Clinic Secretary, Family & Child Guidance Service, Royal County of Berkshire; County Solicitor, Royal County of Berkshire; R.J. Ewing, Bircham &

Co, solicitors; Jonathan Barker and Alastair Niven, Literature
Department, the British Council, London; Michelle Appleton,
the British Council, France; Clare College Archive, Cambridge;
Mark Nicholls, Department of Manuscripts and University
Archives, Cambridge University Library; Timothy H. Duke,
Chester Herald, College of Arms; Naomi da Silva, Family
Proceedings Department, the Court Service, Somerset House;
P. Hatfield, Eton College Archivist; Mike Waller, Gallerie
Moderne; P. Berney, Registration Directorate, General Medical
Council; R. Simpson, Supervisor, Glasgow Necropolis; Avril
Gordon, Glasgow City Council; Mark Jones, Deputy Librarian,
Gray's Inn Library; Nadene Hansen, Company Archivist at
Harrods; Peter Hunter, Librarian, Harrow School; the
Insolvency Service; Elizabeth Stratton, Assistant Archivist,
King's College Library, Cambridge; T. Shepherd, Regulatory
Enquiry Services, the Law Society; Office for National Statistics;
N.P. Willmoth, Senior Financial Services Officer, Life &
Investment Services, NatWest; Colin Matthew, editor of the *New
Dictionary of National Biography*; Jean Rose, Library Manager,
Reed Book Services Limited; V.J. Baxter, Local Studies Librarian,
London Borough of Richmond upon Thames; Royal Air Force
Personnel Management Agency; the Sandhurst Collection;
Scottish Record Office; S.J. Berry, Senior Archivist, Somerset
County Record Office; Anthony Howard, Obituaries Editor,
*The Times*; Jonathan Smith, Manuscripts Cataloguer, Trinity
College Library, Cambridge; J.P. Rudman, Archivist, Uppingham
School; Le Secrétaire Général délégé, Vernet-les-Bains; Patrick
Mclure, Secretary, Wykehamist Society.

To Sarah Johnson, who is now the only person in the world
who can read my handwriting, especially when it appears
between the lines of my typing, I owe special thanks for putting
everything on to immaculate disks. I am also grateful to Philippa
Harrison for her editorial sensitivity and thoroughness, to
Caroline North, and to Kate Truman. Finally I thank my wife

Margaret Drabble who went with me on many of my travels. To her much of what follows will be familiar and a little, perhaps, surprising.

Quotations from *Eton Renewed: A History from 1860 to the Present Day* (1994) by Tim Card are reproduced with the permission of the publisher, John Murray. Lines from Nevill Coghill's translation of Geoffrey Chaucer's *Troilus and Criseyde* are reproduced with the permission of Curtis Brown Ltd, London, on behalf of the Estate of Nevill Coghill. Copyright Nevill Coghill 1971.

Title page: a design for a glass light fitting by the author's father, Basil Holroyd.

# *List of Illustrations*

**Section II**

# PART I

# 1

# Two Types of Ambiguity

Towards the end of the nineteen-seventies I asked my parents to let me have some account of their early lives. I had never been interested in my family. My career as a biographer probably arose from my need to escape from family involvements and immerse myself in other people's lives. 'We don't go to Heaven in families any more – but one by one.' I remember how struck I was when I came across this sentence in Gwen John's correspondence. That was certainly how I felt. I also remember quoting in my first biography Hugh Kingsmill's aphorism: 'Friends are God's apology for families,' and feeling a chord of agreement.

My parents, who had long been divorced, and gone through a couple of subsequent marriages, each of them, as well as various additional liaisons, were by the late nineteen-seventies living alone in fragile health and meagre circumstances. They appeared bewildered by the rubble into which everything was collapsing. After all, it had started so promisingly.

The accounts they wrote were very different. This did not surprise me. They had seldom agreed about anything, not even the date of my birth. As a gesture of tact I preserved two birthdays forty-eight hours apart, one for each of them. This had begun as a joke, grew into a habit and finally became a rather ageing conceit which will enable me to claim by the year 2000 the wisdom of a 130-year-old.

My parents' marriage was something of a mystery to me. What did they have in common? After the age of six I seldom saw them together and could imagine few people more dissimilar. What few scraps of memory I retained brought back echoes of reverberating arguments that floated up to me as I lay in a dark bedroom in the north of England – echoes that, to gain popularity, I would later assemble into dramatic stories for the school dormitory. A breadknife flashed in the dark, a line of blood suddenly appeared, and we shivered delightedly in our beds. But I have few actual memories of my very early years, few recollections of my childhood I can trust, and not many of adolescence. There were probably good reasons for this erasure, though I am hoping that some events may stir from their resting place and rise to the surface as I write.

I was born in the summer of 1935. My mother was Swedish, and my father thought of himself as English, though his mother actually came from the south of Ireland and his paternal grandmother was Scottish. All I knew was that my parents had met on a boat in the North Sea, got along fine on water, then fairly soon after striking land, dashed their marriage on the rocks. I had been conceived, my mother once remarked as we were travelling by bus through Knightsbridge, at the Hyde Park Hotel where King Gustav of Sweden (calling himself Colonel Gustaveson) often stayed. I remember her laughing as we swayed into Sloane Street and travelled on. At another time, in a taxi, she pointed to the Basil Street Hotel with a similar laugh before turning into Sloane Street.

I was largely brought up in the Home Counties by my paternal grandparents and a tennis-playing aunt. But there were irregular intervals, sometimes at odd places abroad, with unfamiliar step-parents who, like minor characters in a badly-managed melodrama, would introduce themselves with a flourish, a bray of trumpets, and then inexplicably disappear. Perhaps the peculiar enchantment that sustained and integrated narratives, enriched with involving plots, were to hold for me sprang from my sense of being brought up by so many characters – parental, step-parental and grand-parental characters – who seldom met, showed little interest in one another, and apparently possessed no connecting story.

In some respects my father had a 'good war', or so I believed. But he could not adjust to the peace afterwards. Though increasingly impoverished, he somehow found (I never knew how) the money to send me to Eton College because he had been there himself at the end of the First World War. He spoke of his time at Eton with unconvincing jollity and was evidently looking forward to a second, vicarious, innings there.

My mother didn't mind where I was educated. She did not have an ideology and simply wanted me to be happy, preferably without too much trouble. She never regarded education, which was full of awkward exams, as an obvious route to happiness. But probably such things were different for men.

They certainly appeared different to my father who had the air of a man acting responsibly on my behalf – as, he implied, his own father should have acted for him. By the time I was sixteen, he judged the moment had come to take me to one side and explain the main purpose of my education – which was to retrieve the family fortunes that would otherwise descend on me, he revealed, in the form of serious debts. Eton was providing me with many valuable friendships that could catapult me, he believed, to success. It did not occur to me to ask why Eton had not provided him with such vaulting associations. He gave the impression of someone who had overshot success and landed somewhere else. In the event, I failed comprehensively in this romantic quest he had assigned me (my average income between the mid-nineteen-sixties and mid-nineteen-seventies was to be £1,500 a year). I did not even know how the exotic family fortunes I was to rescue had originated or where they had gone. Was it all a mirage?

Lack of money was very evident in my parents' last years, when my father was living in a rundown flat in Surrey and my mother in a one-room apartment in London. I thought that the exercise of exploring happier years and travelling back to more prosperous times might bring them some release from their difficulties. From being their only child, the sole child from five marriages, I was to become their guardian and a barely-adequate protector. Having, as it were, commissioned them to write for me, I proposed paying them some commission money. After hesitating, my mother accepted the money with eager reluctance. She had always associated men with money, but understandably had not associated me with it, and was worried that I did not have enough. But times were improving for me, as if I were sitting on the opposite end of a seesaw from my descending parents. My *Lytton Strachey* had eventually been brought out as a paperback and after one very good year, when my *Augustus John* was published, I settled down at the end of the nineteen-seventies to annual net income of between four and five thousand pounds. I could afford to hand over a little money. Besides, I explained to my mother, she would not take my request seriously unless it was put on a business basis. Desperately needing the money, she gave me a kiss and took it.

But my father would not take anything. He wanted to give money and receive praise: he found it almost impossible to receive money or give praise. He felt deeply humiliated by his poverty. 'I certainly wouldn't dream of allowing you to pay 1 cent for anything I write about the family,' he notified me. I

remember reading his letter with exasperation. He was so difficult to help. The truth was he felt embarrassed by my offer
which, he wrote, 'made me feel very ashamed of myself. I am not
yet as down and out as you may imagine.' Now, re-reading his
letter after his death, an unexpected sadness spreads through me.
It was true that he had been 'down' many times, 'down' but not
quite 'out'. Cursing the foul blows delivered on him by politi-
cians, he would somehow pick himself up each time – just in
time. But in his late sixties and early seventies, with only a State
pension and a couple of hundred pounds from a mysterious
'Holroyd Settlement', though he would still speak with anima-
tion of things 'turning up', my father had in fact settled into
involuntary retirement. The game was up. 'I find that time is
heavy on my hands,' he had written to me. That was one of the
reasons I had inflicted this homework on him. Nevertheless I
emphasised that it was for my sake rather than his own that I
was asking him to write an account. And perhaps there was
more truth in this than I realised. For after my father and mother
died in the nineteen-eighties I began to feel a need to fill the
space they left with a story. Neither of them were in the front
line of great historical events: their dramas are the dramas of
ordinary lives, each one nevertheless extraordinary. From their
accounts, from various photograph albums and a few clues in
two or three boxes of miscellaneous odds and ends, I want to
recreate the events that would give my own fragmented upbring-
ing a context. Can I stir these few remnants and start a flame, an
illumination? This book is not simply a search for facts, but for
echoes and associations, signs and images, the recovery of a lost
narrative and a sense of continuity: things I seem to miss and
believe I never had.

I had to distance myself from my parents while they were
alive, not out of hostility to them, but from a natural urge to find
my individual identity, my own route. 'When a writer is born
into a family,' wrote Philip Roth, 'the family is finished.'

Inhabiting their worlds as a child and then an adolescent, I felt invisible; after which I traded somewhat in invisibility as a biographer. But following my parents' deaths, when they became invisible and I was seen to have attained my independence, my feelings began to change. I was drawn into the vacancy their deaths created, needing to trace my origins. It is an experience, I believe, that possesses many people in these circumstances: to ask questions when it is apparently too late for answers, and then be forced to discover answers of our own.

The unexamined life, Saul Bellow tells us, is meaningless. But the examined life, he adds, is full of dangers. I have found wonderful freedom in that maverick condition which can be described as meaningless: a freedom in not being tied to social contexts or engulfed in family chauvinism. My identity was shaped by what I wrote, though this identity was concealed behind the people I wrote about – concealed I think from others, and also from myself. But now I must go back and explore. My parents, my family scattered over time and place, have become my biographical subjects as I search for something of me in them, and them in me. For this is a vicarious autobiography I am writing, a chronicle with a personal subtext, charting my evolution into someone who would never have been recognised by myself when young.

# 2

# *With Virginia Woolf*
# *at Sheffield Place*

My father wrote with a ballpoint pen on blue Basildon Bond paper. I remember thinking that, his name being Basil, this was almost a pun – especially since he was largely playing the history don in this investigation, the don he occasionally felt he would like to have been. The handwriting, as always, is wonderfully clear: thirty lines to the page, three hundred words, as regular as a marching soldier – quite unlike my own unformed and erratic writing.

He had probably prepared this fair copy from an earlier version. It stops suddenly in mid-sentence, at the foot of the thirty-eighth page, leaving him in his truncated schooldays during the early nineteen-twenties suffering from double pneumonia. But there are a couple of stray white pages, numbered 19 and 20, and a fragment of 21, that contain a variant text. They allude rather tantalisingly to 'the only indiscretion' of his own father, the 'real start of our financial disasters', and a 'Holroyd Settlement'.

There are signs that in his fair copy my father somewhat held back. Perhaps he remembered an attempt I had made to write about the family ten years earlier and the drama it caused. It had been an attempt at using my family to find a career of my own rather than following one of the uninviting professions they were urging on me.

My father started his saga in its first version in the eighteenth century and moved fairly rapidly on to his parents – my grand-parents at whose house in Berkshire I had passed much of my childhood and adolescence. But coming across a privately-printed history of the family prepared in 1879 by Thomas Holroyd, High Sheriff of Calcutta, for his son in Australia (later brought up to 1914 by Caroline Holroyd, Thomas Holroyd's daughter, also for her brother who was by then a retired judge of the Supreme Court of Victoria in Melbourne, Sir Edward Dundas Holroyd), my father had been able eventually to reach back into the sixteenth century. That privately-printed history had been largely taken from Burke's *Colonial Gentry* and Foss's *Lives of the Judges*.

My father believed that the 'royd' in Holroyd came from a Yorkshire word meaning stream. I do not know where he picked up this piece of learning. In the opinion of a Yorkshire local historian, Hilda Gledhill, 'royd' was actually a Norse word meaning clearing or place which had been introduced by the Vikings after landing at Durham in the eighth century and making their way south west into northern Wales. When sur-names became more common, people were often called after the land where they lived, Holroyd being someone who occu-pied a hollow place or valley. My father enjoyed history, and had he come across a rare volume, John Lodge's *The Peerage of Ireland*, published by James Moore in 1789, he might have liked to read that the Holroyd family is 'of great antiquity in the West-Riding of the county of York, and derives its name from the hamlet or estate of Holroyd, or Howroyd, as it was pronounced, in Bark-Island six miles from Halifax, which they formerly possessed'. According to John Lodge, who provided a pedigree going back to the thirteenth century, the word Holroyd 'signifies, when applied to land, such as was barren and uncultivated . . . The origin well suits the soil and situation of Holroyd . . . which joins to the mountainous country separating Lancashire from Yorkshire, called Blackstone-edge.' It is spacious country with vast skies and steep valleys full of clinging mists; also deep green fields marked out by granite and millstone walls, and miles of brown windswept moors, dramatic and desolate, round which, in the teeth of the weather, the people of the South Pennines quarried out their lives.

For several centuries Yorkshire seems to have been crammed with these Holroyds – butchers, clergymen, clothiers, farmers, landowners, soldiers, yeoman of all kinds. It was as well my father did not gain access to all this early material or he might never have reached the twentieth century at all.

He began his story with two brothers, George and Isaac Holroyd, in the seventeenth century. From these brothers, he wrote, 'our particular branch of the family is descended'. The elder brother was the great-great-grandfather of the first Earl of Sheffield, now remembered as the friend and patron of Edward Gibbon, or 'Gibbons' as my father rather endearingly called him. This Earl of Sheffield, John Baker Holroyd, is one of only two members of the family to have appeared in the original edition of Leslie Stephen's and Sidney Lee's *Dictionary of National Biography*. There his political career is described, his three marriages noted, and the price paid (£31,000) for the house and grounds at Sheffield Place in Sussex recorded (the purchase of which my father, who was having trouble with his central heating, ascribes to the climate of Sussex being more congenial than Yorkshire 'for his family seat'). There too are listed Sheffield's various Irish and English titles (Baron of Dunamore in the County of Meath, Viscount Pevensey etc.) and a bibliography presented of his observations, reports, and editing of Gibbon's posthumous works. There is scarcely a hint of what Leslie Stephen's daughter Virginia Woolf was to call, in her biographical pastiche *Orlando*, 'that riot and confusion of the passions and emotions which every good biographer detests'.

Virginia Woolf wanted to 'revolutionize biography in a night'. She wanted to free the imagination of the biographer from that tedious parade of dates and battles, that dubious weight of notes, indexes and bibliographies which remove it from the common reader. She wanted to introduce riot and confusion, passion and humour. And then she also wanted to clear those forests of family trees planted from father to son in the colonising territory of male culture. Such dreams lie between the lines of an essay she wrote in 1937 called 'Reflections at Sheffield Place'. At the end of this essay she follows not the male heirs (through the first Lord Sheffield's grandson, an idiosyncratic patron of cricket who took the first English team, including W.G. Grace, over to Australia and founded the Sheffield Shield competition), but a daughter and then on to her granddaughter Kate Amberley who was the mother of Bertrand Russell. If you hop on to the right line it can take you almost anywhere.

For Virginia Woolf, the great gardens at Sheffield Place, with their series of descending lakes, came to reflect something too intimate to find its way into works of historical reference. 'No place was more like home to him [Edward Gibbon] than Sheffield Place,' she wrote, 'and he looked upon the Holroyds as his own flesh and blood.'

Virginia Woolf hands over the telling of her story to Sheffield's daughter, 'the soft and stately Maria', as Gibbon described her. Only she could bring understanding to this devoted friendship between the Peer and the Historian, or 'the Gib' as she sometimes calls him (my father would have liked that). It was a friendship based on opposites, an attachment that (like biography itself perhaps) enabled them both to live lives each could never have lived simply in his own person. In the headstrong figure of Sheffield, Gibbon found someone caught up in those sorts of political and military affairs that, from the calmness of his study and over great distances of time, he sat composing into the sonorous sentences of his *Decline and Fall*. With his friend Sheffield, he was able to slip off his purple language and become quite racy and colloquial. In matters of the heart, where Gibbon was so ineffectual, Sheffield appeared recklessly extravagant. This emotional extravagance troubled Maria who looked to Gibbon for support. For though he was ridiculously vain and prodigiously fat, over-dressed and top-heavy, a waddling indoor figure of a man, 'rather testy too, an old bachelor, who lived like clockwork and hated to have his plans upset' (this must have brought her friend Lytton Strachey to Virginia Woolf's mind), yet he was also 'le grand Gibbon' whom Maria could not help liking. She saw how only in deference to Gibbon would her father check the self-destructive riot and confusion of his passions, and she felt grateful.

In 'Reflections at Sheffield Place' Virginia Woolf was indicating the change she wanted to see in historical biography, 'changing as the furniture changed in the firelight, as the waters of the lake changed when the night wind swept over them'. It is a turning away from the general narratives of history, with their wheeling armies and splendid processions that pass through the gorgeous tapestry of Gibbon's pages. It is an attempt, in miniature form, to put into practice Samuel Johnson's advice to biographers not to dwell on 'those performances and incidents which produce vulgar greatness, but lead the thoughts into domestic privacies': an eye-level rather than the overall view of our past.

This is what has attracted me to biography: the idea of an 'intimacy between strangers', a closeness growing up during the acts of writing and reading between an author, the reader and their subject, all unknown to one another before the book began coming into existence. For I do not think of biography as being an information-retrieval exercise: information, now the fruit of technology, has little fascination for me unless it takes root in my emotions and grows in my imagination into knowledge. What increasingly absorbs me is the unconscious process of learning. While writing I forget myself, and when I return to my world I sense that I am someone slightly different. The effect of these working holidays is of course cumulative, and perhaps there is significance in my having two birthdays. I was born the son of my parents, the grandson of their parents, and so on; and then, as it were, reborn the child of my writings – for it is they that have taken me round the world and shaped my adult existence. Now I must sit at my desk and see if I can bring together these two people who were consecutively, and who are cumulatively, myself.

# 3

# *The Swedish*
# *Experiment*

My mother's beginning was dramatic. In 1916 her parents were living at Örebro, 200 kilometres west of Stockholm. They had been married three years, had a two-year-old son Kaja-Åke, and my grandmother was over five months pregnant with her second child. On 19 November Kaja-Åke was playing in the kitchen where his nurse was cooking – simply boiling water it seems at the fireplace. Some say the child knocked over an oil lamp and started a fire; others that he tipped the boiling saucepan over himself. He was rushed to hospital, lingered there almost three weeks, then died on 9 December. The shock caused my grandmother to give birth prematurely to a tiny daughter on the day after the accident and in the hospital where her son was dying. They called their daughter Ulla. This was my mother.

I knew none of this until my mother wrote it down for me. I am not certain how much she knew of it herself before then – perhaps it is the sort of knowledge we suppress. But while

preparing her account she told me that Greta, a neighbour of her
mother in Stockholm, 'is trying to pump her without her knowing so, to keep her mind off her health – let's see what we'll get.'
In other words Greta was doing what I was doing.

What we got was to be one of the main sources of my
mother's rapid narrative. She wrote on lined paper, twenty cen-
timetres long, and with forty-six narrow lines to the page
which her fast-flowing handwriting often overlapped. She
wrote in pencil, suggesting the impermanence of the past, yet
with great speed and dash, almost violence, underlining
words – names, dates, countries, towns, as well as words that
needed special emphasis such as <u>all</u> and <u>dead</u>. Her writing
appears full of activity, as if responding to the urgency of these
events which streamed confusingly in and out of each other
until they came to an end at the top of the thirteenth page.
Then she started again, from somewhere near the middle,
ending this time with notes of her various dogs: another fourteen pages. My mother had little time for the past. What
absorbed her was the eternal present. Nevertheless, as she
wrote, and then as I read, an unusual interest in these events
seemed to grow up between us.

She noted that her father, a major in the Swedish army, had
died in 1945. That surprised me. I had thought it was very much
earlier. Only when I came to write this book did I realise he
actually died several years later. I never met him. Nineteen forty-
five was the year I began making regular sea-journeys with my
mother to visit our Swedish relatives in Borås and Stockholm,
Göteburg and a holiday island nearby called Marstrand.

My understanding at the time was that, despite being in one
of the country's safest professions, the Swedish army, my grandfather had died young. I imagined him, sword in hand, falling
gloriously from a horse during hectic manoeuvres in a northern
forest.

From my mother's notes I see that he was the son of Knut

Johanson, a director of the Växjö Match Company in southern Sweden and his wife Amanda Hall who came from a family that ran the Kruger Match Company. On her marriage certificate my mother was to give her maiden name as Ulla Knutsson-Hall. Evidently her father took, or was given, his father's first name, a second syllable to remind us that he was the son of his father, and finally his mother's maiden name. He is Karl Knutsson-Hall.

Karl (or Kalle as he was usually called) had a good voice and had once dreamed of being an opera singer. He did sing in a few amateur productions, but his parents wanted him to take over the family's match empire. Eventually, by way of compromise, he went into the army which was thought to provide a respectable career.

My mother's maternal family had come from southern Germany, and her great-grandfather, Gustav Jagenburg, worked in Moscow early in the nineteenth century before settling down with his wife at Rydboholm, near Borås. He was a textile manufacturer and his son Rudolf was said to have invented a wondrous dye that never faded. In the eighteen-eighties Rudolf married the daughter of the prison priest at the Castle of Varberg. The second of their six children was my grandmother. Her formal name was Karin though we all called her Kaja.

How Karl and Kaja first met I do not know. But I do know that the Jagenburgs considered themselves superior to Karl's matchmaking family, which probably means they were richer. They strongly opposed the marriage of this handsome couple on the grounds that Kaja could do better for herself. There was no money to be made in the army and Karl's excellent horsemanship did not particularly impress them. But Kaja in those days was a headstrong, passionate girl. A photograph of her in her early twenties among my mother's possessions shows a sweet face, with watchful slanting eyes, a rather sensuous but determined mouth, her expression provocative and full of character. No one was going to tell her whom to marry. She was in love with this charming officer, and that was enough.

So, in 1913, she married Lieutenant Karl Knutsson-Hall and went up to Boden in the north of Sweden where he was stationed. She was twenty-one and could marry without parental consent; he was four years older.

It seems probable that the marriage never recovered from the burning to death of their infant son Kaja-Åke at the end of 1916. They had no more children after my mother Ulla and by the nineteen-twenties, when the family moved to Stockholm and my mother was old enough to notice things, Karl was spending more time with his brother officers than with his wife. They seemed to regard him still as a romantic bachelor. 'A more gentlemanly officer than Karl Hall could not be found in 1920s Sweden,' wrote one of his subordinates who recalled this 'idyllic warrior' during their company's 'legendary manoeuvres in Trosa during 1922 . . . and the merry ball in Trosa's grand hotel where Karl Hall reigned over the dusty recruits and young beauties . . . a generous, chivalrous heartbreaker.'

Ulla went first to the Margaretta School in Stockholm and then to a French lycée at 9 Döbelnsgatan where she began to learn her many languages. In the holidays she often went to Växjö where the Hall family had a large country house. Her most enduring memory was of twin earth-closets in a red building with white gables where 'I used to sit with my cousin'. Her father being the eldest of nine children, there were plenty of these cousins with whom to play. At the end of the garden stood a lake where they would all swim ('trod on a snake once on the way down the slope', my mother wrote). What she most enjoyed were the children's suppers by this lake in the endless summer evenings – sandwiches made from newly-baked brown bread with delicious fillings. 'I once ate 15!' my mother boasted. 'A record.' She was looked after during those early holidays by

Karin – not her mother (who disliked the Hall family and didn't often go to Växjö) but one of her in-laws whom she thought of as her 'nanny'.

At the age of twelve Ulla was sent to a French family in the Haute Savoie for three months to practise her French. But there was another reason for removing her from Stockholm. Her parents had decided to separate. This was not a friendly arrangement but a stubbornly-fought duel that lasted almost four years and according to the family was to lead to a change in the Swedish divorce laws. Up till that time 'we lived in various nice flats', my mother wrote. But after she returned from France everything changed. Mother and daughter moved rapidly between small apartments and boarding houses pursued by Karl. Sometimes at night there were drunken brawls in the street and on one memorable occasion Karl staggered towards them shouting and waving a revolver.

Kaja was determined to win her divorce. But though Karl was apparently drinking heavily and had, Kaja told her daughter, contracted venereal disease from an extra-marital liaison, there seemed no way for her to obtain a legal divorce unless her husband consented to it. His condition of consent was a million kronor, which he calculated Kaja's father (he of the miraculous unfading dye) could afford to pay him. There was a prolonged and bitter feud that my mother found unnerving. 'I suffered,' she wrote. But what struck me as strange when reading her brief account was that she didn't appear to blame her father for those dreadful years. Perhaps she romanticised him, not knowing him so well, and missing him. Kaja had never been very 'understanding' with her as a child and was, Ulla felt, too 'demanding' with her husband.

Eventually Kaja won the divorce battle largely because one of her uncles was Riksmarshal of Sweden (equivalent to Lord Chancellor in England). After 'Lex versus Hall' was settled in 1932 it became easier for women to get divorced in Sweden.

Following their divorce Karl retreated into a home for alco-
holics where he was nursed by the daughter of a priest (the
home was apparently managed by the Church). Then in her
mid-twenties, Marianne was half Karl's age, but 'understanding
and kind which was what he *needed*', my mother insisted. So
they married. As a bonus, she was 'very good-looking', my
mother observed. This suggests that she must have seen
Marianne, but she gets her name wrong (Margareta instead of
Marianne) which suggests she did not actually know her.
Perhaps they met only at Karl's funeral. In my mother's speedy
narrative, the happy couple are disposed of rather brutally: 'My
father died of T.B. and god knows what else,' she wrote. 'He
caught T.B. from his wife who was later killed by being squashed
by a lorry against a wall whilst walking with a girlfriend in
Stockholm – 5 years after Papa died.' This must have been based
on what Kaja was telling her neighbour, Greta. In fact Karl's
cause of death is given as a respectable heart attack ('Infartus
cordis kardiosclerasis').

In her 'teens Kaja had done some sewing and cutting in her
father's textile workshops in Borås. Then, arriving in Stockholm
as a married woman, she persuaded her father to introduce her
to Countess Margareta von Schwerin, known as Marg, who in
1927 was to open the celebrated fashion house Märthaskolan
where elegant ladies had their dresses made. Before long Kaja
became a consultant there and was coming into contact with
Swedish high society. She took her work seriously and, she
would tell her daughter, was never late, not even by five minutes,
for an appointment. 'I can see Kaja entering the salons well
aware of the impression she made, so sure of herself and her
beauty,' a friend of my mother's wrote to me. 'Everyone had to
admire her, and then entered Ulla, pretty, laughing and much
more warm at heart, everybody felt.'

Kaja soon floated free from the disreputable business of her
divorce and settled into her work as a couturier for

Märthaskolan. This was a school of dress as well as a fashion house and in those days the greatest single influence in the creation of Swedish femininity. The Countess Margareta von Schwerin herself was really a fashion reporter with strong opinions as to what would be useful for young girls. She travelled widely and dealt with most of the French couturiers. But she did not promote a single style or confine her interests to high fashion. She was an ambitious woman and wanted to dress all women in Sweden, whatever their age or status. She saw herself as an educator. Her mission was to give Swedish women confidence in the home and at work by the way they presented themselves.

Among the bits and pieces my mother left after her death are a few photographs of our trips together to Sweden from the late nineteen-forties and the nineteen-fifties. There I am sitting on the floor with my pretty cousin Mary. She is smiling, blonde and lively; I, aged nine or ten, am blank-faced and bird-like, decked out in foreign tailoring, with blue and yellow Swedish cufflinks, a frilled handkerchief and bow tie (my God! What would my schoolfriends in Surrey have said?). Behind us, sitting and standing in rows, a contingent of the family has formed up for the photograph. I can recognise my grandmother Kaja, a formidably handsome woman looking frankly at the camera; and I can see my mother, unsmiling, with a similar gingham frock and hair neatly arranged like my grandmother's – she is on her very best behaviour. But I cannot identify anyone else. Which is Elis? Where is Inga?

But with my mother's written account before me I can at last make some sense of this family group. My grandmother was in her mid-fifties at the time these photographs were taken, though she looks younger. And these are her brothers and sisters, their wives and husbands and children, who have lined up before the camera. There is a bank manager, an engineer, a doctor, a businessman: all respectable middle-class people. Of course there are some lapses from respectability. One of the brothers, for example, an import–export manager, imported syphilis from a Hamburg brothel and has never quite recovered. My grand-mother believes it must have addled his brain – why else would he have married a waitress from a Borås hotel? My mother likes Kristina, her waitress-aunt, who has always been kind to her. But my grandmother cannot stand her and makes pointed remarks such as, when Kristina comes into the room with some drinks: 'You must be used to carrying trays.'

My grandmother is a snob. Snobbishness is her form of authority. It cows other people, and this suits her. That is why she looks so young in the photographs and my mother so ill-at-ease. My grandmother believes in appearances and, living up to her beliefs, she appears splendidly superior.

Kaja always walked, sat, spoke and generally carried herself with soldierly precision. She had the unquestioning air of an officer – more so than her ex-husband. She assumed the posture of high command, straightened her back, raised her chin, yet somehow retained her attractiveness. This is a determined and successful couturier we see in the photographs.

Kaja revelled in this work and felt proud of being part of the Countess's team at Märthaskolan. She allowed herself one acknowledged admirer, Biryer Sandström, a middle-aged gentle-man with a brilliant white moustache, whose presence breathed respectability. He escorted her to parties and she employed him almost as a fashion accessory. It was a discreet arrangement which became easier to manage after 1934 when Ulla sailed for England.

# 4

# *Links in the Chain*

I like to think of Virginia Woolf having used one of my ancestors to plead the revolution in biography. Unfortunately my father had not been strictly accurate when claiming that our branch of the family was directly descended from the two sixteenth-century brothers George and Isaac Holroyd. The first Earl of Sheffield's direct ancestor was George, but we succeeded from the younger brother Isaac. Isaac's most illustrious descendant was Sir George Sowley Holroyd, a Judge of the King's Bench. Like Lord Sheffield he was painted by Joshua Reynolds, and was the second Holroyd to gain entry (a more modest entry) into the original *Dictionary of National Biography*.

My father used to say that most of our family during the eighteenth and nineteenth centuries had been lawyers or soldiers, and that the judges were far more deadly than the generals. I imagined a gallery of hanging judges. But George Sowley Holroyd appears to have been an exceptionally mild man. In an essay for the *Edinburgh Review*, Lord Brougham emphasised his humour and gentleness, the elegance and ingenuity of his arguments, and the lightness with which he employed his learning. I began to notice as I read this eulogium how I was beginning to compare my own circumstances with this distinguished forebear and, like the reader of an astrological chart, take possession of flattering items. 'To whatever branch of investigation he had devoted his life in that he would have eminently excelled.' What an investigative biographer this special pleader might have made!

QUEM TE DEUS ESSE JUSSIT ('What God has commanded you to do'). My father quoted these portentous words at the head of his narrative (though he did not provide a translation). This was a family motto which, with Arms showing Five Roses in Saltire, the Crest a Demi-Griffin, Wings Endorsed and holding between its claws a Ducal Coronet, appeared as an armorial bookplate, framed in black, which hung in the lavatory of his flat in Surrey. On the opposite side of the water-cistern, also registering my father's reduced position, was suspended another framed bookplate which, perhaps because of its complexity, he left without comment. I needed the assistance of the Chester Herald himself to record these Arms correctly. They are: Five Pierced Mullets in Saltire impaled on the Arms of Virginie, daughter of General Mottet de la Fontaine of Compiègne in Picardy, which should properly be blazoned Argent à Chevron Azure between in chief Two Roses Gules slipped and leaved Vert and in base a Mound Sable on a chief of the second Three Mullets Or. The motto below this paraphernalia was COMPONERE LEGIBUS ORBEM ('To build a world with laws') which George Sowley Holroyd had apparently chosen. But the name beneath this Motto, Arms and Crest is that of his eldest son, George Chaplin Holroyd, a naval officer who passed most of his life in India, married Virginie (daughter of the Governor of Pondicherry), and finally returned to be buried in Exeter. With this man's third son, my great-grandfather Charles Holroyd who was born in Hyderabad in 1822, the family finally comes into view. For, in a cardboard box marked Six Cod Steaks 24 × 12 oz among my aunt's possessions, there is a photograph of Charles Holroyd with his three children taken at Eastbourne in the late nineteenth century.

Charles Holroyd passed most of his life on the Bengal Military Staff in Assam. During the Indian Mutiny of 1857, he unravelled a plot to massacre the European tea planters in Upper Assam. In heartfelt thanks for saving their lives they presented him with 'a very handsome silver salver', and more significantly perhaps, also gave him an interest in their tea gardens.

Five years after the Mutiny, at the age of forty, Charles married a widow, Mary Hannay, who had two sons by her first marriage. But nine months later, probably when pregnant, she died of apoplexy. Charles, who continued bringing up his stepsons, did not marry again for another nine years. His second wife, Anna Eliza Smith, the daughter of an indigo planter, was Scottish. She gave birth in Calcutta to two boys in 1874 and 1875, Patrick Charles (called Patrick or Pat) and my grandfather Edward Fraser Rochfort (called Fraser); and then a daughter, Norah Palmer, who was born in 1877 at Eastbourne in Sussex, where Charles had retired with the rank of Major-General. According to the privately printed family tree, Anna died three years later. But I can find no record of her death in London. Then I see in an Eastbourne newspaper that she was buried at the Glasgow Necropolis. So I write to the General Register Office for Scotland in Edinburgh which sends me her death certificate.

Is it possible to be shocked by something that happened over a hundred years ago? I do feel a jolt as I read that Anna Eliza Holroyd, my great-grandmother, committed 'suicide by carbolic acid' at 29 Arlington Street, Glasgow, on 7 January 1880. She was aged thirty, that is twenty-eight years younger than her

husband. This Arlington Street address was the home of her
uncle, William Smith, an accountant, and his wife. But the
'informant' on the death certificate two days later is Charles
Holroyd, her husband. This suggests that she had travelled to
Scotland alone and that he went up from Eastbourne on hearing the dreadful news, leaving his two sons, Pat and Fraser,
aged five and four, and his daughter Norah, who was a couple
of weeks short of her third birthday, at home. Were they ever
told of their mother's suicide? No whisper of it reached my
father, I am sure, or came down to the rest of the family. There
is no photograph of her anywhere.

Carbolic acid was used as a strong domestic disinfectant
which cleaned by its caustic action. Anna would have died
through internal burning. What can have driven her to do such
an unimaginably painful thing, to kill herself when she had three
very young children? There is no report of her suicide in the
Scottish newspapers (there was a more dramatic suicide in
Glasgow that day by an unnamed woman who threw herself
from a bridge in Jamaica Street on the stroke of midnight). Nor
is there any fatal accident inquiry concerning Anna on record.
She left no Will or inventory, no testamentary deeds. There is
simply no living memory of this tragedy, simply a trail of speculation.

Having lived most of her life in India, Anna may well have
found it difficult to settle at Eastbourne where she knew no one.
The prospect of spending the next twenty years or so as the wife
of a retired soldier nearly twice her age cannot have been very
appealing. By the beginning of 1880, she could well have been
pregnant again and she may have been subject to unrecognised
post-natal depression, the prospect of which renewed her feelings of guilt. All this is possible and could form a contributory
cause of her death. But none of it provides a convincing explanation for killing herself so appallingly. Where no easy
explanations were available, many women who did not have a

tenacious hold on life and who found it eventually intolerable were considered to be mentally unstable. I have been unable to find evidence of her being in love with another man, or having had any connection with that other woman, with dark brown hair, whose body was recovered by lowering a boat from the Carrick Castle that January night. Nor is there any evidence of her husband having ill-treated her – otherwise her uncle would surely not have summoned him to Glasgow, or her mother, years later, have sent a wreath 'in affectionate remembrance' when Charles Holroyd himself died.

Anna Eliza, 'the Beloved Wife of Major Gen Charles Holroyd', was buried at the Glasgow Necropolis on 10 January 1880. And that must surely be the end of her story. But it is not quite the end. Over seventeen years later a man was buried beside her. His name – one I have never seen before – was John Stewart Paul and he died in June 1897 at the age of sixty-one. Who was this mysterious man? On the grave-stone it is written that he was the 'brother in law of Major Gen Holroyd'. He turns out to be Anna's uncle by marriage (the husband of her mother's sister) who had christened his younger son Charles Holroyd Paul. What can this tell me? It appears that Anna's family wished to retain the connection with her husband Charles, and that no blame was laid on him for her suicide. In 1901, Anna's mother was buried in the same plot, and so in 1914 was her aunt, Janet Stewart Paul. In Lair 59 of the Necropolis, the four of them lie together with their secrets.

The Eastbourne photograph shows the widower and his three children a few years after Anna's death. They are formally grouped as if in a studio conservatory. The father, sitting on a stone bench, is attired in morning clothes; the two boys (one sitting on the ground balancing a tennis racket, the other standing next to the bench) are dressed in Eton jackets and collars, with buttoned waistcoats and sober spotted ties. Norah, their sister, is perched on the back of the bench, aged about ten, wearing a long-sleeved pleated dress with a high lace collar and lace cuffs. What struck me most when first examining this picture is how old the father appears in comparison with his children. He *is* rather old to have a ten-year-old daughter – in his mid- to late-sixties. But, with his bald head and full white beard, half-closed eyes and melancholic expression, he seems nearer eighty. It is as if his wife's terrible death has marked him for ever. The two boys themselves have somewhat wary and solemn expressions matching their father's. Only Norah, from her superior position on the back of the bench, confronts the camera direct. She is not smiling, but she has a modern look. She appears forthright and freer than the boys.

The four of them were living at a large, rather sombre flint house called The Links built in 1869 close to Beachy Head in the Meads district of Eastbourne. The house itself stood in extensive grounds out of sight of the sea and protected by a high flint wall. Behind this wall, on naturally-sloping, partly-levelled grounds shaded by beech and yew trees, ilex, chestnut and Cedar of Lebanon, lay a sunken garden with a large expanse of lawn over which crying seagulls would sail – a good place for games. During his twenty years there, Charles Holroyd enlarged this property considerably. His Will refers to outbuildings, cottages and pleasure grounds as part of his land. He employed a gardener (who lived with his family in a cottage on the grounds), cook, parlourmaid, housemaid, house parlourmaid, coachman and a governess, Mary Easlea, later described as a companion.

The Major-General makes his appearance in the local newspapers as someone who 'took no part in public affairs, for like other residents who have served their country in distant parts of the world, he came to Eastbourne in search of quiet and rest'. He was a Tory and a member of the Church of England, worshipping at St John's on Sundays and going to the Sussex Club twice a day during the rest of the week. The two boys were 'rather in awe of him', my father writes. But as the tennis racket in the photograph suggests, there was an escape through sport. Both boys had guns, made their own cartridges, and would go rough shooting on the Downs. There were also the adventures of bird's-nesting, moth- and butterfly-collecting, and fishing expeditions at sea. Eventually there was the more permanent escape to boarding school.

But none of these escapes were available to Norah. Her chief pastime seems to have been stamp-collecting. Though she did have friends to stay – the 1891 census lists a fourteen-year-old visitor from Paris, Georgette Backellery – Norah's life appears to have been somewhat solitary. She was educated at home under the supervision of Mary Easlea and remained at The Links with this middle-aged companion until after her father's death at the end of the century. Despite her forthright look in that family photograph, she was said to have been delicate. 'How much this state of health was a state of mind it is impossible to say,' my father wrote, adding that he never heard his own father refer to his sister Norah when talking of his boyhood.

Charles Holroyd was educated at the East India Company's college at Addiscombe, and his father and grandfather had been Harrovians. His choice for Pat and Fraser was Uppingham, a tiny, unsalubrious, sixteenth-century grammar school in Rutland which, under its evangelical headmaster, Edward Thring, was recognised as one of the most progressive public schools in the country. Thring was a powerful personality, 'quick and articulate, charismatic, quarrelsome', the school historian describes him. It was he, rather than Dr Arnold of Rugby, who today appears the radical pioneer in mid-nineteenth-century education. Arnold had been at Winchester and Oxford; Thring at Eton (under the brutal regime of Dr Keate) and Cambridge. Arnold emerged a pessimist, Thring an optimist. Thring was also passionately egalitarian, insisting that 'every boy in the school must receive equal and full attention', and that 'ordinary boys needed as much time as the brilliant'. This inclusiveness contrasted strongly with Dr Arnold's regime of public expulsions and private removals founded on the belief that, boys having 'an essential inferiority' as compared with men, 'the first, second and third duty of a schoolmaster is to get rid of unpromising subjects'. In Thring's opinion, Dr Arnold was 'a very great man, but a bad schoolmaster'. It was true that he had added mathematics, modern history and languages to the school course; but so had Thring added them – as well as chemistry, drawing, carpentry and music too. Both were ordained clergymen, driven by a sense of moral purpose, but Thring's temperament was far less morbid than Arnold's. He was a New Testament man and his sermons never lasted longer than ten minutes. Above all he was a genuine innovator, establishing workshops, laboratories, an aviary and gymnasium at Uppingham, emphasising the skill needed even in elementary teaching, discouraging the multiplication of prizes as motives for work, and campaigning on behalf of a liberal education for girls.

When Thring came to Uppingham in the early eighteen-fifties the school contained twenty-five boys. Thirty years later there were over three hundred boarding in eleven houses, and thirty masters. It could have grown still more but, believing that most public schools were too large, Thring restricted the number of boys to a maximum of 320 with no more than thirty in each house.

My great-grandfather was one of the last parents to interview Thring who died in the autumn of 1887. Six months later the Major-General's elder son Pat arrived at Uppingham, and he was followed a year later by his brother (my grandfather) Fraser. Within these eighteen months Uppingham had grown to almost four hundred boys and in one respect at least begun to change. Thring argued that 'organised games received excessive attention'. Though he encouraged games at which masters could play in the teams – this being a good way for everyone to get to know

one another better – he disliked the worship of competitive ath-
letics which he considered unfair to the ordinary boys. A year
after Thring's death, however, rugby football began to be played
at Uppingham and the spirit of Dr Arnold entered the school. The
great man there in the late eighteen-eighties and early eighteen-
nineties was H.H. Stephenson, the legendary cricket coach, who
had captained the first English team to tour Australia.

I occasionally heard my grandfather speak of Stephenson as
we drank our cider together in the evenings. His tone was rev-
erential, for we were after all discussing one of the great heroes
of the game and 'the best cricket coach at any school'. I loved
these stories of my grandfather, but generally he was too barri-
caded by worries to entertain me with them, though I sometimes
pleaded with him and made him smile. Only at moments would
he bow down his head, hush his voice, and whisper, 'Ah!
Stephenson!' Such an exclamation conveyed more than any
inventory of facts. I would stare into the past and nod my understanding. I got the impression that he venerated Stephenson
because he had received from him all the attention and encouragement he missed at home. He may even have received special
attention on account of being a kinsman of Henry North
Holroyd, third Earl of Sheffield, the great cricket patron of those
days in whose grounds at Sheffield Place the Australians always
opened their tour of England.

As a result of intensive coaching, my grandfather did pretty
well at Uppingham. Stephenson noted in 1892 that he was
'developing into a good run-getting bat', though he 'did not
punish the loose balls with sufficient severity'. Also, Stephenson
added in Fraser's last year, he was perhaps 'rather nervous'. This
nervousness, his lack of aggression, and the sad fact that he was
'not a safe pair of hands' may be said to have marked his later
life beyond the cricket field.

Nevertheless, my grandfather was one of the stars in the new
philathletic era. This was a vintage patch in Uppingham cricket,

full of masterly innings, decisive victories, sensational fight-backs, astonishing records (Fraser making his contribution to all this brave achievement with a 75 against Uppingham's deadly rivals Repton). He quite outshone Pat, one of the ordinary boys for whom Thring had been concerned, and immediately took precedence over him in class, *Holroyd mi* being placed in a higher form than *Holroyd ma*. Perhaps it was this paradox that helped to gain for my grandfather a reputation for academic brilliance in the family years later. We would have found it difficult to believe that 'Uncle Pat' was actually a long way below average, that Fraser himself never reached the upper division of the Classical Sixth where the scholars clustered, or that he won no medals, distinctions or prizes. He appears in several photographs of Constable's House, the school prepostors, and the cricket eleven. All the boys look far older than similar groups in the twentieth century, and no boy looks older than my grandfather. I can quite easily recognise the man I knew in his seventies and eighties – indeed he already looks nearly half that age, weighed down with a Johnsonian heaviness. I find these photographs curiously disturbing. No one is smiling. Between this solemn young boy seen with his family at Eastbourne and the prematurely-aged prepostor of Uppingham, did my grandfather have any carefree childhood and adolescence? What I have discovered suggests that his youth was much delayed.

Pat left Uppingham after three years and went on to the Military Academy at Sandhurst. That, at any rate, was what my father understood. But 'Uncle Pat' did not go to Sandhurst and does not turn out to have been the professional soldier who, with five medals blazing on his chest, marches across my father's narrative. He was an amateur soldier in the auxiliary military force called the Militia which was enlisted locally, sometimes paraded for drill and could be called on in wartime. A photograph taken in the mid-eighteen-nineties at Eastbourne shows him in his uniform, a mild and handsome face with a well-designed moustache nicely waxed at its tips.

While Pat was drilling with the Royal Welch Fusiliers, Fraser went to King's College, Cambridge. My father writes enthusiastically of his playing there against the two most brilliant cricketers of the times, C.B. Fry and Ranjitsinhji. In fact he seems to have given up cricket and did not get a Blue. My father also believed that 'he was an excellent mathematician, worked hard, finally taking a First'. The printed register of King's admissions records him as having been awarded a Third in the History Tripos of 1897. As something starts going wrong, so the gap between ascertainable fact and family legend widens.

Though my father liked to picture Fraser making lifelong friendships in the glamorous atmosphere of Cambridge, he suspected there had been some setback and attributed it to varicose veins (which he himself had), brought on by the 'tight elastic garters' Fraser was obliged to wear. This rumour of illness took many forms and I remember hearing how my grandfather's brilliant prospects as an oarsman had been blighted by his hernia. The truth appears to have been more complicated.

Towards the end of 1894 Fraser was given what the Major-General indignantly describes as an 'arbitrary order, compelling him to give up Classics and take up History' by his college tutor, Alfred Cooke. Cooke was an Old Etonian Classics scholar with a bewildering medley of occupations – he was a priest, a famous versifier, a conchologist and a talented footballer. Early in 1895, Fraser is asking his friend Oscar Browning for advice as to what he should do. The prolonged difficulty in getting tuition lost him 'a full year'.

This friendship with Oscar Browning is surprising. A hugely fat socialite and friend of Oscar Wilde, he had been dismissed as an assistant-master at Eton 'on unsubstantiated charges of misconduct' and then returned to King's as a lecturer in history. A notorious 'character' and (in the words of E.F. Benson) a 'genius flawed by abysmal fatuity', Browning inhabited a world I had never remotely associated with my grandfather.

By the summer of 1896 my grandfather, having crammed two years' work into one, seems to have had some kind of breakdown, raising in the examiners' minds a question of whether he should be allowed to stay on and complete his studies. While they were deliberating, his father sent him out to Cape Town with his brother Pat (the two of them were good friends) 'in the hope the entire change would keep him from brooding over his misfortunes'. But 'the wound still rankles', he reported. What was this wound? The Major-General wrote in confidence to Oscar Browning with some attempt at an explanation.

> He was not well at the time of the examination: shortly before it commenced he heard of the sudden death of his Godfather who was his best friend, and a great help to him. He was working 8 to 9 hours a day, & at night unable to sleep brooding over his loss . . . He is not of a nature to confide in others, & keeps his feelings to himself. I am about the only one he confides in. I do not think Mr Cook [sic] understands him in the slightest, & I do not imagine he would take the trouble to do so . . . he has not met with much consideration since he has been at the university, excepting from yourself, of whom he always speaks in the warmest praise.

It is obvious that Fraser was unhappy at Cambridge and not prospering there. The contrast with those simple sunlit days at Uppingham must have been dismaying. He had entered a far more ambiguous world.

When the decision was made to allow my grandfather to stay on for his third year, the Major-General wired the happy news to Cape Town. So that autumn, Fraser returned to King's, dividing his vacations between Eastbourne and an apartment in London at 22 Montague Place, near the Reading Room of the British Museum.

But it was a gloomy time. In a letter sent from The Links shortly before Christmas 1896, the Major-General wrote that 'it would have been a great pleasure' to invite Oscar Browning to lunch or dine (he had apparently tried to invite himself), 'but my Daughter is so poorly I regret I cannot ask anyone to the House'. So the family rumour of her illness had been based on fact. But what was wrong with her? Had she found out about her mother's suicide? Was she suspected of having inherited through the female line some mental instability? There were whispers of a scandal that my own father picked up when a child on the only occasion he saw her. He refers to 'some story the details of which I never heard, about some awful experience that Norah had at the hands of some man . . . whom she was visiting'.

During 1897 and 1898 The Links became something of a sanatorium. 'Progress is very slow, almost imperceptible, & it will take a long time before, if ever, I am myself again,' the Major-General wrote in a very shaky hand shortly before Norah's twentieth birthday and when he himself was in his seventy-fifth year. According to the *Eastbourne Chronicle*, he had suffered a stroke and was partly paralysed. As for Fraser, 'I hope he has prospered,' the old man wrote to Oscar Browning: 'it will be a crushing blow to him if he has not for he has . . . I know done his best.'

In February 1897 my great-grandfather made his Will. He leaves The Links, its grounds and contents ('furniture plated goods linen glass china books ornaments manuscripts pictures prints statuary musical instruments and articles of vertu . . . and all wines liquors and consumable stores and all my plants and garden tools') in trust to his elder son Patrick. The property is given to him under the condition that, until he reaches the age of twenty-five (when it becomes his own absolutely), he allows his brother and sister to live there if they wish, so that The Links can 'be maintained as a home for my family'.

'The watches jewels trinkets and personal ornaments belonging to me at the time of my death', many of which must have once belonged to Norah's mother, he leaves to Norah herself. The residuary estate is to be divided equally in trust between his three children.

There are pages of instruction designed to protect his daughter from fortune-hunting men. Her third part in the estate is to be retained by trustees 'for as long as she shall remain unmarried and whether she shall be competent or incompetent to give legal discharge'. In the event of her marriage, this Holroyd money shall be for 'her separate use free from marital control and without power of alienation'. The one-third interest in the estate then becomes vested in her and the capital eventually passes to her children after they come of age. It is evident that her father had given much thought to these provisions, considerably more than to his second son who is bequeathed nothing beyond his one-third share of the residuary estate. But after Fraser was awarded his degree in the autumn of 1897, his father added a codicil to the Will leaving him various exotic Indian debentures and securities, including 92,500 rupees at the Bank of Bengal and a thousand shares in the fabulous Rajmai Tea Company, the sound and substance of which were to echo down the years – and were still echoing strangely through my childhood, more sound than substance then.

A second codicil Charles Holroyd signed on 14 July 1898 leaves all his staff an extra year's wages because of the burden placed on them by his long illness.

Six weeks later Patrick marries. His wife Coral is the daughter of another Major-General, and the wedding takes place on 7 September 1898 at the parish church of St Mary's in Bath. Fraser is present, but no one else from Patrick's family. The husband and wife then go off for their honeymoon, and Fraser returns to

The Links. His father was now dying. The cause of his death was given as thirty-two hours of cerebral haemorrhaging with convulsions leading to a coma and eventually culminating in respiratory paralysis. My grandfather was present during this final agony of illness and he is named as 'informant' on the death certificate, dated 19 September.

The funeral was held four days later at St John's Church, and the body was interned at Ocklynge cemetery. Fraser was there, also Pat and his wife Coral with her father, Major-General Montague. Colonel and Mrs Hannay were listed among the mourners. A friend from India, Richard Magor, connected with the Rajmai tea plantations, came to the service; so did numerous nephews, nieces and in-laws, as well as Mary Easlea, but not Norah Holroyd, the dead man's daughter. There were special wreaths from the coachman, gardeners and indoor servants, as well as from his late wife's family. There was none from Norah. But there is one 'in ever loving memory of my dear father, from his heart-broken Fraser'.

Probate was granted at the end of October, and the Major-General's estate was valued at £80,913 8s 10d. A hundred years later such a sum would be roughly equivalent to four-and-a-half million pounds.

On 4 June 1899 Patrick was twenty-five and The Links became his absolute property. He immediately sold the house which was converted into an expensive 'Ladies School' – among its pupils were to be Edwina Ashley, god-daughter of Edward VII, later to gain fame as Lady Mountbatten; and the Marchioness of Bath who, as Daphne Fielding, was to write a celebrated autobiography, *Mercury Presides*. Later, The Links was bought by the Methodist Guild, and became a Christian Holiday Centre, its interior partitioned and sub-divided by the tortured geometry of fire regulations.

The Militia was to do good service in the Boer War and Lieutenant Patrick Holroyd was one of those who volunteered to embark for South Africa. He took his wife Coral, and there, in the summer of 1900, their son Ivor was born. Fraser, who accurately described his occupation as being 'of independent means', had meanwhile fallen in love, a complaint that was to carry him off to Ireland. But while the two brothers were abroad what became of Norah? There was a family rumour that she died young. But my father wrote of having seen her once when he was aged about six – 'someone lying down who was very gentle to a little boy' and who (my aunt recalled) had 'beautiful hair'. That must have been approximately in 1913. So I went in search of a death certificate.

Birth, death and marriage certificates were still held in 1996 at St Catherine's House in the Aldwych. The National Statistics Public Search Room there looked like a medieval place of torment. I joined the panting crowds of fellow-researchers, sweating, glazed, cursing as we bumped against one another, jostling with decades of unwieldy volumes and staring at the lists, and more lists, of the dead. All of us apparently were hunting for our family stories. But I could find no death certificate for Norah Palmer Holroyd. Had she secretly married? She seemed to have vanished.

I had no other information about her, except a whisper my father had picked up from among the grown-ups that she lived with a Dr Macnamara. The family whispers had it that he was a Svengali, with an uncanny hold over this unmarried girl, plotting to get her money. There appeared to be no way of checking this. The trail had ended.

Then I had an idea. Maybe Norah made a Will. Wills and certificates of divorce were then lodged at Somerset House which was just the other side of the Aldwych from St Catherine's House. The crowds are less dense there and the torture more refined. No one who searches for a Will was allowed to take off his or her overcoat in winter lest it contain high explosives. The central heating was kept high, very high, and all the staff worked in shirtsleeves. In this unbalanced atmosphere I began my hot pursuit. I started in the year 1913, tracking backwards and forwards, and came across a Will Norah had made in 1907. This revealed that she died, aged thirty-six, on 22 October 1913. There had been no death certificate because she died at Vernet-les-Bains, a spa town in the far south west of France that was popular among British travellers in the late nineteenth century. Evidently she had visited her brother Fraser, and met her nephews and niece, shortly before setting out on that last journey.

Norah's Will fills a few of the empty spaces in her life and plants some signposts over this lost territory. Whatever immediately happened to her when The Links was sold late in 1899, she was according to the Census living at Beaufort House at Ham in Surrey at the beginning of 1901. The house was occupied by a Dr William Simpson Craig who was replaced as its occupant by his son-in-law Dr Macnamara in 1907, the year Norah made her Will.

When probate was granted in the summer of 1914, Norah's estate was valued at £11,992 16s, which would be equivalent to approximately half-a-million pounds at the end of the century. The chief beneficiaries were indeed Dr and Mrs Macnamara who continued living at Beaufort House until 1920. But Norah's Will gives a good reason for allowing what money she controlled to pass out of the Holroyd family. For fifteen years she had been able to 'enjoy the income' of a one-third share in her father's residuary estate. But because she was dying unmarried, her capital would pass to Pat and Fraser. For this reason 'I do not consider it necessary,' she writes, 'to bequeath to my said brothers or either of them any portion of the savings accrued or which may accrue in my lifetime in respect of the income of the said share and I have for that reason made the dispositions hereinafter contained without reference to my said brothers.'

But there is no malice against Pat and Fraser whose sons and daughter are each left a specific gift – for one nephew 'my gilt Empire clock'; for another 'my sleevelinks and tie clips'; and for her niece 'my gold watch and chain'. All of them receive £100 on their twenty-first birthdays. But my father, who was born four days before his aunt made her Will, is not mentioned; and, since there was to be no codicil, nor did Pat's daughter born in 1908 receive anything. The implication is that Norah's contact with her brothers' families had grown more distant during the last six years of her life.

Her largest legacy of all – £1,400 – goes to 'my friend Frances Mary Macnamara wife of the said Eric Danvers Macnamara' who is himself merely given 'my gold ring set with two diamonds and my crescent scarf pin'. Unless Norah's solicitor had advised against the impropriety of leaving the bulk of her estate to a married man, the conclusion any reader of this testament reaches is that the special friend of this woman with the watch chain, tie and cufflinks, was not the doctor but his wife.

Dr Macnamara was a well-known psychiatrist who practised in Harley Street. He 'devoted his life to mental disease', his obituary in the *British Medical Journal* states, '. . . even his domestic life had many associations with his special study'. Norah Palmer Holroyd was almost certainly the subject of one of the papers he published in medical journals and encyclopaedias on neurological and psychopathological matters – on paralysis, insomnia, the use of morphine and what was called 'functional insanity'.

Whatever he believed her to be suffering from, her death certificate at the Marie de Vernet-les-Bains in the Pyrenees provides no cause of death. It is as if she simply gave up living. She died at four o'clock in the afternoon of 22 October 1913 at the Hôtel du Parc, an 'établissement thermal'. There appear to have been no friends with her. The note of death is of a life unlived, 'célibataire', 'sans profession', signed at ten o'clock the following morning by two local Frenchmen and the mayor. There is no more.

After his sister's death, Fraser increased his holding in Rajmai Tea to 1,752 shares, and continued to hold this special number, with a nominal value of £10 a share, until the decline and fall of his own fortunes.

# 5

# *The Breves Process:*
# *Tea into Glass*

In the late eighteen-nineties my grandfather fell into the company of a large, noisy, ramshackle Irish family. The Corbets had been brought up in the Sunday's Well district of Cork and were utterly unlike Fraser's own family – indeed that was probably their principal charm. There were eleven Corbet sisters and one brother who, to compensate for his solitary condition, had been blessed with fifteen Christian names which his sisters were obliged to learn by heart: Roland, Hudson, Sands, De Courcy, Blenahassit . . . He sailed away to the United States, built up a chain of garages and eventually perished under a car.

The sheer femininity of these vivacious Corbet girls, with their waspwaists and prominent busts, their bright eyes and lilting voices, seems to have bewitched Fraser after the invalidism of The Links, the heavy male world of Uppingham and his worrying time at Cambridge. Though apparently penniless, these

Corbets were always laughing. My grandfather was enchanted
by their happy-go-lucky ways.

He had been introduced to them by a new friend Stephen
(nicknamed 'Nipper') Anderson who was to become a partner in
the Magor family's tea merchant company. 'Nipper' Anderson
was on the verge of being engaged to the beautiful Alice Corbet
and would take several years advancing to the verge of marrying
her. When Alice came over from Ireland to see him, she brought
with her a selection of her sisters: Iley, who played the piano so
delightfully; Ida, who had escaped from a convent and gone on
the music hall stage; Lizzie, the jolliest of the lot of them, famous
for her punctuality (she once turned up for a train half-a-day
early, fell asleep in the waiting-room, and missed it); Lannie,
who would one day emigrate to Australia; and the very pretty
and petite Adeline.

Their parents were both dead. If you spoke to Ida she would
tell you that their father Michael Augustus Corbet had been a
dedicated physician, and how her mother had died transporting
medicines on horseback through the snows of winter. If you
questioned Adeline, she would whisper of their father's unmiti-
gated brilliance as a poor professor at Cork University. Each
sister had her own story; and all relished the others' repertory of
stories. On Adeline's birth certificate – she was born at 6 Lower
Janemount in Cork on 13 July 1876 – her father's profession is
given as 'Traveller' which means neither gypsy nor hedge
scholar, but commercial traveller.

The eldest of these Corbet girls is Minnie. She has married the
huge and friendly Tom White, director of a pharmaceutical company, and lives in Bray, County Wicklow. They have no family of
their own but act *in loco parentis* to Minnie's unmarried sisters,
the delicate Atty, the mysterious Sloper and others. But these sisters are rapidly getting married. When 'Nipper' Anderson
hurried over to Ireland soon after Fraser's father's death to meet
the rest of Alice's family, he took Fraser along with him. It was

a holiday he needed. There were picnics by the sea and sunny days at the races, trips up to Dublin, walks around the magical waters of Glendaloch, and always the congenial company of this tumultuous family teeming with enjoyment.

Alice, as we know, is to be engaged to 'Nipper' Anderson. Lizzie has recently married and, as Mrs Parsons, gone to live in Bristol. Ida's career as a singer in the music halls is being brought to an end by some passionate love letters from an older man, William Temple, whom (despite the disapproval of his mother, 'old Lady Temple of Leeswood') she suddenly marries. Even the youngest sister of all, Lannie, will soon be engaged to a champion cyclist and billiards player. Romance is in the air and there seems no time to lose. Fraser's attention is caught by the next youngest sister, Adeline, a slip of a girl with a sensuous curving mouth and elaborate, altitudinous hair. She is called 'Bang' by her sisters: Fraser they call 'Josh'.

Bang and Josh were married on 4 April 1899 from Lizzie's new home in Bristol (her husband acting as one of the witnesses). Bang took only one year off her age (making herself a romantic twenty-one instead of twenty-two) on the marriage certificate, and gave her late father's profession innocuously as 'Gentleman'. There is no evidence that she went to Eastbourne and saw The Links which was being sold that summer. She was soon pregnant and living in her new home, the Red House, at Datchet, near Windsor in Buckinghamshire. They had chosen Datchet because her sister Ida now lived there.

On 7 January 1900 Bang and Josh's first child was born – a son whom they named Desmond Sowley Holroyd. But after sixteen weeks he was to die of bronchial pneumonia. Fraser, who was with his son when he died, was once again the 'informant' and signed the death certificate.

Two years later Adeline gave birth to a daughter. She and Fraser had gone down to stay with Bang's sister Lizzie at Bristol for the birth, and Yolande Phyllis was born at Lizzie's home in

Victoria Square, Clifton, on 22 April 1902. The house was alive with Corbet sisters, and Alice won the contest to sign Yolande's birth certificate as one of the many 'present at the birth'.

Everyone agreed that it was 'unfair' to have only one child. Lizzie had three; so did Lannie; and also Ida. Adeline's next child, a son whom they christened Kenneth De Courcy, was born at the Red House on 16 December 1903. And that, Adeline decided, was enough. Of course married women were expected to have children – it was their duty. But Bang was in many ways hardly out of childhood herself and never really would be. She was not naturally a loving mother. Her children got so much in the way of the exciting social life she was beginning to enjoy in England. She employed a young Welsh nurse, Kate Griffin (whom the children called 'Nan'), to look after Yolande and Kenneth; and in 1906 the family left the Red House and moved nearby to Meadowcroft, a house in Bolton Avenue, New Windsor, not far from the castle. But then something unexpected happened. 'It was here that I was born in 1907,' writes my father, '– an evident mishap.' The date of his birth was 20 October 1907, and after some debate they named him Basil De Courcy Fraser. What comes through a close reading of my father's account, written near the end of his life, is his sense of being unwanted: an outsider at home, a reject at school, an exile during later life, and inferior to his elder brother and sister. 'I was a sickly infant with a pidgeon [sic] chest and a frail hold on life,' he wrote. 'Nan sat up night after night looking after me, and there is no doubt that I owed my continued presence in the world to her. I saw little of my mother.'

The photographs of him at Windsor from infancy through childhood show him more ill-at-ease than ill. Aged one month he lies awkwardly on a cushion between Yolande and Kenneth who are more interested in the photographer than their new sibling. Later he is being held in place on a pony between the others' smarter horses; and later still he perches precariously on a *chaise-longue* to make a pretty threesome. For these are studio portraits which the proud parents will pass round their friends. Kenneth puts up with this business quite well – he is like someone holding his breath until the ordeal is over, yet still in command of himself. Basil's round face looks vulnerable and bewildered – but then he is the youngest. It is Yolande who appears in her element. She 'makes eyes' at the camera, puts an arm round her younger brother, sits elegantly on her horse. Or she poses alone, bare feet dangling from a podium. And there she is again, reclining on a sofa, studying a flower, standing small and defiant on a bench in the garden. Like her Aunt Norah she focuses, she comes alive, while her brothers look rather wooden or lost.

The children saw a good deal of their mother's sisters and their husbands over these early years, but little of Uncle Pat and his family. He had come back from South Africa with his wife Coral and their son Ivor, been appointed a captain in the Militia in 1903 and gone to live in Hampshire. Here, on 17 November 1908, his daughter Verity was born. My father could not remember going to Ropley Manor, his Uncle Pat's home in Hampshire, and he believed that his Aunt Coral disapproved of Fraser's marriage. The two brothers maintained a rather furtive friendship despite the gap that was appearing between their two families and that would widen over the years.

However, there were plenty of Corbet aunts to entertain the children. Aunt Iley, the pianist, was living not far away at Reigate in Surrey; and jolly punctual Aunt Lizzie they would sometimes visit in Bristol. But my father remembered most vividly going to play at Datchet where his Aunt Ida, the ex-music hall singer, and her husband from the zoo lived. Were the paddocks there really 'full of Zebras, Giraffes and Wildebeasts' as he imagined? 'There was an awful lot to see if one was lucky,' he insisted. There were those bright birds flying in the aviary and animals at the end of the garden ('small ones of course and I've forgotten what they were now'), and a big pond flashing with red and yellow fish in the sunlight. 'Halycon days!' he exclaimed, recovering with his childhood excitement his authentic childhood spelling.

There were three Temple daughters with whom my father sometimes played at Datchet. One, prim and religious, later married a man connected with cigarettes ('Passing Clouds' they were called) and had numerous daughters herself; another took after her father and devoted her life to horses and dogs; while a third, reviving memories of her mother's music hall days, travelled far, gambled long and had, we were told, a child by Rex Harrison. Not a bad family record.

Fraser and Adeline would occasionally leave Nan in charge of the children and go to Ireland where they became 'Josh' and 'Bang' again. There are some exuberant pictures of these holidays with the Corbet sisters, showing them on bridges and rocks against a waterfall or the sea, then in woods with their bicycles and in jaunting carts with horses. And there is one of Josh in his three-piece suit and watch chain, a pipe in his mouth, jumping high in the air. He loved these trips to Ireland and was thinking of buying a house called Greystones near Minnie and Tom White at Bray.

The family sometimes kept photographs but never letters and seldom postcards unless the pictures took their fancy. There is one postcard from this period, kept because the picture was drawn and coloured in by my Aunt Yolande. Written from Brocket, a large, newly-built house at Maidenhead into which the family moved in 1912, it was posted to her mother in Ireland. It tells of an air balloon which 'came right over our house. Nanny was so excited and called Yolande so many times that I thought the house was on fire.' The card is addressed to 8 Prince of Wales Terrace, Bray, and was probably written early in 1914 when Josh still had ideas of moving to Ireland. But the

Great War changed his plans, and a little later Tom and Minnie White came instead to live near Maidenhead.

They came with one of Minnie's sisters, Lannie (my father's favourite aunt) whose husband went off to Australia to make his fortune. He took with him their second son who prospered there and before long was employing his father; but he left in Ireland their elder son who did rather well in the IRA before, things getting too hot for him, he joined his father as a fellow-employee in his brother's Australian business. Lannie's daughter Joan, the youngest child, went with her to Maidenhead and was my father's chief companion in these war years. 'She was certainly closer to me than my own brother and sister,' he writes. One thing they had in common was a lack of confidence. Waiting for the fortune her father never made in Australia and for the call to join him that never seemed to arrive, Joan grew up as a poor relation wearing the cast-off clothes of her cousins, all of whom she hated 'except perhaps myself', my father adds.

The happiest days of my father's life 'were certainly those between the ages of five and eight – before I was sent to school', he wrote. 'I was spoilt by the old Nurse, had a small companion to play with and few worries. Exciting things happened too.' On good days he and Joan would play together among the flashing birds, amazing fish and small animals at Datchet. On bad days the two of them used to be dragged out from their hiding places and sent together to dancing class, Basil shamefully dressed in black velveteen knickers 'which showed every mark if one slid around on the floor for a few happy minutes', Joan in some frock that Yolande or one of her other cousins had discarded. Basil knew how she felt as he had inherited his brother's rotten toys.

Far better were their games outdoors such as drinking a special brew from an old tin and being tremendously sick. Joan often came to play at Brocket. The gardens there were 'the nicest part of all', my father wrote. They were laid out in three tiers with a drop of six feet between them, like a giant's staircase, and made a magical playground. Along the back of the house ran a stone-paved terrace and against its wall were apricots, nectarines and peaches facing southwards to the sun. The top level of the garden next to the house was the adults' play area, which is to say it was largely occupied by a grass tennis court, several formal rosebeds and three willow trees overlooking the second garden below. Flanking the tennis lawn, descending pathways followed the line of two boundary walls against which grew fig, pear and plum trees. On the second level lay the kitchen garden, its fruit and vegetables arranged in big squares and with a central path arched with apple trees that joined two curving flights of steps to the third level. Here stood three long hothouses crammed with black and white grapes and exotic flowers. At this lowest level there were also chicken houses with some fifty chickens wandering in and out of the potting shed, garage and coal yard with its wonderful mountain of black coal, perfect for climbing.

These gardens at Brocket 'were as good as many of the walled gardens in large country houses', my father wrote. From 'asparagus to onions, from gooseberries to quinces we had it all!' He especially liked the black, red and white cherries that gave their fruit in rotation and 'could have fed a small army of children'. Nevertheless he and his brother would sometimes balance themselves on the top of the potting shed and, using a butterfly net mounted on a long bamboo rod, steal some of the horribly sour cooking apples from the garden next door. 'It is the only intimate thing I ever remember doing with my brother as a small boy unless you can count watching my father start the car on Sundays.'

Compared with Kenneth who was a massive three, almost a monumental four, years older, and Yolande who, being a year older still, was almost an adult, Basil seemed a Richmal Crompton urchin-child. But he was happy. He had his own tomboy friend Joan and he lived in a secure and exciting world until the war – not the Great War, but that 'war of my own' which was fought out at his preparatory school.

Scaitcliffe School had been founded in the early eighteen-eighties by the Reverend Doctor Charles Crosslegh. He chose its rather perilous name after his seventeenth-century family house in Lancashire, taking out a ninety-nine-year lease on Crown land near Windsor Park in which to start a cramming establishment for prospective candidates to the Royal Indian Engineering College. Twenty-five years later it had been bought by Ronald Vickers, a classical scholar who, turning his back on the family armaments and engineering business, converted Scaitcliffe into a boys' preparatory school for Eton, Charterhouse, Wellington and other prominent public schools. His family was wealthy – several of them had been painted by John Singer Sargent – and he ran a private school 'because he liked doing it', my father observed. By the time Basil arrived in 1917 the school had some forty boys and was very much a Vickers family enterprise.

My father's difficulties at Scaitcliffe were largely caused, he felt, by his brother. Kenneth had actually left the term before Basil arrived, but his reputation stayed on. He had been a great success: doing wonderful things on the cricket and football pitches, excelling as an intrepid diver into the school plunge, performing miracles in the gym and, despite only scraping into the lowest form at Eton, gaining the approbation of the headmaster. This was not easy. Ronald Vickers was 'a remote austere figure, despite his underlying care and interest', his son Richard admits in the school history. '. . . Discipline was extremely strict.' Except for his academic record, Kenneth 'was everything I wasn't!' my father exclaimed. 'At first my life was absolute hell. I was scared stiff of the bigger boys and when frightened I talked my head off instead of being quiet. I was the butt of the school bullies. My locker was ransacked, my belongings stolen.'

This glimpse of rampageous school life differs from the picture of an extended family presented in the school history. There is no illustration in this book of the most visible Scaitcliffe master, Edgar Ransome (nicknamed Rampoo), but there is a fine description of him which contrasts rather dramatically with my father's boy's-eye view at the age of ten. Richard Vickers writes:

> Despite his great size – he weighed over 20 stone – he was
> a slow bowler of considerable skill who regularly
> attended nets each morning of the summer term. He was
> also a fine amateur pianist, whose rollicking songs were
> always an amusing interlude on winter evenings. His class
> presence was truly formidable, so woe-betide any boy
> who was slow to learn his tables or whose writing strayed
> from the line during copy-book exercises.

Certainly he must have had a lasting effect on my father whose writing never strayed from the line until his final illness. Ransome was the junior form master at Scaitcliffe for twenty-six years before retiring to be a tobacconist in Basingstoke. To cover his bald head he always wore a cap, and became 'pre-eminent' among the 'great characters of the school's early years'. But my father greatly feared and disliked him. 'I never quite understood how Ransome got a job at Scaitcliffe,' he wrote.

> He was a particularly coarse old man with a large
> stomach and a big fleshy hooked nose from the end of
> which hung a permanent dew drop. He couldn't even
> speak correctly, so heaven knows why [Ronald] Vickers, a
> purist, came to engage him.
>   One of my worst recollections of Scaitcliffe was being
> made to stand in the corridor for bad behaviour. Should
> Vickers happen to come along the culprit got six sharp

cuts with the cane. Edgar Ransome, who took the lowest class of very small boys, loved to inflict this form of punishment. His classroom was opposite Vickers's Study door, so the unfortunates were particularly vulnerable.

Basil could not wait for the holidays. During the war, the family spent more time at Brocket, but because of school he was seeing less of Joan. By the age of twelve his best friend had become his dog, a mongrel officially named Pat whom he called 'Woorah' – 'I don't know why.' Looking back at this period he was to write: 'I loved my dog dearly but did nothing for him. Nan [Kate Griffin] fed, sometimes bathed and generally looked after all our animals. My contribution was to reckon up how long he could live and imagine there would be no world for me when he died. And now I can't even remember how he died or when.' Knowing as I do his last solitary years with his dog, this passage has for me an almost Johnsonian tone of self-recrimination.

My father's last year at Scaitcliffe was more tolerable. Memories of his glamorous elder brother were receding and he himself was a bigger boy now – not someone who could easily be bullied or have his locker ransacked. He was playing cricket and football not too badly. He had escaped from Ransome's form and there were fewer beatings. He had even learnt when to be quiet and not talk his head off. 'I wasn't too unhappy,' he concluded. 'I kept out of the way.'

I have no photographs of my father at Scaitcliffe, only one of a school group taken in the grounds shortly before he arrived, with my Uncle Kenneth standing eyes half-closed in the back row, and the formidably handsome Ronald Vickers seated at the centre, the solitary adult, with a cricket ball in his hand: an intimidating figure.

Between the ages of seven and eleven my father didn't notice the Great War much. The same seemed to hold true for Fraser. His brother Pat, having been transferred to a regular battalion of the Royal Welch Fusiliers in 1915, made his Will and went off to fight in France. By 1917 he was back with the reserve battalion and retired after the war while in his forties. It was said in the family that he suffered, this amiable man, from shell-shock and that this was aggravated by domestic warfare. Certainly his career was modest by the standards of the two major-generals, his father and father-in-law, and he seems to have been a disappointment to his wife Coral who, according to my father, taught both their children (in particular their son Ivor) to despise him.

Coral already despised Fraser who took no part in the Great War allegedly on account of his varicose veins. So how, apart from fathering his three children and being 'of independent means', did my grandfather occupy himself in the first twenty-five years of his marriage before the big disaster?

At the beginning he seems to have had a notion of taking up the law. On 22 November 1899, some seven months after his marriage, he entered Gray's Inn (where George Sowley Holroyd had been admitted the previous century), enrolling at the private college run by the Bar Council. The Register of King's College, Cambridge, has a note of his studentship, and the Uppingham School Roll notes that he went on to qualify as a barrister. Actually he took no law examinations but shortly after the death of his first son he left the college to look after Adeline.

Over the next fifteen years he seems to have done very little but look after Adeline. She needed looking after – indeed she insisted on it. All the children could see what was going on. Their mother got more attention at home than any of them did. She was their rival. Whenever she didn't get her own way, she would have violent hysterics – like firework displays they were – and Fraser, who was a naïve and kindly man, was pricked with self-reproach. For he had really married the Corbet family, and the barometer of his happiness shot up whenever he was among them *en masse*. Bang wasn't allowed any of her tantrums when her sisters were around – they teased her too much. 'What's the difference between a man and an umbrella?' her sister Lizzie called out at one of Bang's bridge parties. All the card players stopped and looked up. 'Really, Lizzie, whatever are you talking about?' Bang answered. 'I'm sure I don't know.'

'Well, you damn well ought to – you've been under both of them.'

The implication was that sex was as enjoyable for Bang as a rainy afternoon. She lusted instead after a refined life. When none of her sisters were at Brocket, Adeline would put on operatic performances, crying out that she was not long for this world, that people would miss her when she was gone. She would send up many quivering Hail Marys and pray for the good Lord to take her – she was still playing these scenes fifty years later when I was among the audience. Alarmed by her mysterious illnesses, Fraser sent her to many specialists. They gave her their most expensive attention, but the mystery of her illness remained unsolved.

In 1900, after leaving Gray's Inn, Fraser had been made a director of the Rajmai Tea Company and would regularly see his brother Pat at the board meetings. These meetings were pleasant social affairs, spiced with tales from the East. Pat and Fraser enjoyed spending this time together without their wives.

But everything began to change in 1914. Adeline could not compete with the war. All men had to do something then. So what did Fraser do? According to the Uppingham School Roll, he joined the Stock Exchange. The Stock Exchange itself has no record of his membership. But my father remembered that Fraser had got a job with a shrewd German financier called Lowenfelt two or three years before the war. Lowenfelt started a firm called the Investment Registry in Waterloo Place. It was a lucrative business and Fraser made some money by taking Lowenfelt's advice to invest in rubber shares. Unfortunately, he did not take Lowenfelt's advice as to when he should sell the shares, and lost much of his gains after the development of synthetic rubber. Nevertheless he made some profit.

It was probably a mistake for my grandfather to have left the Investment Registry – it was to carry on in Grafton Street and London Wall into the nineteen-sixties. That he did leave was partly due to the uncomfortable sensation of having a German as his partner during this war against the Germans. It had an unpatriotic air. Besides, Lowenfelt was also a Jew which in those blatant days was additionally unpopular in England, though it hadn't told with Fraser before the war. In any event, listening to others, he seems to have persuaded himself that there was something 'ungentlemanly', if not actually illegal, about Lowenfelt's manipulation of the share market. Lowenfelt was a man ahead of his times, and already Fraser was falling behind the times. My grandfather's modest success at the Investment Registry persuaded him that he was 'a safe pair of hands' in business matters. He debated whether to pick up a more suitable business partner or go it alone, and then steered somewhere between these choices. In 1915 he decided to buy a patent cleaner from a naval captain he had recently met. It was a miraculous machine which, Captain Jennings assured him, would revolutionise the world of house decorating. There was nothing, not even the most dulled paintwork or delicate fabric, that this restorative device, filled with its finning formula, could not make new – and so quickly it took one's breath away. My breathless grandfather wanted to call the new company he created round this machine 'Brevis', signifying its amazing speed, but this name had been taken by another company, and so he named it 'Breves' meaning nothing at all, which is what he got. He took premises at the Knightsbridge end of Sloane Street, employed some staff and, as company secretary, chose a charming and penniless old man who had been hammered on the Stock Exchange. He had a long white silky moustache, always dressed immaculately in spats, and was devoted to my grandfather for rescuing him from poverty. Like schoolboys, the two of them would disappear behind a locked door to mix buckets of the secret formula which were then reverently handed to the works manager. It took a year, following the unexplained disappearance of Captain Jennings, for them to conclude from the flaking paintwork and faded fabrics that their magic substance, known as 'the Breves Process', did rather more harm than good.

My grandfather was determined to turn expensive failure into expansive success. He acted boldly, moving from 15 Sloane Street to larger premises, Imperial Court, between Harrods and Harvey Nichols, round the corner in Basil Street. Here he sought to develop the business. In the nineteen-twenties directories, Breves is listed as 'builders, decorators, electrical, heating and sanitary engineers, furnishers, designers and manufacturers of panelling, parquet floors, upholstery, carpets, bedding, curtains, blinds, picture restorers, vacuum cleaners, removals'. In short, Breves did everything and, like a circus performer, did it all at once. It made a small loss each year.

But my grandfather was still a man of wealth. Brocket, his home at Maidenhead, was an imposing, red-brick, Edwardian house with attics and cellars full of servants. The family owned a carriage and pair and, after 1908 when Fraser bought an Enfield Allday, they had a car. The ex-coachman, Thatcher, drove it during the week and my grandfather took over the wheel at weekends. Then there was my grandmother Adeline, 'one of the most accomplished backseat drivers in the country', according to my father. Fraser himself did not drive for long: the new technology did not suit him. The Enfield Allday, for example, having no self-starter, had to be 'wound with a starting handle', my father remembered. 'There was too a petrol tap which had to be turned on to allow the petrol to flow from the tank to the carburettor. This small point my father always overlooked. My brother and I used to hide behind the garage and listen to him trying to start the car. It was rare entertainment.'

My father's time at Scaitcliffe ended abruptly. In his account he wrote: 'When I was twelve Vickers made me sit for the Common Entrance examination. He did so, he said, to accustom me to sitting an exam. He made it abundantly clear that I hadn't the faintest chance of passing, so it was to everyone's dismay that I achieved the bottom form at Eton.' He was still in the lower half of Scaitcliffe and had been there little more than two-and-a-half years. He had obviously longed to get away, but did so just as he was beginning to enjoy the place.

What he had endured at Scaitcliffe, he now endured again at Eton, only it was worse because his brother was not simply a glowing memory but a very obvious presence in the school – 'one hell of a big fellow'. And he was not pleased to see his younger brother turning up so unexpectedly. Kenneth was 'in the library' which meant he was among the elite of their school house. He played for the 'twenty-two' (Eton's second cricket eleven) and also had his Field colours (which meant he was in the top team of that peculiar Eton game which somehow fails to combine the qualities of soccer and rugger). Above all Kenneth was a member of the fabulous Eton society known as 'Pop' which meant he could wear fantastically coloured waistcoats and 'stick-up' white collars that dazzled younger boys. In the school hierarchy it was impossible for such a swell to talk to a lower boy. Not understanding the social oligarchy of the school, Basil was hurt that his brother with whom he sometimes stole apples from the potting shed roof at Brocket had no word for him at Eton. 'My brother actively disliked me and avoided as much as possible having anything to do with me,' he remembered. He obviously embarrassed Kenneth. 'As usual when nervous I gave my half-witted display,' he concluded with a Thurber-like touch, 'and set a seal on my misery.'

In his diaries, the novelist Anthony Powell, writing some seventy years later, remembers being in the same division as my father, whom he described as being 'red-faced, hearty, one would say boring'. But he adds that he 'did not know him at all'. Since there was two years' difference in age between them, this Holroyd seems more likely to have been my uncle who was closer in age to Powell and, by Etonian standards, far more boringly successful.

Basil forgot the trick he picked up at Scaitcliffe of keeping 'out of the way' and reverted to his nervous habit of talking 'my head off'. That was the voice my mother was first to hear on board the *Suecia* when she sailed to England, the voice which was so raucous on bad days and, on good days, could 'talk anybody into anything'. That he did not relearn the discretion of his late Scaitcliffe period may have been due to his removal from Eton after a little over two years. 'I got double pneumonia and was taken in an ambulance to Brocket.' After an examination by the family doctor and a period of convalescence looked after by Nan, he was sent to Leysin in Switzerland. 'I was pronounced in good order within a few weeks,' he wrote. 'Then came the question of whether I returned to Eton or not. My mother, still convinced that I was ailing, opted for a Swiss education. She found the story of my fight for life very tellable at her weekly bridge parties. So I was sent to Chillon College.'

There my father's narrative stops. The difference between Chillon and Eton 'was immense', he wrote. 'I had spent most of my time loathing Eton.' Yet he would have preferred to return there than remain a prisoner of Chillon. Kenneth had now left for Clare College, Cambridge; so Basil had survived the bad years, and happier times lay ahead. I never heard my father speak of Chillon College which must have been near Geneva but which no longer exists (neither the Municipalité de Leysin nor the Fédération Suisse des Ecoles Privées has any knowledge of it). It was evidently one of those private boarding schools that specialise in educating American, British, French, German and Italian nationals, some of whose parents work in Switzerland, others of whom are sent abroad to be 'finished'. For my father it represented exile, under the shadow of failure at Eton.

He remained in Chillon for the best part of two years. But now that people could travel abroad again in the early nineteen-twenties, his family was able to visit him, starting their holidays in Switzerland and travelling leisurely back through France. It was at Dinard, the fashionable watering-place in Brittany, my father remembered, that during one of these journeys Fraser first saw a display of Lalique glass. Later, in about 1926, he went to a Lalique exhibition mounted at showrooms in Great Portland Street. It had been brought over to London by the Curzon family following a grand exposition of decorative art in Paris. Though the glass did not attract great attention in the British newspapers, it impressed my grandfather who went over to Paris the following year, saw René Lalique and tried to get himself appointed sole agent for the glass in 'Britain and the Empire'. He was just too late, the agency having been acquired by 'a likeable rogue' called Keir. But Fraser managed to pull off a deal with Mr Keir. He now had the magical ingredient, like the earlier 'Breves Process', necessary for success.

Between the mid-nineteen-twenties and the mid-nineteen-thirties my grandfather pursued an extraordinary strategy. He sold for cash, or lodged with Barclays Bank as a means of raising loans, all his Rajmai Tea shares – indeed he got rid of ninety more shares than he actually possessed (these ninety shares were 'sold' to his friend 'Nipper' Anderson and must have been part of a 'gentleman's agreement'). He then acquired another 1,000 shares and used them to get more loans. By these means he raised the equivalent today of almost one million pounds. What was so strange about this programme is that it went against everything in which he believed. He disapproved of selling shares, most especially Rajmai shares, because it struck him as an act of disloyalty. It was this rapid buying and selling, this playing of the market, that he had disliked in Lowenfelt. Also, tea was doing rather well in the nineteen-twenties before the government placed a fourpenny tax on it. The Industrial Fatigue Research Board had come up with the finding that 'a cup of tea aids efficiency and curbs industrial discontent'. It was patriotic to drink Indian tea in Britain. You drank it for prosperity as you would later dig vegetables for victory. A survey in 1927 showed that the British were drinking more tea and less beer – and also that birth rate figures were falling.

But Lalique glass dazzled Fraser and, though they did not guess why he had taken this dramatic change of direction, it seems to have been uniformly popular in his family. Adeline liked having it around the house; Yolande thought it beautiful; and the two boys, Kenneth and Basil, saw a future for themselves in this new family business – a far brighter future than on a tea plantation. René Lalique, then in his mid-sixties, had become recognised as a pioneer in this Age of Glass. He was an astonishingly versatile artist who exploited its texture and colour, using motifs from nature (flowers, fish, birds, animals) in the jewellery, sculpture and ornamental tableware he designed in his Paris studio. Fraser gazed at this glass as if it were a magic crystal. He looked about him – there were hunger marches, miners' strikes, lengthening dole queues and street demonstrations protesting against unemployment throughout Britain; there was the Wall Street Crash in the United States, civil disobedience in India, the Japanese invasion of Manchuria, revolution in Argentina, revolt in Peru, the rise of Hitler in Germany and Mussolini in Italy, and throughout the world an economic crisis – Fraser looked and saw, reflected in his glass, that all was well. The omens were good, he decided, for further business expansion.

The Basil Street offices were converted with a Chinese-style background into glittering showrooms by 1928. A gallery, with beige carpets, walnut veneers to the showcases, and brown walls paling into ivory at the ceiling, was prepared during the early nineteen-thirties in New Bond Street. A special lighting division was set up in Newman Street, off the Tottenham Court Road. There was also a smart office in Brown's Arcade near Oxford Circus and an apartment in Carlyle Square in Chelsea, where orders were dispatched and drinking glasses, salad dishes, scent bottles, flower vases, car mascots, glass sparrows, fish, cocks, horses, eagles and other amazing objets d'art sent out on approval. The Breves Lalique catalogues during the late nineteen-twenties and the nineteen-thirties show the wonderful range of goblets, bowls and plates, jugs and decanters, stat-uettes, paperweights, ashtrays that became available, decorated with leaves, dragonflies, peacocks, beetles, swallows, sunflowers, cupids, water-nymphs – a witty, decadent array.

My grandfather gave a magnificent fancy-dress party in Knightsbridge for everyone associated with 'Breves Lalique Galleries'. It was opening time in the West End. The lights were switched on, and all stood dazzled and ready for the boom which my grandfather sensed would sweep through the business world, bringing prosperity to the nineteen-thirties and a well-earned peace into which he could retire in the nineteen-forties.

This was to be my father's future. Meanwhile, the School Clerk's records at Eton have him going up to University College, Oxford, in the summer of 1925. But if that was his intention he did not carry it out. Instead (and to my surprise since he never referred to it) he turns up as a pensioner (that is, an ordinary student without financial assistance from the college) at Trinity College, Cambridge, in the Michaelmas term of 1926, having passed one paper in mathematics for the ordinary Bachelor of Arts degree in Easter that year. The examination he took was called 'The sun, the stars, and the universe'. But as he studied only one subsidiary course, 'I do not think that your father was intending to take an ordinary B.A.,' writes Jonathan Smith from

Trinity College Library. 'Your father's social life here is a bit of a mystery. Unfortunately he does not show in our personal names index to club and society records, nor does he make an appearance in the *Trinity Review*.'

What a contrast to Kenneth at Clare College! He appears in pictures of all sorts of clubs, teams, societies with a sheen of maturity spread over his rather blasé handsome features, so resplendent in his gleaming blazer, so sophisticated with his casual cigarette. And he had worked a bit too. He is listed in the third class for parts I and II of the Architectural Diploma, and in the second class for part III. It is not a bad record for someone who had entered the lowly Third Form at Eton.

My father stayed only four terms at Trinity and 'left without a degree'. He had left Scaitcliffe early by accident; he had left Eton early through illness; why had he left Cambridge early too? No one has the answer to this until I happen to mention it to one of Kenneth's stepsons. He tells me that my uncle (his stepfather) revealed that Basil had celebrated his return from Switzerland by amassing spectacular gambling debts at Cambridge.

It must have been shortly after my father went down from Cambridge that Fraser, having paid off all his debts, made him and Kenneth directors of Breves Lalique in the late nineteen-twenties. 'In my brother's case it could have been all right,' my father commented, 'but in mine it was madness.' Yet it was a fine madness, and nothing is so becoming in Fraser's career as his championing of Lalique with his two sons in the decade before the Second World War.

# 6

## *The Coming of Agnes May*

To all but his children, Fraser had kept his marriage looking reasonably harmonious all these years. But he was deeply unhappy. Why was Adeline so discontented? Was it his fault? He was always buying her costly trinkets – surely she had everything she wanted? And that was probably the trouble: she wanted such unrewarding things and did not know why they failed to satisfy her.

Of all the Corbet sisters, Adeline had probably made the best marriage – or so it seemed. Yet she was the one who always complained. While she was crying out that she was at death's door, it was the others who actually died. And when she prayed to God to relieve her of some disaster, it seemed that these disasters were visited on her sisters. Two of these sisters, the delicate Atty and the mysterious Sloper, had passed away very young and long ago in Ireland. Then the beautiful Alice, having finally married 'Nipper' Anderson, was drowned while sailing away with him for a new life in the United States. Iley now had Parkinson's Disease – they would put her hands on the piano and she would play a few bars, then stop: and soon she stopped altogether. Lizzie's life was also clouded by an awful tragedy, one of her twin sons having been run down and killed in the road outside her house. Her brother-in-law, the jovial Tom White, had grown enormous – over eighteen stone – and on medical advice taken up golf (though it was said he could never see the ball). He and his wife Minnie (a mere sixteen stone) would play together at Maidenhead. One day Tom broke his club and seemed to explode. He was presented with his death certificate on the sofa afterwards at Brocket. Minnie went on playing rather half-heartedly, but did not long survive him. Lannie had by this time received her passage money to Australia – had in fact received it more than once. But she would not go, even though her beloved daughter Joan, now living with her lesbian girlfriend in England, had quarrelled and refused to see her anymore. But after her 'protectors' Tom and Minnie died, she could no longer stay. So finally she went, and was given a pittance by her son and restricted access to her grandchildren over what was to be a lonely exile in Australia.

That was how life had treated those delicious Corbet girls who, in my grandfather's eyes, appeared to possess the very secret of happiness.

Fraser had attempted to shield Adeline from such disasters. Perhaps he had shielded her too much. Was there some extra apprehension that called forth his protection – a fear of the unknown, untreatable by her doctors? So much was unknown to Adeline. She had learnt little at school and little from her married life. No one had really bothered to teach her anything, and her imagination never came alive except when sensing danger. The world was teeming with danger: a shopping trip to London, a matinée in the theatre, lunch at a restaurant – all had their risks. Being uncertain of so much, she pretended and was perceived as being pretentious. She did not really love anyone, was loved neither by her husband nor her children, and never realised what was lacking or how she might attract it. All she knew, as she went on with her bridge parties each week and giving attention to her dogs, was that life had turned out a disappointment.

Adeline and Fraser had been together for over a quarter-of-a-century, and perhaps theirs was no worse than many marriages. People did not get divorced so easily then. But the times were changing. They were to change for Fraser and Adeline after the General Strike of 1926.

After the war my grandfather used to be driven by Thatcher in his Lancia each day from Maidenhead up to Basil Street in Knightsbridge. Passing through Hammersmith in the second week of May 1926, he told his chauffeur to stop the car and give a lift to a woman who was standing on the pavement – many people were giving lifts during the General Strike. As a courteous gentleman Fraser must have thought it his duty to help this voluptuous-looking, well-dressed young woman in distress, with her fine eyes, full lips and welcoming smile. It was the very least he could do – indeed he desired to do more. In the car, they got talking and by the time they reached their destination in the West End they found that they had not exhausted all they had to say to each other. So they arranged to meet that evening and continue their conversation . . .

The lady's name was Agnes May Babb. She was thirty years old – that is twenty years younger than my grandfather – though she admitted to being only in her late twenties. And she was married – in fact had already been twice married, though it seems unlikely that my grandfather knew this. Agnes May's first husband had been a young accountant called William Reynolds Lisle. He was made a Second Lieutenant in a London regiment shortly before she married him in 1916. Both of them gave their address as Rose Cottage, Barrow Green Lane, Oxted, in Surrey. He was the son of a solicitor (who had recently died leaving him a nice inheritance) and, on the marriage certificate, she agreed that her father too had been a solicitor, and was also dead.

Rather curiously she gave her Christian names as 'Maimie Archie' – almost as if she had not been quite sober at the time. But that perhaps was understandable as her husband was off to fight in the war. Against the odds, Second Lieutenant Lisle survived the war. In his petition for a divorce, which came to court towards the end of 1919 and was made absolute on 19 July 1920, his wife's name is correctly given and she is cited as respondent. But there is no co-respondent which suggests that she deserted him almost immediately after the marriage.

Then she went up a couple of ranks. Eleven days after her divorce came through she married Thomas George Symonds Babb, a thirty-three-year-old, previously-unmarried Captain in the Royal Engineers. Both gave their address as 187 Ladbroke Grove, a large late-Victorian terraced house some three hundred yards from where I am writing this book.

Thomas Babb was the son of a hotel proprietor in Minehead, and on the marriage certificate Agnes May agreed that her father too had been a hotel proprietor. As soon as they married they left London, but six years later she is separated from her husband and back in London, standing on the pavement in Hammersmith, waiting for a lift.

How much of this past history my grandfather got to know I cannot tell. Certainly Agnes May's two husbands were not meant to find out that she was the daughter of a humble glass-grinder, Joseph Bickerstaff, from St Helens in Lancashire – her sophisticated voice showed little trace of a north country accent. She was unlike any other woman my grandfather had known, a fast smart modern woman of the nineteen-twenties as thrilling to him as the Corbet sisters had been thirty years ago in Ireland. He quickly became infatuated with her. But what was he to do?

What he did shocked everyone – it was so dramatically out of character. He left home and put himself up at the Royal Automobile Club's palatial Edwardian hotel-and-headquarters in Pall Mall (sometimes called 'the Chauffeurs Arms' by members of senior clubs). And he bought a twenty-one-year lease on an apartment a few hundred yards away in Piccadilly into which Agnes May moved in the summer of 1927. From the second floor of Berkeley House, 81 Piccadilly, on the opposite side of the road from the Ritz Hotel and not far from Lord Palmerston's old house, her rooms looked pleasantly across Green Park towards Buckingham Palace. The yearly rent of this love nest was £1,250 – equivalent to no more than £40,000 a year in the late nineteen-nineties.

But this was not my grandfather's only fresh expenditure. He had to make separate provisions for his wife and children. This he attempted to do by means of a legal arrangement, the trustees of which were his old friends 'Nipper' Anderson (who had of course been married to Adeline's sister Alice) and his partner in the tea business, Richard Magor, whose father had befriended Fraser's father in India.

It was on his 'Indian fortune' that Fraser was relying to support his new way of life. From 1 July 1927 he covenants to pay his trustees, for the rest of his life, one-half of his income from the Rajmai Tea Company for the benefit of his wife and three children. Rajmai Tea shares are not the sort of happy-go-lucky shares that are bought and sold by anyone and everyone on the open market – the sort of shares from which Lowenfelt made his dubious profits for the Investment Registry. On the contrary, they were shares in a private company, reliable shares owned by one or two families and their loyal friends that had the same nominal value of £10 a share as they had when Major-General Charles Holroyd listed them among his assets in the previous century. Of course, if they somehow did make their way on to the Stock Exchange, there is every reason to feel that by now they would fetch considerably more than £10 apiece. But there is no need for them to be traded in that fashion: they are rock solid, part of Britain's undented tradition. The nominal value of Fraser's shares is a little under £30,000. But their true worth is incalculable. They are, in the Holroyd family's legend, priceless, invaluable, beyond dreams.

Apart from this income Fraser allows Adeline and their children the occupation of Brocket and the use of its contents. In the event of his death there are binding guarantees reaching into the next generation. But he retains the right to sell his Rajmai Tea shares if 'he shall in his absolute discretion think fit', then reinvest his fortune and divide the renewed income in the same proportions.

My grandmother made it clear that she would never consent to a divorce. After all, she was an Irish Catholic and knew her rights and duties, knew what was proper, knew that the shock of it all would kill her and that her husband would forever have it on his conscience. But that Fraser, who for thirty years had given every appearance of being ruled by conscience, could so far have forgotten himself flabbergasted her. She had thought him such a safe pair of hands. She did not keep quiet about the catastrophe. She told everyone. She wrote letters to Ireland and Australia; and she made terrific and terrible scenes in Maidenhead. Everyone at Brocket was familiar with her ascending Hail Marys, her dramatic pleas for wingèd death to carry her off; but their repetition and the increase in their volume chaffed at the children's embarrassment. They wished she would shut up, though reluctantly recognising that this time she had some justification.

Yolande, Kenneth and Basil all preferred their father to their mother. His was the more sympathetic presence, and yet they were not really close to him. 'He is not of a nature to confide in others, & keeps his feelings to himself,' his own father had written to Oscar Browning, and that was how he remained. The

Archbishop of Canterbury was soon to announce his approval
of free sexual discussion. But such a thing was absolutely impossible for my grandfather and his children. The only intimacy
they really shared was one of English awkwardness. Yolande,
Kenneth and Basil were in their early twenties, easily shocked,
quick to judgement. 'We were horrified by the slur cast on the
family name,' my father wrote in the fragment of his account.
'How could we ever hold up our heads again? How could he
have done it?'

It seems that Fraser told them almost nothing, that he could
not bring himself to speak of such things, could not even bear to
see his children. They were left in a vacuum. 'We cannot judge a
man,' one of Yolande's friends wrote to her, 'as their tempera-
ments & everything are so different from ours & they do things
hastily.' Among the family at large there was general incredulity.
'I'm absolutely lost for words to say about Uncle Joshie,' wrote
a cousin from Australia. 'It all sounds to me like a dream as
Uncle Josh was the one man in the world that I believed in . . . I
think that temporally he must be unbalanced and that sooner or
later he will realise the great mistake he is making . . . he was
such a model I simply *can't* convince myself that it is true. If my
own father left, heavens I would be singing a hymn of thanks-
giving . . .' But none of Fraser's children were thankful he had
left. And none of them seemed capable of understanding what
had happened.

Except for the allusive couple of pages my father wrote fifty
years later and a strange legal document, there was nothing to
mark or record the break-up of the marriage. The few photograph albums among my Aunt Yolande's possessions suggest an
uninterrupted passage of smiling summer holidays. There are
groups of the family with dogs and tennis rackets at Brocket;
and snaps taken on trips to Greece, Turkey and Sicily – the
Acropolis at Athens, the Sancta Sophia and Blue Mosque at
Constantinople, the Chapel of the Royal Palace and the

Monreale Monastery at Palermo, all visited in 1927. But mostly there are holiday shots of Yolande in the South of France: at Antibes in 1928; Juan-les-Pins and Cap Ferrat in 1929; Monte Carlo between 1930 and 1932. There she is sunbathing and picnicking on the beach. I am astonished to see her water-skiing behind speedy motor-boats. She still takes almost as good a photograph as she did when she was a precocious child, and she looks happy with her friends Cathie and Cynthia and Freda, though this is the period of her father's decampment. Clearly these holidays, longer and more luxurious than at any other time, are designed as an escape from this distressful family break-up. In the background occasionally, and sometimes in a group posed on deckchairs, Adeline appears; but of course Fraser is never to be seen, nor are Kenneth and Basil often there. They have their own friends elsewhere, and besides they are now directors of the famous Lalique enterprise on which the family fortunes, including the continuation of these holidays abroad, will depend. Apparently it does not occur to them that their father's change of business life may be part of his emotional and sexual change of life. They do not see the disposal of the Rajmai Tea shares as a letting-go of his family past, or the purchase of Lalique glass as his embracing of Agnes May's contemporary glamour. But then they do not know that Agnes May's father had been a glass-grinder.

Kenneth and Basil themselves kept almost nothing from their past, and among Yolande's three or four cardboard boxes there is little except the photograph albums of people and dogs – the people, if not the dogs, usually unidentified. There are a few papers, but they are mainly notes for the milkman, old cheques for tiny sums, reminders from the Eastbourne Mutual Building Society, a newspaper cutting on 'the ABC of Purchase Tax', a receipt for shoe repairs (3s 6d) and an advertisement recommending analgesic tablets. Some of these items are stuffed into a torn and ragged evening bag of soft red

morocco. There are several old letters too, among which is the
one already quoted, from a cousin in Australia, dated 20
December 1926, expressing amazement at Uncle Joshie's temporary madness. Otherwise the creased and faded bits and
pieces belong to later years. But in the lining of this dilapidated
red bag I find three or four extra papers that cannot have seen
the light for more than half-a-century. One is apparently in
code. It is scribbled in pencil and difficult to make out even
with a magnifying glass in sharp light. I call in a second opinion, my wife's. As part of her biography of Angus Wilson, she
has been doing research on the codebreakers at Bletchley Park,
and after a few minutes she solves the puzzle. We are reading a
special recipe for de-worming dogs. The other pages come
from three short letters written by Fraser and sent to Yolande
from the Royal Automobile Club in October and November
1926.

My grandfather's handwriting has not altered greatly since he
wrote the only other letter I have seen – to Oscar Browning in
1895 – which is in the library at King's College, Cambridge. He
has a clear, handsome, flowing hand with, nevertheless, the odd
word regularly crossed out. The first letter is simply a note to be
delivered by hand:

> I have been very seriously ill and am not yet in a
> condition to stand further worry.
>    With all my love
>        ever yr fond & devoted Dad.

This serious illness, whatever its exact nature, recalls his
breakdown at Cambridge. The other two notes his daughter
kept are also written from the RAC apparently one month later,
and both are incomplete. The shorter of them concerns some
money for Yolande's wedding. 'I enclose a cheque value £20 to
pay for your wedding clothes,' he writes. 'Early next month

£175 [£150 has been crossed out] will be paid into your a/c making £275 since last June.' This amount (equivalent over six months to £8,000 in the late nineteen-nineties, or presumably £16,000 a year) is an allowance the details of which, her father adds, can be better explained by a Peter Rawlins of 45 King William Street, London Bridge. The handsome Peter Rawlins had been an admirer of Yolande's Aunt Lannie in the days before she went to Australia. So Fraser is keeping everything, as it were, in the family. Yolande has evidently been sending letters to her father at the RAC, and eventually he agrees to see her. He also agrees that, as a wedding gift, 'you can certainly have a piece of Lalique'. The note ends at the foot of the page without a signature. 'My love and affection for you have not changed & I am not the character some may wish you to believe.'

Perhaps the separation between husband and wife had been too long postponed. In any event it seems to have been peculiarly bitter, and whereas the unpleasantness of it all paralysed Fraser, it released a hailstorm of recrimination from Adeline. Her husband is now a wolf in sheep's clothing. The children cannot credit this. Certainly they do not want to, but they do not know what to believe. The worst that can be said of him, they think, is that he is weak. For years they have seen how weak he has been with their mother. Is he now being weak with another woman?

Yolande's pressing letters to her father are obviously not unsympathetic but they express her bewilderment. What were the facts? Surely it must be possible to put everything right by a family discussion about it all? Fraser's last note is his reply to this suggestion.

Discussions more especially on subjects where I am
unable to make concessions are distressing, & when I
know that your minds have been poisoned by
misrepresentation & the withholding of important facts.
    I am grieved that you have felt the strain of the

position – your letters were greatly appreciated – but because I am not for the *moment* able to confide in you please trust me & do not believe all you hear. Time will I am sure show that your belief in me is not misplaced & this will I hope repay you for the sorrow you have suffered.

I have been wronged for years and it was only my love for you three children which enabled me to endure so long.

You are & will always be in my thoughts – I have no wish to ostracise . . .

And there the letter stops. There is no mention of the woman in the case. Perhaps, by staying at the Royal Automobile Club, Fraser was concealing her presence in his life for as long as possible. But by the early summer of 1927, after he bought her the flat in Piccadilly and made his legal Settlement with Adeline and his family, the truth must have been known to them all. It was the old story. Adeline was aged fifty and Agnes May thirty. Adeline had given birth to four children; Agnes May apparently had no children. She was a glaringly attractive woman – an expensive tart, my father irritably thought when he eventually met her, whom Fraser insisted on treating as a great lady. But she was also sympathetic and understanding, sexy and loving to Fraser who believed that Adeline's loveless complaints over the years had worn away all good feeling and were the real cause of their failed marriage. At any rate, he could stand no more. He had that special sensitivity to women that some men whose mothers die early retain all their lives. The fact that his mother had killed herself may have acted on him as an inhibition – though I do not know whether he was ever told that she had killed herself. In any event, his need had grown so acute through neglect that he was driven to actions which people who thought they knew him found incredible.

But what had attracted Agnes May to Fraser? He was in his early fifties, six feet tall but rather bent, with ears that stuck out as if straining to understand what was going on, and bald though his face was decorated with what, after the rise of Hitler, was to be known as a Hitler moustache. He was a generous but not a glamorous man, a gentleman in the Edwardian style who, though desperately wanting to be young, could not shimmy or foxtrot or even 'Tip-toe through the Tulips'. He would have liked to belong to the new generation with its jazz and tangoes, its naughty sentimental songs, but he could not really join in. His moment of youth had been too long delayed; and what Agnes May gave him, however vital and necessary, was probably as much part of his imaginative as his physical life. He did not care much for nightclubs and cabarets, *thés dansants* and musicals. Also he felt guilty at being unable to 'do the right thing' and offer Agnes May marriage, and did not object when she called herself Mrs Holroyd.

The affaire lasted four years altogether, during three of which Agnes May lived in Piccadilly as Fraser's mistress. Then he had grown tired and she had become bored. The arrangements for their separation were spelt out in an extraordinary Deed of Covenant dated 5 May 1930 and drawn up by a solicitor in Clarges Street, round the corner from Berkeley House, representing Agnes May. In consideration of 'past services' and from 'motives of concern for her interest', Fraser states that he is 'desirous of securing to her' the payment of £33 6s 8d each month – or in other words £400 a year (equivalent to £13,000 seventy years later). The first payment has already been made on 1 April, and these monthly payments were to continue for ten years or during the joint lives of them both 'whichever of two such periods shall be the larger'.

But there are conditions attached to these payments. Agnes May must lead a chaste life. If she 'returns to cohabitation with her husband' Thomas Babb, or divorces him and remarries, then

THIS **DEED OF COVENANT** is made the *fifth* day of May One thousand nine hundred and thirty **BETWEEN EDWARD FRASER ROCHEFORT HOLROYD** of Berkeley House, 81, Piccadilly, London, W.1., (hereinafter called "the Grantor") of the one part and **AGNES MAY BABB** c/o Stanley Attenborough & Co., of 4, Clarges Street, London, W.1., (hereinafter called "the Annuitant") of the other part **WHEREAS** the Grantor in consideration of the past services of the Annuitant and from motives of concern for her interest is desirous of securing to her the payments hereinafter mentioned **NOW THIS DEED WITNESSETH** as follows:-

1. The Grantor for the consideration aforesaid hereby covenants with the Annuitant that he the Grantor will

provided and on conditi... Arbitrators or an umpire whose decision shall be absolutely conclusive and binding on all parties and this shall be deemed an agreement for a reference within the Arbitration Act 1889.

IN WITNESS whereof the parties hereto have hereunto set their hands and seals the day and year first above written.

SIGNED SEALED AND DELIVERED by the above named Agnes May Babb in the presence of :-

*Agnes May Babb*

the monthly allowance will be forfeited. And there are other things she must not do: she must not call herself Mrs Holroyd any longer; she must not 'come to reside within two miles' of Fraser's family house at Maidenhead or 'hold any communication' with his family; she must not lay claim to 'his Lancia car' or become a bankrupt (though there seems more likelihood of him entering bankruptcy than her). If these conditions are met, the allowance will continue to be paid to her on the first of each month, and she agrees to inform Fraser through his solicitor of 'her exact place of residence' every three months – providing that he does not disclose this address to his family as she does not want to be molested by them.

This strange document has lain for many years with a small bundle of my father's out-of-date Wills, divorce and tenancy papers, long ago forgotten. 'She faded out of the picture with a minimum of fuss,' he wrote of Agnes May in his brief account. 'I suppose she was given some money but I've no idea how much. At the end of it all we were very broke.'

The Deed of Covenant is signed by Agnes May Babb in a spiky, slightly backward-leaning hand. I touch it with my finger. It is this signature alone that has given me her name and provided a small crack in the dark, enabling me to find out more about her.

By trawling backwards over the years at the Public Search Room at St Catherine's House I came across Agnes May's previous marriages and her birth certificate. Now I travel forwards to find out whether, after she had separated from my grandfather, she remarried. From my grandfather's point of view the good news (since it put an end to his monthly payments) is that she did marry again on 15 February 1934. Her husband was a thirty-year-old divorcé and 'company director', Reginald Alexander Beaumont-Thomas.

Agnes May Beaumont-Thomas (formerly Babb, previously Lisle and initially Bickerstaff, who for two or three years adopted the name Holroyd) calculates her age on the new marriage certificate as thirty-six (which is only two years short of her actual age) and she describes her father as a hotel proprietor which she remembered having copied down on her certificate of marriage to Thomas Babb. Her father appears to have had a biblical ability to die and come alive again fairly regularly. At the time of her first marriage, she writes that he is 'deceased' as her husband William Lisle's father was; but he was alive four-and-a-half years later when she married Thomas Babb (whose own father was alive), and had died again by 1934 now she was marrying Reginald Alexander Beaumont-Thomas (whose father was also dead). Actually he did not die until 1942. He died intestate, so there is no mention of a daughter. Despite her wealth, his estate, which went to his widow, was valued at only £207 3s 6d.

The Beaumont-Thomases are married at Biggleswade in Bedford and Agnes May gives her address as 'The Red Lion Hotel, Sandy'. But to have remarried, she would have had to get divorced. The decree nisi had been granted on 13 June 1933, and the bad news for my grandfather is that he has been named as co-respondent – though it is more than three years since he has been living with her. Perhaps this is no more than a legal convenience since his name is written with no great accuracy on the divorce proceedings – Edwin (instead of Edward) Fraser Rochford (instead of Rochfort) Holroyd. It seems unlikely that damages would have been sought against him but he may well have had to pay the court costs. What is surprising is that even an inaccurately-named co-respondent has been necessary, since husband and wife were living apart for more than eight years (had she gone back to him, her adultery with my grandfather would have been condoned). The speed with which she marries again is spectacular – even quicker (three days versus eleven days) than her first remarriage. For this was a very good marriage she was making. Her late father-in-law, Reginald Alexander Beaumont Thomas (the name was not then hyphenated), a steel and tinplate manufacturer of Brynycaerau Castle, Llanelly, had left £419,285 18s 9d to his three children on his death in 1917. Such a sum would be worth £14 million at the end of the century.

For two years Agnes May Beaumont-Thomas continued living with her company director husband in Campden Hill Gate. Then they leave London – perhaps to one of the properties he had been given in Gloucestershire, perhaps abroad (his first wife had been French and they had married in Paris). I can find no further trace of them. So Agnes May disappears from my story, like an alarming comet passing over the night sky.

*

But was there nothing more I could discover about the ramifi-
cations of this affaire? Suddenly I recalled the mysterious
'Holroyd Settlement' my father had mentioned in the account he
wrote for me of his early years, and which still provided him in
his old age with a couple of hundred pounds or so a year from
the National Westminster Bank. This Settlement had occasionally been spoken of in hushed and hopeless whispers during my
early years. I remember my mother telling me how she and my
father took me, aged six or so, to the home of a famous lawyer,
Sir Andrew Clark, who had been a friend of my Uncle Kenneth's
at university. He was reputed to be the cleverest barrister in
England and was much disliked for his arrogance (he later
gained fame for a brilliant investigation into the Ministry of
Agriculture known as the Crichel Down Inquiry, and also for
cutting off his daughter with exactly one shilling when she married an unacceptable man). My mother was terrified that I
would smash one of the precariously-placed objects in his drawing-room as I wandered happily from table to table and my
father appealed to him to release us from the iron grasp of our
family Trust. I broke no china that afternoon, nor was the Trust
Deed broken. My grandparents, my uncle, my aunt, everyone
wanted it broken: and yet it could not be broken. The letter of
the law was too strong. Somewhere in its legal depths, like treasure in a long-sunken wreck, lay the money we so desperately
needed. It remained as if in a chest whose key is lost, its contents
slowly disintegrating.

But what the origins of this complex affair were I never knew. At
my request the National Westminster Bank now sent me the documents from its vaults and I could see what I had begun to suspect:
that the 'Holroyd Settlement' was the legal arrangement made by
my grandfather in 1927 after he left his family, together with a
Supplemental Deed dated 27 May 1932 which reveals something
of what happened over those five years. It is a ruinous story.

Two properties are identified in this Supplemental Deed. The first is Agnes May's expensive love nest in Piccadilly, the lease of which did not expire until June 1946. The second is an oddly-crenellated, nineteenth-century town cottage with a small garden. It resembles a gate house to some grander building. Auckland Cottage, 91 Drayton Gardens, in unfashionable Fulham, is where my grandfather retired in April 1930. The rent on this house was £200 a year (equivalent to £6,000 in the late nineteen-nineties) and the lease did not expire until March 1944. These two properties Fraser handed over to Magor and Anderson, his trustees, in place of his Maidenhead house. They were to sell or sub-let them once he returned to Maidenhead so that his payments to his wife and children, promised in the principal deed, could be kept up. All his Rajmai Tea shares were now in other hands. A small design shows the details of these loans and overdrafts he had so far secured.

| Amount owing | Name of Bank | No. of shares |
|---|---|---|
| £24,500 | Mercantile Bank of India Ltd. | 1,000 Transferred to the name of the Nominees of the Bank. 100 Collateral. |
| £8,000 | National Bank of India Ltd. | 227 Transferred to the name of the Nominees of the Bank. Guaranteed by Messrs. Geo. Williamson & Co. |
| £10,000 | Major Holroyd (He owes Lloyd's Bank for this amount.) | 300 In Major Holroyd's name. |

| | | |
|---|---|---|
| £5,000 | Barclays Bank Ltd. | 125 The amount of £5,000 is being repaid at the commencement of June. |
| Total number of shares | | 1,752 |

All the family were required to sign this new Deed, Basil getting as his witness the British Consul in Venice where he happened to find himself in the early summer of 1932.

But he was back in England that July and accompanied Fraser to a nursing home near Blandford in Wiltshire where his Uncle Pat had gone following an operation. My father hardly knew his uncle, beyond recognising him as a handsome, mild-mannered man with a liking for drink. In the account he wrote for me almost fifty years later, he recalled 'finding my Uncle Pat tiptoeing down the stairs at Brocket when he was staying a few days with us. It was one o'clock in the morning and he was on his way to the dining-room for one more whisky.' According to my father it was whisky that killed him at the age of fifty-eight. He was suffering from a duodenal ulcer, an infected appendix, a blockage of the intestinal canal and chronic constipation. That was how Fraser found him at the nursing home. As with their father, and with his son who died in infancy, Fraser is again 'present at the death' on 15 July 1932. Even Basil's regular high spirits temporarily drooped, those high spirits on which he depended to overcome his sense of being unwanted, 'an evident mishap'. He never forgot that awful white room in the nursing home and 'my father's great distress at his brother's death'.

On the death certificate issued three days later, Fraser gave his address as Brocket, Maidenhead. The signing of the Supplemental Deed that summer of 1932 had been his act of negotiation back home. But it cannot have been a happy return.

His two sons lived mostly in London, and Brocket was a household of squabbling women – even their dogs quarrelled. Yolande by now hated her mother, and her mother hated Nan who had stayed on after the children grew up despite Adeline's many high-pitched invitations for her to leave. All Yolande's filial affections seemed to have been transferred to Nan. Between the three of them there were incessant plots and counter-plots, and much yapping at the ankles.

But Fraser was a man of illusions. It was to these illusions we were responding when retrospectively we pictured him as a brilliant mathematician, barrister, athlete and so on. Though his romantic illusions might be shattered, his financial illusions still glimmered in the city of glass he had attempted to create in the West End of London. His optimism shone blindingly forth. Were there moments of panic and doubt? In any event, there was nothing for it but to go on and hope for the best.

When my father had his signature witnessed by the British Consul in Venice on 18 May 1932, he was endeavouring to sell glass to the Venetians. Over the next couple of years he talked Fraser into forming a new department for glass light fittings: table-lights, wall-lights and hanging lights which were sometimes inverted fruit bowls suspended from the ceiling by ropes, decorated with opalescent shells, and fitted with flared flames of frosted or tinted glass. These had several seasons of popularity and were installed by some famous restaurants including Quaglino's and Claridge's. But they were not profitable because of the breakage when drilling the glass to the metalwork. One of his designs appears on the title page of this book.

But Basil was keen to develop this side of the business and made contact with a German glass manufacturer called Stensch which, following the Anglo-German trade agreement of April 1933, appointed Breves Lalique as its British agents. Early in 1934 Basil went over to Berlin to meet the Stensch family, and made friends with their twenty-year-old son Rudi, who had been

sent down from Bonn University. Being a Jew, he explained to
Basil, he had been 'retired' from Bonn as a result of the national
boycott on Jewish professions introduced by the new Chancellor,
Adolf Hitler. Possibly the non-completion of a university career
did not strike my father as so very grave a matter. In any event
it was his easy-going habit to offer anyone he liked a job in
Breves Lalique. He had come over with one of his cousins from
Australia (the one who had begun so promisingly in the IRA)
and together 'these two exuberant, extrovert fellows painted the
town of Berlin red', Rudi remembered. '. . . For us Jews, then
being very subdued under the first impact of nazidom, it was a
wonderful tonic.' Their air of innocence, their very ignorance,
was appealing. For they lit up the hope that this anti-Semitic
phenomenon would soon blow away almost as if it had never
been, like an illness that passes, leaving no marks, and is forgotten.

Rudi took my father and his cousin to Leipzig where they
were to make a reconnaissance of Germany's major commercial
trade fair. 'I particularly remember when we all went to the local
firemen's ball,' Rudi wrote to me, 'and your father and his
cousin insisted on driving our car right into the hall and in the
centre of the dance floor. They then snatched the helmets of the
worthy firemen, donned them on their heads, appropriated the
buxom partners of these firemen and began to dance some weird
Scottish jig. The impact of these young blades on the oh so
German "Spiessbürger" [petit bourgeois] was quite sensational . . . Heinrich Himmler, you should have been there to
watch it!' For a moment the world of P.G. Wodehouse rode triumphantly over the Nazis' campaign against decadence.

After a week Rudi returned to Berlin and a few days later he
received a telephone call from Basil who sounded in deep trouble. 'In a muffled voice he told me that he was at the Eden Hotel
in Berlin and would I please send him immediately a wire saying
that I had heard from London that your grandfather [Fraser]

Major General Charles Holroyd with Norah, Fraser and Pat, a few years after their mother's suicide. Eastbourne c. 1885

Constable's House, Uppingham, c. 1892. My grandfather is seated, centre

The Corbets off picnicking in Ireland

January 1975
Family Tree Jagenburg

Rudolf Jagenburg (my grandfather)
Born at Rydbo holm (outside Borås — Sweden)
1865 — 1943

Children: Elis 1890 — 1969 dead
Karin 1891 — (my mother)
Elsbeth 1893 — 1974 dead
Hans 1896 — 1968 (dead)
Lmt 1898 — ____ Göteborg
Åke 1900 — ____ Borås

Married to Ida Peterson
Born 1865 — 1938? in Gränna
Sroeder

Elis married to Kristina Liljå×
born 1889 — living alone in Borås now
was a waitress in Borås "Stads Hotel"
never liked or really accepted by the
family although extremely good to
her husband in quite...
as he had o...
syphilis, acq...
Hamburg...
penicillin...
inherited a...
Bronox as hi...
import mostl...
Hard but la...
& made her...
e.g. "You mu...
track" ect...
good — & is...
contact now...
guar... (Ba...
3) Karin
Lieutenant Ku...
Born 1886 —
became mai...

20  Heaven knows why!
It was in "The Red House" that my eldest brother Desmond
Scroxley Holroyd was born. He only lived 4 months.
My mother was greatly upset by this and her second child
my sister Yolande didn't arrive until April 1902 which was
two and a quarter years after Desmonds birth.
By contrast Kennett my elder brother was born in 1903
— towards the end of the year.
We had moved to Meadowcroft — in Bolton Avenue — Windsor
by then. And it was here that I was born in 1907 — an evident
mishap from my Parents point of view.
My mother had been catapulted into a life entirely unlike
anything she'd been accustomed to before.
A big house — servants — a carriage and pair and all
that went in those days with those who were comfortably off.
She wrongly assumed that it befitted her new status to
adopt a dictatorial tone to her servants and a condescending
air to those who for one reason or another she adjudged beneath her.
In those early days the impact of her new role in life was at
least deadened by the presence of some of her family. Ida lived
only a mile or so away. Lizzie was down at Bristol which,
although quite a journey was within range. Sly lived over at
Reigate in Surrey. The lovely glamourous Alice was already dead in America.
When she was with any of them or when any of the others,
still living in Ireland were over on a visit she was much
more natural.
It would be wrong however to assume that she wasn't
thoroughly enjoying the social life that had now opened out

My mother's and
my father's accounts

My grandparents c. 1900

Kaja, Stockholm, c. 1913

Major Karl Knuttsson Hall 1930

Kenneth, Basil and Yolande c. 1912

My grandparents with their children at Windsor

Kenneth and Basil before the First World War

Kenneth and Basil between the wars

Yolande c. 1905

Ulla, my mother, when she arrived in England c. 1934

had been taken very ill and would Basil please return post haste. I would get an explanation later.'

My father gave his explanation next day at a *thé dansant* on the roof of the Eden Hotel. It appeared that he and his cousin had become involved with two young women they met at a Leipzig bar, and all four of them spent the night at a hotel. The cousin promised to take his companion to Paris the next day. This gave my father no option but to add that he would take his lady to Stockholm. But next morning he woke to find his Australian cousin had gone in the night. He was left with a girl on each arm and two hotel bills. He paid off the bills and saw that one of the girls got home in a taxi, while the other girl – who appeared in the daylight to be a dramatically painted woman with a loud Saxon voice (a veritable Saxhorn) – he took by train to Berlin. The fake telegram arrived and 'the histrionic performance of your father when he explained to the girl that, alas, he could not proceed with her to Sweden and how all his life his greatest pleasures were being spoilt by quirks of fate, was masterful', Rudi wrote. 'We both took her to the station and put her on the train to Leipzig.' Then the two young men went on to another railway station in Berlin's working-class northern district, where my father was to catch the train to Stockholm. Over a few drinks while waiting for his train, Basil repeated his offer for Rudi to come over and work as a trainee for Breves Lalique in London. 'At that time I faced the problem of many young German Jews whose careers had been suddenly aborted – what to do with my life,' Rudi remembered. 'So I accepted with alacrity. I had been in London once before as a schoolboy and had felt at home. If I had to become a refugee there was only one country I would choose.'

It was in the autumn of 1934 that the great Lalique galleries finally opened at 4 New Bond Street. 'The ornamental glass associated with the name of M. René Lalique deserves recognition as the first attempt in Europe to explore the full possibilities of glass as a plastic material, and Messrs Breves, its agents in London, are to be congratulated on the general effect of their new galleries,' wrote *The Times*. 'A plain shopfront faced with travertine, with the name in white metal above, opens to a deeply recessed window which allows a clear view of the whole interior. As far as possible all the working features such as doors, and the decorations of the new galleries are constructed of Lalique glass, in association with stainless steel.' René Lalique himself, a shy seventy-three-year-old with a white moustache, arrived from Paris hidden in an enormous overcoat, almost two hours late, missing the ceremonial speeches by the French Ambassador and the Mayor of Westminster. But he was not too late to avoid a reporter from the *Manchester Guardian* who noticed him among the guests (including everyone from Lady Oxford to Princess Bibesco) and described his 'somewhat brisk military appearance suggestive of Cheltenham rather than the Champs Elysées'.

About this time my mother arrived from Sweden.

# 7

# A Triumph and
# Disaster

Ulla was pleased to be getting away from Stockholm. She had an adventurous spirit and she loved travel. Nor did she mind leaving her mother. It was not that she and Kaja didn't love each other, but they needed to be independent. Living together, they were like two dancers each treading on the other's feet. Ulla's feelings for Kaja were a world away from anything Yolande had ever felt for Adeline, yet both daughters had their difficulties. Adeline liked to stop Yolande from going to parties in London. But when Ulla said she was going out to a party in Stockholm, Kaja would dress up and go along too. And what a power dresser she was! The rustle of her dress before she entered a room and the lingering perfume in the air after she made her exit were potent spells that lodged in many imaginations. She had such a sharp eye too and was still so strikingly smart that her presence grew immensely oppressive to Ulla. The trouble was that Kaja, then in her early forties, seemed so terribly old to her daughter, yet she simply refused to behave like an older person. She was delighted when people took the two of them for sisters. Because she preserved such a strict manner at home, it was only gradually that Ulla realised what was going on. Though her mother kept a single gentleman admirer, the distinguished-looking Biryer Sandström, famous for his cravats, who escorted her through the high places of society, she also kept company at other times and in lower places with all sorts of amusing bohemian artists. One of them painted her in a fur coat, earrings and lace bodice (I have the painting in London). It was also rumoured that Picasso – or was it Picabia or even one of the Pissarros – had become infatuated with one of her feet while she was travelling abroad. It was usually Picasso in these stories and part of Kaja's foot was said to appear in his *Guernica*. Her own collection of pictures, near masterpieces all, hung like trophies on the walls of her apartment, the names of the painters – 'Fragobard', 'Valminc', a rare 'Edouard Monet' – echoing discordantly their famous reverberations (she left me a small 'Verner' and what looks like an unusual 'Whatho'!). The distraught Biryer Sandström found himself obliged to fire off many agitated telegrams.

'What a mother! What a daughter!' exclaimed one of Ulla's schoolfriends. Stockholm seemed too small to hold them both. So Ulla was not unhappy to be escaping. She would be particularly pleased to miss that one day a week when her father was allowed access to her. She didn't mind being taken to the opera by him and felt proud of his musical knowledge (though she was embarrassed when he started humming – and besides, opera was not the sort of music she really liked). But what she hated were the evenings he came to dine with her and Kaja. There was absolutely no conversation at all, simply an icy silence and then dreadful bickering.

Ulla had been to France but never to England before. Her English was not bad and under the pressure of events would quickly get much better. Of course she felt a little apprehensive, but on the whole she was excited. It was the summer of 1934, she was seventeen, and she wanted to have fun.

On board the *Suecia* as it set off from Göteburg, Ulla sat at the Captain's table – Kaja had arranged that. Everyone dressed for dinner, there was a formal toast, and a dignified atmosphere prevailed – at least it would have done had there not been so much noise from one of the other tables, in particular from one persistent raucous English voice. 'I was annoyed and kept turning round,' my mother remembered. On the second evening a man swayed up to her table and with exaggerated correctness requested the Captain's permission to ask Ulla for a dance. The Captain assenting, she found herself waltzing with the ghastly-voiced Englishman. He explained that he had been smoking too many Gauloises, and then went on jovially talking. 'He could talk anybody into anything,' she later wrote. He told her he had recently been in Germany and then gone to Sweden to meet important people in Kosta Glass. He spoke brilliantly of the beauties of Lalique and his own rich future in glass. Before they reached Tilbury, he had talked her into giving him her address and telephone number. And also a promise to see him in London. This man was to be my father.

Ulla's first experience of England was a shock. She was living at Beckenham in Kent with a Mrs Malmburg who received pupils for English language tuition. No. 48 Coper's Cope Road (a name which struck her as incredible – it came from a handsome eighteenth-century house with quoins and a pediment on giant pilasters at the end of the road) was partly a guesthouse, partly a small school. The regime was deliberately English and included kippers for breakfast at 7.30 a.m. which made my mother sick. She was pleased to get an invitation from the man on the boat, asking her to lunch with him at the Grill Room of the Hyde Park Hotel. But Mrs Malmburg felt anxious – until Basil spoke to her on the telephone. By the end of their conversation, she was convinced that Ulla could hardly be in more distinguished company than this Old Etonian director of Lalique.

So Ulla went up to London. She was worried over this first journey by train and bus to the capital. The Hyde Park Hotel, which flew the Swedish flag whenever King Gustav stayed there, was only two minutes' walk from the elegant Breves showrooms in Basil Street with their 'Chinese' wallpaper and permanent display of Lalique. At the Grill Room, Basil ordered Ulla what she took to be a lemonade but was actually Jimmy the barman's speciality, a Gin Fizz. After the first shock, she found it delicious and had to be driven home by car. But she had sobered up by the time she reached Beckenham, and Mrs Malmburg, impressed by her description of the Hyde Park Hotel, was happy to let her go on seeing Basil. Ulla was allowed to spend weekends at Maidenhead which, to Mrs Malmburg, sounded a pretty safe and proper place. Here Ulla met the amiable if rather distant Fraser, the baffling Adeline (a small figure with tall hair), Yolande dashing everywhere in her short tennis skirts, and Kenneth encircled by his aristocratic friends. Thatcher, the family chauffeur, had retired and his place was taken by Frederick who would drive Fraser, and sometimes his sons and their friends, up to London on weekdays. Ulla used to wonder what he did there until it was time to drive back again. She was always wondering things like that.

Ulla's English had improved, though she still found the English Js awkward and would speak of waving a 'Union Yak at the You-billie'. Basil taught her some slang and several naughty words, and he and his friends started calling her Sue or Suzie instead of Ulla which rather stuck in their throats. She was becoming quite anglicised, and picking up extra English culture from her visits to Brocket – the weird offerings of hot-water bottles, the ritual of early-morning tea, the ceremonious walks with the dogs, and the strange procedures when everyone sat down to dinner.

Brocket was then in the last phase of its glory. The lease had come to an end in 1933 but Fraser, still hoping for good things, renewed it year by year. 'It was a lovely brick house,' my mother remembered, 'covered with green ivy, a drive and two gates.' It had been designed by a young architect called Clifton Davy who became well-known for his domestic work along the Thames Valley. The upper part of the building was built of solid oak half-timbering with herring-bone brickwork, and the house itself divided from Boyn Hill Avenue by an ornamental brick wall. Above the heavy oak front door two quotations had been cut into the stone: 'Through This Wide Opening Gate None Come Too Early None Return Too Late'. And, more conventionally: 'Welcome The Coming Speed The Parting Guest'.

My mother was obviously impressed by Brocket. The large hall with its light oak panelling, its beamed and rafted ceiling, was a perfect place for parties. The French doors opened on to a veranda some six feet above the tennis court and, when the evenings were warm and the lamps lit, there was no better place for sitting out between dances. It is not difficult to imagine how exciting these dances and parties were for my mother now that she was not under the watchful eye of Kaja.

Ulla wrote regularly to Kaja who was delighted with her daughter's progress into British society. These Holroyds with whom she was spending so much time appeared to be a wealthy and well-appointed English family, with some Irish and perhaps Scottish ancestry as well as an Anglo-Indian chapter in their history. Basil himself, curiously christened after a herb, recommended himself as an Old Etonian and a Cambridge man whose central names (De Courcy Fraser) had to Kaja's ear a reassuringly rare Anglo-Saxon elevation. Kaja was pleased that her daughter was enjoying herself. It was all most satisfactory.

But events were to move with a speed and unorthodoxy that took Kaja aback. 'You must have been conceived,' my mother hazarded, 'on the canebacked sofa in the drawing-room at

Brocket' – which rather puts paid to her speculations over my conception at the Hyde Park or Basil Street hotels. Perhaps it was that same sofa on which Norah Palmer Holroyd had lain, her pretty hair spread out, before her final journey into France in 1913; and the sofa on which the enormous frame of Tom White expired after breaking his golf club in the early nineteen-twenties. Dr Johnson once boasted that he could write the life of a broomstick, and it would need him, or Virginia Woolf, to tell the common reader the story of a sofa.

My father was twenty-seven on 20 October 1934 and my mother celebrated her eighteenth birthday on 20 November which was probably also the date of my conception (but since I was apparently born almost a month off schedule it is difficult to tell). The two of them were then secretly married at the Registrar's Office at Bromley, not far from Beckenham on 15 December 1934. One of the witnesses was the taxi-driver who drove them there and then took them up to London through the rain (it was pelting down that day according to the Meteorological Office). They spent their honeymoon at the Basil Street Hotel, which had some good Lalique glass in its art deco interior (it was only a few yards from the Breves showrooms). Then they went off to spend Christmas in Stockholm where, rather belatedly, my father asked Kaja for permission to marry her daughter. Kaja answered that she wanted them to have a decent period of engagement, which was awkward – no one thought of consulting Ulla's father Karl whom Basil never met.

To set things off correctly Kaja took Ulla to be fitted for her white wedding-dress, at which stage I can make out the word 'Calamity!' in my mother's handwriting, dramatically under-lined as she underlined other decisive words such as 'pregnant!' and 'married!' There was no hiding the pregnancy from Kaja's sharp eyes. Ulla was too sick for that; after which there was no point in hiding the marriage. Had they intended to stage a second marriage in Sweden? I believe they had. It would have been a good joke: and everything still had the air of a joke. But Basil now admitted to the marriage – and his wife's pregnancy. It was certainly not what Kaja had had in mind: a Registrar's Office in Bromley. For a time, a rather short time, she looked severely about her, then relented. 'I think Kaja was glad to see me "happily settled" as she thought,' my mother wrote, 'since she herself was busy with poor old Biryer Sandström.'

The white Swedish wedding was called off and the married couple sailed back to England in January 1935. After Basil had brought his parents up to date, they settled into 91 Drayton Gardens, the cottage in Fulham to which Fraser had retired after leaving Agnes May. My mother's labour pains came on that August in the Fulham Forum, the cinema at the end of the road. She was taken to the London Clinic and Kaja arrived from Sweden just in time for my birth at 4.20 p.m. on 27 August. My father, who had been playing golf, was late – which may account for him assigning me a birthday two days later.

Kaja stayed on in England for the autumn and came to visit us again in 1936. The regime at Drayton Gardens seems to have been pretty comfortable. There was a Danish housekeeper called Vera who looked after my parents; and a nanny who looked after me – 'she fell in love with the milkman & had to have all her teeth out (nothing to do with the milk)', my mother explained. There were also two small town dogs, Snaps and Popples (which sounds like a breakfast cereal or perhaps a circus act), a tabby cat that discovered things and was called Christopher Columbus (he had been bought from the grocer for one penny by my mother who believed that it was 'bad luck not to pay for a cat'). We also owned two goldfish, Dalgeish and Pullen, named after a couple of architects my father knew.

All this was agreeable enough, but what my Swedish grand-mother liked most were her visits to Brocket. English society might be incomprehensible, but its incomprehensibility was impressive. What for example could she have made of the family

Arms and Crests and Latin mottos – those Demi-Griffins Wings Endorsed, those Roses Gules and Pierced Mullets in Saltire that occupied a more prominent position at Brocket than the lavatory of my father's flat in Surrey that was to be their hiding place years later? Whatever she made of them, I feel sure she was glad they were there. Only they should not have been there. What Kaja could not have known, since no one else knew, was that none of these Holroyds, not Fraser nor his father Charles, nor even their eminent forebear Sir George Sowley Holroyd, nor the first Earl of Sheffield himself, had established through the correct registers and pedigrees, the right to ancestral Arms by inheritance. So this parade of exotic Conquerfoils, that Fess Dancetty Argent, those many Escallopes Gules, diamonds and lozenges, the very Pierced Mullets themselves were all assumed without proper authority.

Never mind. Basil took Kaja round the house. Off the hall was a large drawing-room with two silent grand pianos where Adeline held her bridge parties. There was also a cosier 'morning-room' and a rather dark formal dining-room, its refectory table lined with straight-backed chairs. This led on to an Edwardian conservatory full of ferns and garden furniture. Down some stairs by the side of the dining-room were the kitchen quarters – a pantry and spacious kitchen off which stood the cool larder and a scullery where vegetables from the garden were prepared. Basil introduced Kaja to the staff in the Servants' Hall, but did not take her of course to their rooms which were on the top floor and reached by the back stairs. Kaja's own room when she stayed at Brocket had once been Kenneth's, and contained a magnificent Hepplewhite four-poster bed. It was on the first floor, as were Fraser's and Adeline's bedroom and their two dressing-rooms (one of which, with its separate door on to the passage, had by now become Fraser's bedroom). At the south west corner of the house, overlooking the garden, was Yolande's bedroom which no one else entered. There were three other

guest bedrooms and along one side of the corridor two bathrooms, as well as a spare room that had once been the children's
nursery.

Basil ended his tour where they had come in downstairs, at
the entrance hall with its medley of sticks and umbrellas, and its
two lifesize figures of a black man and black woman that had
fascinated him as a child but that somewhat perplexed Kaja. Yet
it was the quality of her perplexity that was important. Indeed
she exaggerated the grandness of life at Brocket and when
offered a pot of Russian caviar at lunch, served by the parlourmaid on a silver salver and with a silver spoon, she took the
whole pot and had to be corrected by her daughter in Swedish.

Another foreign visitor to Brocket and to Drayton Gardens
was Rudi. He had first come over as a trainee at Breves Lalique
for a few months in 1934. The following year the Nazis introduced conscription and he had to submit himself for a medical
examination. Standing stark naked before a panel of senior officers, he was congratulated on his excellent health and asked in
what arm of the services he would prefer to serve. Surprised, he
replied that, as a Jew, he was surely ineligible for any service, but
was told by the presiding Colonel that the new 'Reichswehr'
(German army) needed strong 'Burschen' (members of the student fraternity) like him, and that he should not believe all he
read in the newspapers. It was this incident that finally decided
him to seek his future abroad, much to the chagrin of his father
and his 'Aryan' partner who were both convinced that the Nazi
nightmare would soon be over.

By 1935 the United Kingdom immigration laws had been
tightened. No one could arrive and simply look for a job. Only
prominent people – capitalists who brought money to invest –
were welcomed and given a home. Rudi's grandfather had
recently died leaving him £750 (equivalent to approximately
£25,000 at the end of the century). This he proposed putting
into a new company my father was starting called Holroyd

(Glassware and Lighting) Ltd. His money, my father promised, would guarantee Rudi a junior partnership. But there was a difficulty. It was impossible to transfer money out of Germany legally, and illegal currency smuggling was now a capital offence.

It was then my father came up with one of his ideas. In the rather kitsch range of table-lamps made by the Stensch factory in Berlin were some with a stem cast in the shape of a gnarled tree with a variety of animals lurking in its shade. Among this odd zoo was a herd of elephants, the largest of which was so big that the front and back parts had to be cast separately. What my father was proposing sounded like one of his innocently dangerous pranks which were becoming less innocent and more dangerous as the decade advanced. Why shouldn't one of these huge elephants convey Rudi's inheritance abroad? Basil ordered six of the table-lamps for his company, and suggested that the loaded elephant should be marked with a scratch on one of its heels. So this was agreed. When the lamps were ready for dispatch, Rudi's father and his partner sent the nightwatchman out on an errand, concealed the fortune inside two of the raw elephant halves, soldered the parts together and put the whole elephant in a patina bath. Then they scratched the prearranged code and substituted this elephant for one of the six already waiting export.

The consignment arrived at London and, instead of waiting for customs clearance and dispatch to the warehouse in Fulham, Rudi went to the docks at my father's suggestion and took possession of the elephant with the damaged heel. 'I was very nervous and in the taxi riding back tried to break the beast open,' Rudi remembered. 'I made such a racket that the Jewish cabbie asked what the hell I was up to. I revealed the secret to my co-religionist, whereupon he took a big spanner and somewhere on the Commercial Road, smashed the elephant to bits, revealing the hoard. Cheers all round: my future was secure.'

My father had one more suggestion. He had changed his

young wife's name from Ulla Knutsson-Hall to Sue Holroyd. Now he indicated to his new partner that the name Rudi Stensch would sound less well in England than in Germany. Forty years later it was Ronald Stent who, having read one of my biographies, wrote to me from Ealing asking for my father's address.

But my father did not now want to give his address. He was getting old, he was poor and he lived very modestly with his dog in Surrey, having been left by his third wife. He could not invite anyone there, and he did not want to go anywhere else or to see people, or write to people, or read what people wrote to him. He simply did not want people. Or even the absence of people. He did not know what he wanted. Or whether he still had wants. He did and he didn't. In any case he was no longer the jovial personality who could 'talk anybody into anything'. When he compared his meagre circumstances to those heady expectations of the early nineteen-thirties, a sense of humiliation spread through him. That was perhaps one reason why he could not continue with the account of his life he had written for me beyond his uncompleted schooldays. Besides he did not wish to be reminded of those mad escapades when he was a damn fool in his twenties. So I learnt of his adventures with Lalique from Ronald Stent who in the late nineteen-thirties used to push my pram along the Hammersmith Road; and also from Hazel Truman and Merle Rafferty who happened to see in a newspaper a picture of my mantelpiece on which stood my Lalique legacy, three glass sparrows. 'I remember meeting your grandfather and your grandmother,' wrote Hazel Truman, 'both of them aristocrats in my opinion. Your mother we (that is the staff) thought was so beautiful and so very young.' 'Basil often appeared with friends to "borrow" a dinner service which came back with breakages,' Merle Rafferty wrote, 'but his father was always long suffering where his younger son was concerned.'

In my library I have a copy of the general circulation edition of T.E. Lawrence's *Seven Pillars of Wisdom* with its curious

subtitle: *a triumph*. It has been inscribed: 'To Mr E.F.R. Holroyd
with every good wish from the Staff. Christmas 1935.' There is
a photograph of them all in their best evening clothes taken the
following year. Fraser wears his white collar and tails, Adeline
one of her long black dresses with a silver fur stole; Yolande sits
next to her in a patterned dress – she is already beginning to
look like her mother; then comes Ulla, a blonde beauty, still
very Swedish, still in her 'teens; and standing behind them is
Basil, smiling in his dinner jacket; and also Kenneth nearer the
centre looking very smart. There are over a hundred people altogether, including Hazel Truman and Merle Rafferty. It is like the
last picture of a royal dynasty before the republic comes in.

Everything moved quickly after this. My parents left Drayton
Gardens (the lease of which was sold to help pay off debts) and
moved to Latymer Court, a block of flats in the Hammersmith
Road. Brocket was given up in the summer of 1937, Fraser dis-
charged most of the servants and took Adeline, Yolande and
Nan off to a much smaller house a few hundred yards away
called Norhurst. Lalique had begun to go out of fashion and the
family business was running into the ground. By the time war
came Fraser had to tell what staff remained that it was all over –
there was no money for anyone.

Ronald Stent, alias Rudi Stensch, was rounded up during the
panic of June 1940 and, along with thousands of other German
Jews and people of alien origin, interned on the Isle of Man. He
had plenty of time to reflect on his half-dozen years with the
Holroyds. They had introduced him to a segment of British society to which few refugees had such easy access. 'Its upper-class
lightheartedness and devil-may-care attitude was in such contrast to my own background,' he wrote, 'and the fraught
surroundings from which I had escaped.

> My education into a would-be Englishman was really an
> amalgam of what the Holroyds showed me, and what I

learned from Speakers' Corner; my spelling of English
had always been better than that of the Old Etonian
Basil; my vocabulary over the years was enriched by the
Daily Telegraph crossword puzzles; but my accent I could
never shed.

Ulla, alias Sue, had also become anglicised and was more
adept at shedding her accent, though she still made mistakes
such as ordering 'two whitebait' for supper at the 'fishmongler'.
She no longer had a housekeeper, though I had a new
Scandinavian nurse, Nanny Tidy, who was so ferociously tidy
and had such emphatic views on hygiene that my parents were
seldom allowed to touch me. 'She was much too strict,' my
mother admitted, 'but I was only nineteen and had to take her
advice.'

The war threatened my mother with what seemed to her a
more terrible internment than any imposed on 'enemy aliens' on
the Isle of Man. Against the rising note of the first air-raid warnings, Basil announced that it would be too dangerous for them
to go on living in London. He had given up the lease of their flat
in Latymer Court and they were moving down to the safety of
Norhurst, his parents' new house in Maidenhead. My mother
realised that he was thinking of my safety, and perhaps also of
hers, but she objected to being informed of decisions in which
she had no part. My father insisted on treating her like a child.
'He never really told me anything,' she wrote.

So the three of us moved down to Norhurst 'lock, stick and
barrel', as my mother wrote. 'Disaster!' she added dramatically.
'<u>End</u> really of life.'

# INTERVAL

# 8

# *Literary Lapses*

At the beginning I was no different from anyone who wants to write poetry, novels and plays. Being a solitary child, books soon became my friends and the means by which, from the privacy of my bedroom, I travelled all over the world and off to other worlds in my imagination. I much preferred these voyages to actual journeys, full of anxiety and incomprehension, I was obliged to make with my parents.

I also liked having stories read aloud to me. My Aunt Yolande would take on this duty, reading to me beside the Aga cooker in the kitchen. She read from a thick, tattered, black-boarded volume with drawings which she had loved in her own childhood. It was full of the adventures of a racy girl called Mathilda. I could not get enough of her exploits and, when we had gone through them all, I craved to hear them just once more, every one of them, and then all over again from the beginning to the end – if only they would never end.

During the war my aunt drove a library van round prisoner-of-war camps in the Home Counties. She was then approaching forty and it was her first job. She often used to take me, aged six or seven, on these exciting expeditions to our enemies. I remember wondering whether they ever escaped. They never did, apparently, and I picked up the notion that my aunt's choice of thrillers, romances and detective fiction, held them captivated behind the friendly barbed wire.

I owe much of my early interest in books to my aunt. Though I never actually caught her reading – she read in bed at night, she let it be known, and seldom slept – she was one of those people who are said never to be without a book. Her bedroom was her library – even her bed rested on books. Books were part of our furniture at Norhurst. We used them for propping open doors, supporting windows, balancing tables, reaching things, and also lining the air-raid shelter.

Some years later I joined the new public library at Maidenhead. I lived like a lord there – like little Lord Fauntleroy – with a trained staff and a parade of authors lined up alphabetically before me on the shelves. It was a handsome building in a town not noticeable for its architectural events, and in due course it became my university.

My Aunt Yolande soon grew curious about this place. She herself patronised the private lending library at Boots the Chemist in the High Street where she could pick up a bestseller with her toothpaste and soap. Eventually, her curiosity growing, she followed me to the public library at the end of the town. What she saw amazed her. It was like a palace. Abandoning Boots she became a new member, though she never lost the habit of lightly roasting the books she borrowed in a medium oven for the sake of the germs. Many cautious booklovers did this, and you could tell the most popular volumes by passing the palm of your hand along the spines and bindings and sensing the residual heat from middle-class Aga and Rayburn cookers.

That library became my club, my home from home, my place
of recreation and learning. It was a democratic place – we were
of all sorts, ages and conditions. And it was here, sometime
later, I came across my first biographies: *The Life of Oscar
Wilde* by Hesketh Pearson, and Hugh Kingsmill's *Frank Harris*.
From Hesketh Pearson I eventually learnt something about the
craft of non-fiction storytelling. I read Pearson's biographies in
my 'teens to find out what was going to happen next in the past.
He didn't take you into the recesses of history, but brought his
characters – Walter Scott, William Hazlitt, Henry Labouchère,
Tom Paine – into the present so that they seemed to fill the bedroom where I was reading. He didn't bother with dreary
documentation, but relied on good anecdotes, skilful use of quo-
tation, pen portraits done in primary colours and with solid
underlying draughtsmanship. It was exhilarating stuff.

From Hugh Kingsmill I learnt about the business of serious
comedy. His *Frank Harris* was a small masterpiece, it seemed to
me, of poetic irony. What F.R. Leavis was for many of my generation, Hugh Kingsmill became to me. He was my guide. He
belonged to no school of writers, no literary group or movement. He was an isolated figure as I felt myself to be. And I had
found him for myself. Kingsmill divided the world not into men
versus women, not by colour or class, not geographically or by
politics: in short not by any of the usual categories. He saw the
world as being occupied by two species of human beings: men
and women of will who sought unity by force if necessary (and
so often it was necessary): men and women of imagination who
could detect a harmony underlying the discord of our lives and
used it as their compass. He identified the real struggle in
modern times as being fought out between these two species of
human being over the battleground of public opinion. But all of
us were composed of will and imagination, and were tempted to
externalise the enemy within. The charting of these impulses
was the main theme in his biographies of Samuel Johnson,

Charles Dickens, D.H. Lawrence and Matthew Arnold.

The early influences of Pearson and Kingsmill propelled me towards becoming a biographer. But there were other causes too. The books at Norhurst – volumes of Andrew Lang and Winston Churchill; also dusty romances by Rhoda Broughton and Marie Corelli (which Adeline had devoured long ago) – did not appeal to me. I loved the adventures of Rider Haggard and Conan Doyle, and was astonished when my grandmother told me that Conan Doyle's historical novel *Micah Clarke* was the finest work of fiction ever written. This was especially strange because Doyle's re-creation of seventeenth-century puritanism had originally been rejected by publishers because 'it has next to no attraction for female readers'. The book first came out when Adeline was fourteen, and perhaps she remembered her father reading it in Ireland.

It was my grandfather's opinion that literature had flourished in the age of Shakespeare and pretty well come to an end in the twentieth century, though he granted special status to a few remarkable men who happened to write such as Winston Churchill, Lawrence of Arabia and an American homosexual nutritionist called Gayelord Hauser who, at an advanced age and on a diet of cider vinegar and black molasses, hazelnuts and soy bean oil, was said to have enjoyed an affaire with Greta Garbo. On account of his deep knowledge of Hauser, Fraser was, we all maintained, 'better than any doctor'. We seldom bothered to call in the family practitioner Dr Flew (whose full name, I believed as a child, was Dr Influenza) unless one of the dogs was off colour. But though he had this reputation for learning, Fraser seldom read anything except, with trembling indignation, the newspapers. It was not the author but literature itself that had died in our house. It had been ingeniously recycled into a batch of doorstops, makeweights and steps up to the tops of cupboards.

'What shall we do with the boy?' my grandparents would

ask, and everyone would turn and stare at me. There seemed no answer to the question. Other people, the people I read about, had narrative, it appeared to me, while I hovered in a vacuum. Inevitably I began absorbing the pace and condition of my grandparents, which is to say the regime of seventy-year-olds when I was still seven or eight. It was an odd form of precocity, a jump from early childhood straight into second childhood. Having compensated with book-adventures for the compulsory inactivity in Maidenhead during the war (like living at the dead centre of a storm), I later went one stage further by stepping from my own life into other people's where there seemed to be so much more going on.

But before I thought of taking up biography I tried composing verse, the influence of which veered drastically between Wordsworth and T.S. Eliot. The effect of this upon my father was extraordinary and, by the beginning of the nineteen-fifties, we found ourselves collaborating on a history of the world in verse. I was very much the junior partner in this herculean enterprise which, in its heroic hexameters, extended over a hundred closely-typed foolscap pages. We put a light blue cover on it, sent it off to the publishers Faber & Faber, and waited. And waited. After a long dazed silence, and in response to our eager telephone calls, we eventually received a report which, though congratulating us on our quixotic stamina, concluded that the satire was not sufficiently satirical for publication – a statement that, as we pored over it, struck us as worthy of the Delphic Oracle. Later on I showed our *oeuvre* to the writer and artist Colin Spencer who thought our best chance of success lay in running it as a hilarious serial, illustrated with cartoons, in *Punch*. But by that stage my father and I were moving along very different avenues of literature.

I was hardly out of my 'teens when I began writing a novel largely in the historic present which I had picked up from reading Joyce Cary, though the mood was intended to be Chekovian, and my patterns of writing were partly derived from the novels of Patrick Hamilton who had brought fame to Maidenhead with his thriller *Hangover Square*. I worked on my novel for a long time but could find no way of ending it. A first draft in a thick exercise book marked 'Ideal Series' peters out after 110,000 handwritten words. A second version, this one typed, appears to reach some sort of exhausted conclusion on page 626.

My father, seeing what I was up to, soon joined me in fiction-writing, polishing off four or five full-length unpublished novels and several unpublished short stories. This was all the more remarkable since over this period he had a full-time job as a salesman which involved a good deal of motoring round the country, leaving him only a few evenings and some weekends for novel-writing. But he was growing to dislike his work and, feeling apprehensive over the future, hoped that this book-writing business might rescue him. He acquired a literary agent who liked what he wrote, but sadly never a publisher.

Only one of his novels, an 80,000-word typescript called *The Directors*, survives. It is competently done rather in the manner of C.P. Snow. But since it describes the business world he was anxious to escape, and is rather full of bank managers and solicitors discussing delivery schedules and production returns over dinner, it did not make for glamorous reading. However, it is rather well-plotted and with some editorial pruning, some helpful advice, might have been published. Its weakness is that the men are somewhat undifferentiated and speak with the same voice – which is my father's voice. The women are of two sorts: those who, in their roles of wife or secretary, protect and mother their immature charges; and those who wreak havoc either by their addiction to sex or by provoking unquenchable sexual appetites in the men. Sexual excess rather than business chicanery is the villain of *The Directors*.

My own novel, the incompetencies of which struck one good-natured publisher as marks of originality, was largely autobiographical. It described my grandparents' life at Norhurst, my parents' marital exploits, and my own limping attempts to become a writer. But since I seemed unable to harness these first two subjects to the advancement of the third, I eventually put the manuscript away and turned to what in due course would emerge as a biography of Hugh Kingsmill. Then, coming across the manuscript in the mid-nineteen-sixties, I suddenly saw how I might carve out the first quarter of this spacious family saga and make it a self-contained novella covering twenty-four hours of family life, which I called *A Dog's Life*. Once I had accomplished this I sent the typescript to William Heinemann Ltd, the publishers that were about to bring out my *Lytton Strachey*. My typescript went to the editorial manager, Roland Gant, who was himself a novelist and a translator from the French. 'This is a difficult novel to describe,' he wrote in his report.

> Age and particularly old age dominate it . . . these are not the tragic or coy old people created by novelists. They are comic but not laughable because they are so true to life. Like many old people they have lowered their sights and narrowed their field and live in grumbling contentment within their prescribed limits . . .
>
> As I am usually over-sparing in praise, I could add that reading *A Dog's Life* gave me the same kind of sensation of being in the presence of real talent as did the first production I ever saw of *Three Sisters*, listening to *Under Milk Wood*, and reading *Mrs Dalloway* for the first time.

Heinemann were to offer me an advance on royalties of £500 which was ten times what they had given me for *Lytton Strachey*. Roland Gant did not wish to publish *A Dog's Life* until the two Strachey volumes were out of the way. But since Penguin Books wanted the novel as a paperback and my publisher in the United States also sent me a contract, I was happy.

But my father was not happy. He had given up writing novels by then and assumed that I had done so too. He had read an early draft of my novel guardedly, reassuring himself perhaps that it would never be published. When I posted him the later shortened typescript, his reaction was more sparing in its praise than Roland Gant's. 'The typescript of your book arrived,' he wrote, 'and I read two or three chapters before I was so nauseated that I had to put it down.' Since the first two chapters covered five pages and the third chapter reached the top of page eight, this was not encouraging. Of course he had read more, though he could not bear to finish the book. But he wanted to impress on me as dramatically as possible how dreadful my novel was. When I urged him to complete it (it was not long), arguing that the death of Smith, the family dog, brought out the underlying sympathy of the characters (a sympathy sunk so deep, one reader was to write, that you needed a diver's suit to reach it), he simply refused. He hated everything about it.

> Your formula is evident. Take the weakest side of each character – the skeleton in every cupboard – and magnify them out of proportion so that they appear to become the whole and not part of the picture . . . Surely you could have written a study of old age and loneliness without photographing your own family for the background? Why should they be pilloried? You go out of your way to avoid any redeeming features in anyone's character. One would have thought that you could have waited a few years until we were dead before appraising the world of our misery.

If I went ahead and tried to publish the novel, my father promised to bring legal proceedings against me and the publishers. Publication would, he believed, expose to savage ridicule the whole family, especially himself and Yolande.

As you know I work in a firm with a staff of several hundreds. Were you to publish the book I should have to give up my job. I am too old [aged sixty] to stand the sort of humiliation you wish to heap on our heads. I am also a little too old to get a new job and start again.

In the circumstances – for my sister's sake and my own – I must do everything to prevent this book being published *anywhere* till we are dead, and I am prepared to take whatever steps that are necessary legal or otherwise.

I was appalled by this hostility – as appalled as he was by what he felt to be my hostility. The next four months, during which I tried to negotiate some compromise, were deeply unhappy for us both. When I asked my father what pages he would like changed, he answered rather wittily: 'Why not introduce a few fictional characters? It would of course entail rewriting but you would discover whether you are a novelist or whether – as I believe – you are not.' Here lay one of our difficulties in reaching an agreement. For where I would refer to *A Dog's Life* as a novel, my father insisted on calling it a 'distorted biography'; and where I pointed to inventions, he saw lies. But it was of course true that the first drafts of my characters were closely sketched from life. 'Had you written down the name and address of the family you could hardly have done more to ensure that they were identified,' my father stated. He did not allow that this problem might be solved by my using a pseudonym since he believed, probably correctly, that my identity would soon be uncovered. When I sent him Roland Gant's report and an approving letter from another editor, he merely replied that they were 'not on the receiving end', and repeated that 'the whole family are together in their dislike of this distorted picture you have drawn of them'.

But this was not really true. Adeline, my grandmother, knew

nothing of this book and never would; while my mother, who was now living again in London, described it as 'a hoot' (though it was very far from the kind of novels she really liked, which were big American bestsellers featuring very rich people misbehaving in Cadillacs and swimming pools). Her acquiescence however did not impress my father. 'Your mother may not object to anything you say about her under the misapprehension that – her surname being different – she will not be so easily identified . . . She is as usual generous at others' expense.'

My mother was changing her surname so frequently that I doubted whether any pack of investigative critics could catch her. But I was shocked by the ferocity and unfairness of my father's anger, not realising how many bruises I was pressing on. For example, I called the character based on myself after my Uncle Kenneth. I did not know my father's earlier years had been lived under the shadow of his elder brother. 'Could it be that he is the worldly & financial success you so admire & is therefore not to be offended?' Such a question nonplussed me. For years my father had been accusing me of a lazy disregard for the financial ways of the world. The truth was that he envied Kenneth's success and resented his inability to give me some of it.

Being obliged to reread *A Dog's Life* for the first time in almost thirty years, I do not find it hard to understand my father's dismay. As Henry Farquhar he appears 'inclined to fatness, jovial in manner and vociferous in his denunciations'. He bulges out of his green suit, the colour of which clashes with his complexion (a patchwork of mauve and crimson), and by various means he spreads consternation and panic through the house. At one time he is innocently using up all the hot water for his bath (drowning the clamour of complaints at the bathroom door with his lusty singing); at another he is filling the dining-room with smoke, sparks and a snowstorm of tobacco as he attempts, between terrible volleys of coughing and a blind staggering from wall to wall, to light his pipe.

My father had a rather bullying manner of speech. What left him as no more than an intended hearty pat on the back would land as a telling slap on the other person's face. It was a trick that opened him up to caricature. He would prefix his honest advice with phrases such as: 'Don't be an utter fool . . .', and invite other people's opinions by asking: 'What pearl of wisdom are you about to let fall?' His general conversation was peppered with recommendations to 'Be your age!' or 'Take it from one who knows.' He could not understand the reactions some of this well-meant banter produced. In my novel I tried to catch this tactless style of talk and set it in a more sympathetic context. 'Even at his kindest, Henry somehow contrived to sound offensive. He was shy of his generosity, awkward in exposing his good nature,' I wrote. '. . . For all his apparent robustness, Henry hated the sight of pain or illness, and was far more sensitive than he dared admit.'

Such passages had no effect on my father, if he ever read them. 'I must admit a feeling of great distress when I read your true opinion of me,' he wrote. '. . . I quite agree with your statement that I am a failure. I am well aware of it.' In vain did I tell him that this character in my novel was not a failure in the way he meant – he actually brings off an important business merger on which he had set his sights. The 'failure' lies elsewhere: in the inability shown by each one of the family (including 'Kenneth') to break out of his or her separateness and (except at the moment of tragedy) touch the others. 'After the long-awaited triumph of the merger that he [Henry] could share with no one, after the thrills of the drive that no one wanted to hear, a great weariness overcame him. He couldn't continue this kind of life forever.' Yet we continued. That, it seemed to me, was our predicament.

Heinemann gave me moral support over this difficult period, which is to say that they distanced themselves from the battle, frightened of a Pyrrhic victory. They could not afford, they warned me, to win a court case over a novel. The cost of injunctions, delays, extra storage etc. would be too great. It was therefore up to me to settle matters amicably. Since this proved impossible, production on the book was stopped and *A Dog's Life* never appeared in Britain.

When I asked my father about publication abroad, he replied: 'Of course I agree that were the book to be published in Hindustani or Erse there would be little likelihood of it affecting anyone, but this does NOT apply to the *English Language*.' He relented a little, however, over the United States. 'If you alter the story as far as Yolande is concerned this is all I ask of you,' he conceded. 'She, not I, must be the judge of this.'

I had given the character of my Aunt Yolande the name Mathilda after the dashing young heroine whose adventures she had read to me in the kitchen when I was a child. In the novel I raised her to over six feet tall, made her Henry's aunt instead of his sister (and gave him a special moustache and a naval background). My American publisher then took the advice of a New York lawyer who declared the novel to be potentially libellous if the Holroyd family were indeed in the corned beef business in Canada (my equivalent of tea in India), if my father lived with his family and was 'in celluloid', if my mother was married to an industrial agriculturalist, and so on. In any case, the lawyer concluded, there would be no substantial risk of libel because 'the Holroyd family simply isn't that well-known in this country'.

I decided to go ahead and publish in the United States. I felt I had done what was reasonable to protect everyone, including myself, and no one should be hurt. I did not tell my father or my aunt. I alone was to be the judge.

*A Dog's Life* was published in the United States in 1969, reviewed surprisingly well considering how English it was and, less surprisingly, sold not so well. I was in New York at the time of publication, beginning research for my *Augustus John*. When I returned, bringing with me my advance on royalties due on publication of the novel, I found that my father was in great financial difficulties. Everything he had feared about the future of his business and had once hoped to escape through a new career writing novels, was coming true. So I handed him my advance – the best part of £2,000 – without him knowing that it came from the American publication of *A Dog's Life*.

What then happened remains obscure to me. Some months afterwards I received a letter from the Official Receiver in Bankruptcy. It appeared that my father's new company, Seamless Floors Ltd, was already in liquidation. 'I note that you are named as a party in the debenture created by the company on 6 January 1970,' the Receiver wrote to me. Evidently my father had been interviewed with his solicitor at the Board of Trade offices. Beyond the fact that this was bad news, I understood nothing. There were references in the letter to 'the provisional liquidator', a 'floating charge' and 'Section 322 of the Companies Act 1948'. The letter ended: 'Will you please consider the matter and let me know your views?'

It seemed to me that my views would be without value and were therefore useless. But I must have replied (I have a second letter stating that the contents of my reply 'are noted'). The correspondence has long ago been destroyed by what is now called the Insolvency Service (which is part of the Department of Trade and Industry) and in any case I heard no more. My 'investment' had not been enough to save my father.

It must have been about five years later, when I gave him the American edition of *Augustus John*, that my father suddenly realised my novel had actually been published and also that I had handed him my royalties. There were many ironies in the situation. He appreciated, I think, my fine act of revenge. None of the family had been troubled by its publication, and it all seemed history now. But my father wanted to 'balance the books'. He wanted to 'pay me back'. He did so most ingeniously by means of some far-flung tea shares from a colony of the Rajmai empire that had somehow escaped the liquidation of Rajmai itself in the late nineteen-sixties. I still have these shares. Indeed I cannot get rid of them. Each year I am sent details of the severe local weather, the fresh damage to crops, the lower prices and higher production costs. Some years the directors (who until recently included a member of the Magor family, a new Richard Magor) are unable to recommend a dividend; other years when they do, they are nevertheless unable to pay shareholders abroad because of Foreign Exchange Regulations. I have become the apotheosis of Holroyd business enterprise. The rupee stops with me.

Looking back, it seems to me that my father probably had the better of our long rally (those tea shares were really his aces). But I am left with an unexpected feeling of gratitude to him. He saved me later embarrassment. Also the troubles I had over my novel-writing, though intensely depressing to me at the time, reinforced my desire to tell non-fiction stories by adapting some legitimate fiction devices. Besides, I have my father's novel *The Directors*, and the letters he wrote to me about *A Dog's Life*, which together with the remaining draft of my own unpublished fiction-writing, lay down various stepping stones after his own account ends, and help me to pursue my story.

PART II

# 9

# *Some Wartime*
# *Diversions*

At Drayton Gardens I was a placid infant sleeping in my pram in the garden whatever the weather and waking punctually for my 'meals'. My mother had been unable to breastfeed me because I 'bit too hard', so she gave me 'Cow and Gate' milk from a bottle. It was mixed with water and if the mixture was too rich I came out in vivid spots. One day my mother added a mashed banana. I consumed it, stared frantically at her, and turned blue. She quickly gripped me by the feet, held me upside down and shook me until I started breathing again. But I had made no noise.

At Latymer Court I was a backward baby, literally crawling backwards into the furniture whatever temptations were waved or frisked in front of me. This habit of going backwards across the floor into crevices and corners grew so pronounced that my parents eventually consulted a child specialist. As they explained my curious problem to him I entered the room crawling forwards.

I have no memories of my mother living with what she called 'the old people' at Maidenhead. They seem to inhabit different worlds. But she had two memories of me there. In the first, she is laying me wrapped up and fast asleep on her bed while she goes off to prepare my 'lunch'. When she gets back with the tray I am gone. The window is open and in a panic she wonders for a moment if there has been a kidnapping. Anyway, there is no kid napping. Not on the bed. Where was I? What should she tell the family? Will she ever get me back? She does get me back after a search reveals that I had turned over and slipped off the bed on the side next to the wall and am now sleeping quietly under the bed. The story is satisfying since it explains, or so I like to think, my preference as an adult for low beds to the insecurity of sleeping in high ones.

Her second memory gives a dramatic glimpse of the family as I got to know them and later tried to recreate them in *A Dog's Life*. At the beginning of the war Fraser arranged for a large shelter to be built under the vegetable garden at Norhurst. I can remember the strange hump of the vegetable bed like a stilled wave, or the channel made by a monster worm as it furrowed its way from one side to the other. The interior smelt of wet earth and concrete, and possessed a curious other-worldly aroma that infected all our spirits. I used to play innocently on top of it during the day, but underground it did not seem quite so innocent. My father and our gardener were the architects. At night they had stolen out and returned with wheelbarrows of materials from a road that was being built near by – pioneers of privatisation. Inside, there were concrete slabs to sit or lie on, and hanging oil-lamps, and an enormous stack of tinned foods; but the German Luftwaffe never put us to the test of discovering whether we also had a tin-opener.

Before this hideaway was completed we used a lighted store-cupboard in which to conceal ourselves during emergencies. It was here we would place the large chest full of fragrant Rajmai tea sent to my grandfather from India each Christmas – a comforting companion in a crisis. This small cupboard under the stairs seemed to me a holy place that would surely afford protection from any war as it had previously protected my grandmother from thunderstorms. But we had dug for victory and had our new shelter ready for the Battle of Britain.

Being only thirty miles from London we sometimes heard the buzz and drone of the bombers and saw the night skies crossed by the moving lines of the searchlights. We had been issued with 'siren suits' as the proper clothes in which to greet enemy aircraft, and we were to be given rubber gasmasks which made us look ridiculously frightening and suggested death from suffocation. Among my aunt's possessions is the first draft of a letter and a form which reveals that she had applied for gasmasks for the dogs – my grandmother's bad-tempered sealyham, the few miscellaneous terriers attributed to my grandfather, my mother's faithful scottie Popples, and the various labradors or sheepdogs owned by my aunt herself.

When the first air-raid alarm sounded at night we were more than prepared. My grandmother, who gave the impression of spending most of her nights poised at the door of her bedroom waiting for burglars, rushed straight into my mother's room and snatched me (I was then aged four) from her bed. She was followed by Fraser running from his room without his dentures and quite naked save for the truss he was obliged to wear for his hernia. The two of them began wrestling over me while through a window, mingling with the sustained wail of the siren, could be heard my aunt screaming for the dogs. There was turmoil as everyone fumbled over the zips of their siren suits, hunted for torches, gasmasks and other impedimenta. Then we all struggled downstairs. We unlocked the back door (no easy matter) and made our way over some flowerbeds down the garden, cursing the irregularities of the route, the bad behaviour of the others' dogs, the Germans, and one another. As we tumbled at last over the marrows and cabbages into the shelter, the 'All Clear' sounded, and we began tottering back. 'I was spellbound, but had to follow the "circus",' my mother later wrote in her account for me. 'Back to bed and you really did not know anything about it as you were half-asleep all the time – so was I.' But I do recall the illuminations in the night sky, the cold air, and a general mêlée.

My father was to join the Royal Air Force, and my Uncle Kenneth, who had been in the Territorial Army (he was a member of the Artists' Rifles in Chancery Lane) was immediately made a Captain in the Rifle Brigade. On 20 October 1940, 'being about to leave the United Kingdom of Great Britain and Ireland and to serve for a time in foreign parts', he gave Basil power of attorney over his affairs. My father is still described as being a company director and his address is given as Norhurst, the family home.

While training in the Rifle Brigade earlier that year Kenneth had come across his cousin Ivor (son of 'Uncle Pat') who was a regular soldier. He had been impressed initially by Ivor's devotion to discipline, but soon, seeing how far it went, wondered whether he was 'off his head'. At Maidenhead we always enjoyed these stories of 'mad Ivor' and used to speculate on whether he suffered from early sunstroke or something more devious.

But why, I wondered, hadn't my father joined up at the same time as Kenneth? His service record, which refers to 'rheumatoid polyarthritis noted in 1932', suggests that his entry was delayed by poor health. He did not become a member of the Royal Air Force Volunteer Reserve until the spring of 1941, his civilian occupation during 1940 being given as a sales manager in Birmingham. I never heard him refer to this job (he was probably selling off his glass company there), nor did my mother mention it in the last pages of her account, simply covering this period with a note: 'Couldn't stand the strain.'

It is clear that by the end of 1940 their marriage was pretty well over. At Maidenhead they slept in separate rooms, though this was partly because there were no proper double beds in Norhurst, and my mother always insisted on nine hours' sleep at night – otherwise she had 'no eyes' in the morning and would have to place teabags on her eyelids during the siesta hour. In a Will my father made on 20 March 1941, shortly before joining the Royal Air Force, he appointed his brother and sister as his joint executors and trustees and as my guardians. There is no mention of his wife in the Will, and in his service record he gave his father as his next-of-kin (though in a moment of absent-mindedness describing him as his wife).

Later that year Flying Officer Basil Holroyd was posted to Wilmslow in Cheshire – and my mother went too. It was their last chance together. Once they had settled into a boarding house (the first of four), she came and fetched me from Maidenhead. I had been attending a small nursery school which I was taken to along a lane known as Folly Way. The school was called Highfield and all I can remember now is learning to crochet and 'colour in' surrounded by an indiscriminate noise as the boys rushed around the top of Castle Hill. At Wilmslow I went to a new school of which I recall nothing except a big green field. But my mother wrote about a prize-giving day in the summer of 1942 with crowds of parents in the garden. It was evidently one of those amiable occasions when the sun shines and 'all shall have prizes'. But when my name was called out I was too shy to go up to the headmaster's table, and my father had to collect the prize himself. It was too literal a version of what he wanted from me.

My mother worked at the refreshment bar of the Church Army Canteen inside the RAF station at Wilmslow. Pumping the milkshake machine and cutting the fruitcake passed for glamour in those days – it was certainly livelier than Norhurst. She made several friends, in particular the vivacious Shirley Morton whose husband Ivor became a semi-celebrity playing the piano with Corporal Dave Kaye at the entertainments which included Gracie Fields among the visiting stars. We sometimes heard them on the 'Light Programme' of the BBC too playing chirpy dance tunes, and patriotic songs, 'Roll out the Barrel' or 'Hang out the Washing on the Siegfried Line'. I remember the great hangar where they played against a clatter of plates and cups and glasses in the background. In the evenings, as one of the 'Wilmslow Wheelers', my mother (they still called her 'Sue' in those days) would join the convoy of bicycles off to the pubs. Bicycling back in the black-out on her upright but uncontrollable Raleigh was always a tricky business and there were many spills. Though this was the time when I heard loud arguments at night between my parents, the wartime spirit of forced gaiety and compulsory conviviality in public never seemed to flag. 'Basil was always one over the 8 in those days,' my mother wrote in her idiomatic English.

But my father did not like my mother's new friends or approve of her going out with them at night, leaving me in the boarding house. He was often away himself at RAF stations in the north of England arranging the supply of provisions overseas and would have preferred my mother to go back to Maidenhead, taking me with her. But she would not go. They argued violently. 'We really could not stand each other by then,' my mother wrote. Though she makes no mention of another man in her account, she told me never to mention the name of a certain RAF officer there, and not having mentioned it, I have forgotten the name.

It was at Wilmslow that my mother began having affaires. In his novel *The Directors*, my father wrote: 'Thelma's first affairs hurt him bitterly . . . She was constitutionally unable to exist without the admiration of men . . . She didn't even feel very deeply about any man she went to bed with and usually forgot all about him as soon as the brief intrigue was over. Then the excitement of a new affair would prove irresistible.' I have no doubt that this passage comes from these times at Wilmslow.

During one of the school holidays in 1943 ('it must have been summer', my mother wrote, 'although you were wearing your pale blue overcoat'), my father announced that he was taking me down to Maidenhead. 'But he never brought you back to me,' my mother continued. '. . . After a few months, when the Mortons left Wilmslow, I went with them.' She stayed with her friend Shirley Morton for several weeks in London and then moved to a boarding house in Cresswell Gardens, off Drayton Gardens where she had begun her marriage. I have no memories of this upheaval, only of the repercussions that would follow.

My father, soon to be promoted to Squadron Leader and unexpectedly benefiting from his exile at Chillon College, was being trained as an RAF interpreter. In 1944 he was posted to Paris. Before leaving, he drove me over from Norhurst to begin my first term at Scaitcliffe, the boarding school he had described as 'absolute hell'.

# 10

# Notes from Norhurst

'What shall we do with the boy?' That cry comes back to me whenever I think of my early years at Maidenhead. As if to answer the question, my father, in the intervals from his career in France, would turn up at Norhurst with some devastating present – an air rifle, chemistry set, conjuring tricks or even golf club – and after a few flourishes and gestures, a few words of encouragement and a laugh, leave the fine tuning of my tuition as rifleman, chemist, magician or golfer to my aunt while he returned to fight the Germans or encourage the French. My aunt did her best, but I remember thinking one rainy day as we quarried out some lumps of ice to put on her forehead while waiting for the ambulance to arrive, that we shouldn't have chosen the dining-room to play cricket.

Most of these events passed my grandfather by. He got little sleep at night and would catch up during the day with a series of 'forty winks'. Besides he had his own disasters to occupy him.

The post would arrive, he would shake his head and on the backs of the envelopes begin a sequence of calculations that never seemed to come out well. Distracted, he would suddenly stand up and crash his poor head against some unexpected corner of furniture and then, blaming the government and all its works, stick on another piece of Elastoplast.

This Elastoplast, like the impasto of an expressionist painter, covered the dome of my grandfather's head which, because he was bald and somewhat bent, he appeared to be accusingly presenting to us all. His face too, with its changing surface of bumps and bruises, was something of a battlefield largely because of his shaving habits. He was not a skilful shaver. His chin and cheeks, as well as his nose and neck, were sometimes dotted with tufts of cotton wool and crossed with thin red lines like alleged Martian canals. Late in life my father gave him an electric razor. After some experimentation in the privacy of the garage, he found this gadget easiest to use while standing on the seat of the upstairs lavatory from where he plugged its dangling cord into the overhead light. In the darkness the whole operation lasted nearly half-an-hour, for he sometimes submerged part of his kit in the cistern. It was impossible for the rest of us to use the lavatory over these periods. My aunt, my grandmother, Old Nan and myself would line up outside, rattling the door handle and crying out in exasperation. But he felt protected by the comfortable whining of his machine. Occasionally he would shave the same side of his face twice since there was no soap to guide him. But over a week things would even out.

From time to time, amid panic and pandemonium, my grandfather was required to travel up to London for a meeting of the Rajmai Tea Company, and once or twice I went up with him on the train. When he arrived at Paddington he would hand up his neatly-folded copy of *The Times* through the smoke of the hissing engine to the train driver who touched his cap and nodded his head as he took it. My grandfather always

came back looking worried from these days in London, and the
dogs themselves would sneak into the corners of the rooms.

Part of his difficulties arose from increasing deafness, though
this also afforded him protection from the perpetual squabbling
that filled the rooms at Norhurst. As a child I had the double
experience of my parents' marriage that had unhappily broken
up, and my grandparents' marriage that had been unhappily
kept going. At one point I was to make an attempt to run away
from Maidenhead to join my mother in London; at another
point, I attempted to run back from London to Maidenhead.
The family was baffled: but I do not feel so baffled.

Norhurst was to be my intermittent home for twenty years.
Everyone was very kind to me, but the atmosphere had become
saturated with unhappiness. It was a ritualised unhappiness,
repeated in the same formula of words through the awful succession of meals, housework, and more meals that was our
routine, every day, all year. I can hear their voices still:

> *I declare unto goodness I don't know what's wrong with
> you . . . Are you perfectly potty? Are you insane?
> Sometimes I think you should be certified . . . Shut up!
> You bitch! . . . You are disgusting! How dare you speak to
> me like that? I do have ears you know . . . One can't open
> one's lips in this bally house . . . Sorry! Sorry! Sorry!
> Sorry! Will that do? Or would you like me to go down on
> bended knees? Why don't you arrange for me to be shot
> at dawn? . . . I'm sick to death of you all. I wish I were
> dead! I wish we were all dead, dead and gone.*

Sometimes they shouted all this and more, much more, from
separate rooms. At other times I would come across one of them
practising these same words under her breath. During meals,
above the immaculate reports of wars, natural disasters, weather
and sport issuing from the huge wooden wireless in one corner

of the dining-room, they confronted one another with the same shouted phrases yet again. From another corner of the room my grandmother's parrot 'Mr Potty' (though we realised after she produced an egg that we had got her gender wrong) croaked back to us our shrill invective from her vast cage.

Into this echoing pit of abuse had tumbled 'Josh and Bang' from their heady days in Ireland; also their daughter Yolande who had looked so engagingly bold and lively in her early photographs, so happy with her friends in the South of France; and even the kindly Kate Griffin, the 'Nan' who had nursed my father so carefully through his illnesses and was now called 'Old Nan' by me. It was their collective unhappiness I had tried to recreate in *A Dog's Life* that so distressed my father – and that probably accounts for my avoidance of arguments today. 'They sat around in dismay, bowed, overcome,' I wrote. 'The words came from them mechanically, as though they existed under a spell . . . They had passed and repassed on the same staircase, twisted the same door handles, sat in the same old chairs around the same old table, and heard the same monotonous voices . . . and as time wore on they had somehow grown into strangers – strangers to themselves and one another.'

We lived at Norhurst as if in a capsule. No one visited us – we would never let anyone in. If by some mischance a person came to the door and rang the bell, we suddenly stopped our insults and froze into silence until he went away. When the telephone rang (Maidenhead 336) we panicked, rushing with frightful cries from room to room until it ceased ringing and we could relax again into our hostilities. We were certain the telephone was not 'safe', that the world could hear every syllable we said, though we had nothing to say and could hardly hear what others were saying to us. We did not want to hear. The truth was that we were frightened of the world outside. We had locked ourselves in an awful embrace and forgotten how to communicate with strangers.

And yet, because of its familiarity and my insecurity, I was attached to Norhurst as my father had been to Brocket, which was only round a corner but a generation away. That house lay in sunshine, this one in darkness. On the ground floor the 'morning-room' was without light and occupied by the telephone, like a monster in its cave; in the large hall, like the remnants of a beleaguered army, had been assembled the last cracked pieces of Lalique glass: the jardinière with gazelles and the eglantine powder box; the archer ashtray and the water grasshopper in opal, green and blue; the goblet with dogs and the vase with egrets; the amber carp, the dahlia bowl, the mulberry and mistletoe lights, the cockerel mascot. One or two of these, with a cry and a curse, we smashed each year until there was almost none; at the back of the house a gloomy dining-room gave on to the garden where the sparrows, chaffinches, thrushes and blackbirds waited noisily for their three meals a day; also at the back was the kitchen, the only warm room in the house, and a dilapidated scullery where frightful battles over washing-up raged. Off the landing upstairs stood five small bedrooms and two bathrooms – one for my grandmother, the other for the rest of us. But baths were discouraged. A bath a day was unthinkable. As my grandmother remarked (referring to my mother): 'Some people must be bally dirty if they need *that* amount of washing.' The boiler, which was encased in a shed outside the kitchen and which we fed night and day with coal and coke and much else besides, seemed to have fallen asleep. Whatever mixture we gave it, whatever knobs we twisted or levers pulled, it continued dozing and we got barely enough tepid water for our washing-up contests. The trouble was that we all had contradictory notions of how the boiler should be operated. 'Now look here,' my grandfather would begin, taking out a pencil and the back of an envelope to demonstrate his theories to Old Nan, the only person who was obliged to listen to him (though he would raise his voice so that his message reached everyone). On Fridays a gardener called Western came in to help with the leaves and twigs, enabling the rest of us on Saturdays and for the rest of the week to blame him for getting everything wrong. 'Western must have been putting grass in the boiler again,' my grandfather would grumble, shaking his head mournfully. He was very fond of Western whom he often called 'a damn fool, and no mistake', beaming as he said it.

It was the garden I loved at Norhurst, with its hovering dragonflies and bumblebees, its ladybirds, butterflies, chaffinches, robins. It was a long and narrow garden, divided into three sections. Nearest the house was a lawn which belonged to the crowds of birds except in wartime when we turned it into a vegetable patch. In peacetime, it reverted to green grass with rosebeds, a place in which to savour Rajmai tea on a summer afternoon, and get my aunt to send down her lethal-sounding leg-breaks to me with a tennis ball. The middle section was wilder, incorporating a small rock garden and a dangerous pond with its mighty toad, and a large tree in which I could hide. Further down, where the shelter had been dug, was a sandpit for me to jump in. It lay beside some enormous marrows and elongated hanging beans. At the end stood a garden shed and, over the fence, the peaceful insecurity of All Saints' cemetery.

Though once or twice a cousin was invited to play with me (the boy who was whispered to be Rex Harrison's son and who then suffered from an ophthalmic illness that made his eyes bright red), on the whole I played alone. I hid and found myself in the tree; captured and released myself from the shed; raced myself up and down the length of the garden past the sundial and the dogs' graves; threw a tennis ball high on to the roof and, as it spun down out of the blue sky, caught it; and contrived a complicated game with a ball against the garage doors, simultaneously winning and losing.

The garage, guarded on one side by a peach tree and on the other by a walnut tree, was a sombre fascinating place, an

Aladdin's Cave, piled high with treasures from the past – a broken rocking-horse, a strangely-painted screen, a still-working radiogram, pictures of girls and horses by Lewis Baumer and Anna Zinkheisen, suitcases, ladders, illustrated catalogues and mildewing books, one or two imposing pieces of furniture and large threadbare carpets with faded colours, a bowler hat belonging to my aunt, a walking stick that turned out to be a gun, and bottles of cider that I was sometimes allowed to drink in the evening with my grandfather. It was obvious treasure. There was even room for a car, a little eight-horse-power Ford that my aunt no longer used.

I sometimes sat in my aunt's old car and listened to records on the radiogram. My grandparents had no interest in music and my father seemed actively to dislike it (he could be propelled to his feet if told that a piece from Gilbert and Sullivan was the National Anthem). But my aunt had a collection of 'seventy-eight' records – 'Miss Otis Regrets' or 'Dinner for One Please, James', 'Bye-bye Blackbird', 'It Had to be You', 'Who's Sorry Now', 'Always', and Charles Trenet singing 'La Mer'. They were scratchy but curiously poignant and appealing. My aunt never took them into the house to play – she never played anything. I did not know why. But I played them, and then I played my own records. How I first heard classical music, how I got hold of my records, I cannot remember. I daresay I listened to the wireless and then demanded these records as birthday and Christmas presents. I would take Schubert's *Unfinished Symphony*, Verdi's *Requiem*, Wagner's 'Ride of the Valkyries' out to the garage, and sit there absorbing them in the dark. My favourite composers were Tchaikovsky and Beethoven whose symphonies I got to know by heart. I suppose these garage concerts began when I was aged about nine, and continued for eight or nine years. I would turn up the volume, open the car door, and sit enthralled. Sometimes I could not sit still but had to stride up and down through the dusty bric-à-brac waving my arms, lifting up my voice, joining in. This music, and the imaginary adventures I was led on upstairs by Conan Doyle, Rider Haggard, H.G. Wells and others, were no artistic luxury for me but the essence of my life. I would come in from these hours in the garage, or down from my bedroom, glowing with happiness and fortified against the family warfare that was more real to me than any combat against Germans, Italians or Japanese. I was at the centre of this domestic warfare and regarded the world war as mere orchestration for it.

Though I was an excessively timid child, the boredom that timidity induced would sometimes get the better of me, and I became for a few moments vicariously bold. One day I found some nice fat cartridges inside a desk in the morning-room. Remembering the walking stick that was a gun I took these cartridges to the garage and found that they fitted. I then went off to find my grandmother who happened to be in her bathroom, not having a bath. I showed her the walking stick, put it in her hands, pointed to the trigger and asked her to pull it. She was reluctant to do so, but I begged her and begged her until eventually she did pull it. There was an enormous bang and a hole appeared in the floor through which our feet dangled, emerging, I daresay, like strange stalactites in the garage below.

I got into grave trouble for this exploit and my father arrived back from France to punish me. But really everyone blamed my grandmother. She had become a figure of blame round whom all the irritation in the house seethed and beat itself. The sight of her struggling downstairs, or patting the cushions, or rearranging the chairs, or humming as she sauntered indecisively between rooms, or simply eating, provoked surges of uncontrollable indignation from us all.

In his novel *The Directors*, my father has a breakfast scene in which John Maitland, a distinguished character with 'a Victorian conscience about anyone who is dependent on him', sits reading *The Times* while his wife chatters uninterruptedly without ever gaining his attention. She is an empty person, without occupation or interests, a child in a woman's body, who has become completely dependent on her husband and so made him her prisoner. This is a picture of Fraser and Adeline at Brocket while my father was young. 'John has bought the old Georgian house shortly after their marriage and she had fallen in love with it at first sight. She still loved it when she wasn't feeling bored – which was all too often. Time hung heavy on her hands . . .'

After almost half a century of time, Adeline (whom Fraser now called 'Di', rapping it out like a terminal injunction) makes her appearance in my novel as I saw her when I was young at Norhurst. She is now a 'bent and fragile old woman, bravely pessimistic', with a parchment face, and lips coloured crimson so inaccurately as to make her mouth leer across her cheek like a Hogarthian trull. I pursued her in *A Dog's Life* as she advances to her breakfast.

> Her sparse metallic grey hair lay chaotic and unkempt, crushed by a dilapidated hairnet. From her left ear hung an earring; on her right foot a sober black gumshoe. Around her neck was suspended a fantastic chain of imitation pearls that stretched, as though elastic, far below her waist, and, when she got down from her stool, almost to the floor itself . . . Before her on the table was piled an assortment of articles, reminiscent of a junk shop. There was a ballpoint pen and a bottle of ink, one ball of string, a bottle of aspirin, some soap, a book, two flashlights and a small tin of boot polish. She was prepared for almost anything.

My father did not object to this passage, or to my other descriptions of his mother. 'Strangely enough, you seem to have dealt more gently with your grandmother,' he wrote to me. 'This

I suppose is only to be expected considering she caused most of the misery. It was greatly due to her spendthrift habits that father got into trouble with the banks. Anyone who was dependent to any degree on her paid pretty dearly for the pleasure.'

At various times in the course of her life we had all been dependent on her. Adeline had spent the family money, my father believed, and given the family no love in exchange for that money. Fraser and Basil were consequently 'embarrassed', both in the financial sense and in their vulnerability to attractive women like Agnes May and Sue who, they calculated, did give love for money. My father, who lacked self-esteem, talked women into marriage with glowing descriptions of financial happiness to come. He could not credit that anyone would accept him 'for poorer'.

I cannot believe that readers would find the hunchbacked, haphazard figure of my grandmother, as she appears in *A Dog's Life*, with her meaningless patter and mad apprehension, more sympathetic than the other characters. Her days, I wrote,

> succeeded one another in a dull, identical pattern, each one finding her a little older than the last, a little more tormented by monotony, a little more fearful of the approaching end to her monotony . . . she waited for several seconds listening, but not knowing what it was she expected or even wished to hear. For Anne seemed convinced that there existed some secret in life which she had never discovered, but which was always being discussed behind her back. She hurried from place to place, from one shut door to another, in the hope of a sudden revelation . . .

My father was convinced that his mother never loved him because, being her son, he genuinely was unlovable. And he could do nothing about it except make a million. Then he would be worth something. Money would transform him. Though it was worse for him because she had not even wanted him born, he knew that Adeline had not really loved his brother either, or even his sister, or her own husband, or anyone else so far as he could see. Until now. For she loved me. If Basil 'put a foot out of line just once he heard about it till kingdom come', I wrote in *A Dog's Life*. But I 'could get away with sheer bloody murder', as I almost had done with the gun in the bathroom.

Now that her bridge partners were 'dead and gone' and her wicked pack of playing cards put away, Adeline had nothing to distract her until I came to live at Norhurst. She at once offered me everything she had – everything she had somehow been unable to give her own children. I became another version of herself. 'There's nothing much to occupy a child in this rotten place,' she would say. 'It's all gone to rack and ruin.' She continually gave me things, often really absurd things like extra carrots for the night. She saved up her rations for me, saw I got second helpings of spinach and dried eggs, stood over me as I tried to eat them urging me on, plucking at my sleeve, trying to pull out of me some loving words. 'See anyone you liked better than yourself while you were out this morning?' she would ask. But this was not a promising gambit for a heart-to-heart talk because she never wanted me to go out of the house at all. 'You'll catch your death,' she would say, before warning me to keep clear of strangers. She was terrified when my father arrived with a bicycle, and would endanger her own life leaning far out of her bedroom window looking up and down the road until I wobbled safely back. If I was taken to the Plaza or Rialto cinemas – expeditions that would send me almost ill with excitement – my grandmother would raise up her arms to heaven at the sheer folly of it and then force quantities of formamint tablets on to me in case I 'caught something'. She, who had apparently been so carefree over my father's illness, fretted all the time over mine. 'Your eyes look like two burnt holes in a blanket,' she would greet me in the mornings. She waited vainly for gratitude. 'Now do buck up and be a comfort,' she pleaded. But what could I do? Too often I felt irritation, impatience and the need to escape as she hovered near me, watching, worrying, plucking at my sleeve. 'I declare unto goodness the boy never tells me anything,' she would complain. But I had nothing to tell her. The important things for me were my book and music adventures and they could not be told to anyone. 'Don't waste your time speaking to your poor old grandmother. All right! All right! I'm not going to hurt you. But you'll miss me when I'm dead and gone. "I wonder where she went," you'll say. "She was good to me when she was alive, poor old soul."' And so she was good to me. But it was too late and there was too much distance between us to make something of that goodness.

# 1 1

# *Yolande's Story*

Whatever was to be done with 'the boy', it was usually left to my aunt to do it. Apart from reading to me in the kitchen and playing cricket on the lawn, she would take me to films in Maidenhead. She herself loved musicals and romances which I didn't like; and I loved comedies and thrillers which she didn't like. But in those days there were two films in a programme so we usually came out reasonably pleased. She also took me occasionally to matinées at the Theatre Royal in Windsor. We would get on the bus and rattle through the fields and villages to the theatre that stood under the shadow of the castle, round a corner from the river. These were journeys of painful excitement for me. But I was dreadfully disillusioned by the Windsor pantomime, sitting through the first part with unutterable expectation, and then with awful impatience through the long interval during which trays of tea and cake were passed along the rows of seats in the stalls. I watched the final act with dismay, hating the silly jokes and longing for the entrance of the pandas – for I had got it into my head that I was at a *pandamime*. I have never since enjoyed pantomimes.

My aunt was aged forty in 1943, the year I returned from Wilmslow to Maidenhead. To assist with what was called 'the war effort' she had taken a night job at the telephone exchange. She never told us what she did there, but I liked to imagine her in the dark decoding secret messages. Most of her days were passed 'walking the dogs'. No extremity of weather kept her indoors – she could not abide frowsting with the rest of us. She would start out at a terrific pace, almost running, as if to catch up for lost time, over the Bath Road, up All Saints Avenue, along the playground and across the fields. Then she would strike for home through Maidenhead Thicket. The dogs were exhausted when they arrived back. But my aunt seemed driven by a frantic energy. She never had meals with the rest of the family. She could not bear the sight and sound of us eating, the uproar, the spectacle: my grandfather's loose dentures, my grandmother's regular farting, my own obstinate mess, even Old Nan's insistent chomping. However late we were, she would burst into the house halfway through lunch and was always welcomed by Adeline with: 'We were beginning to wonder where you'd got to.' By way of reply, she would cry out: 'This place is like an oven!' Then she banged open all the windows and, as we cowered at the table clutching our white napkins like flags of surrender, she would turn on us and snatch away our half-full plates of food for the first round of washing-up. Adeline sometimes tried to hold on to her plate, not because she wanted to eat what was on it but because she wanted the privilege of washing it up. 'Now do be sensible, Yolande,' she would cry. 'Do leave everything! You're in no fit state. I'll see to it all later.'

'I'd save yourself the trouble if I were you,' Yolande would spit back. 'I'd only have to do it again afterwards.'

'Leave the whole bally thing alone!' Adeline would scream, as they struggled for the plate.

Old Nan, who sat in her usual curiously tilted position, the top portion of her body bent acutely forward so that it seemed, despite being anchored to the chair by her substantial lower self, that she simply must crash forward, would aim her disapproving cough at Adeline and reach for her sewing or knitting like Madame Defarge beside the guillotine.

Every move in the choreography of this family quarrel was achingly familiar to us. There were of course minor variations. Sometimes my grandmother, taking advantage of my aunt's absence as she ran out to feed the birds, would put some knife or fork under the tap, and my aunt would snatch it from her as she raced back in and put it under the tap again. It was all done with extraordinary anguish and venom.

The only meal my aunt liked was tea which she ate alone at about six o'clock as the bells from All Saints Church began sounding through the garden. She loved sweet things, drinking her cups of Rajmai with plenty of sugar, and eating biscuits and cake. Then she would disappear off to the telephone exchange or into her bedroom with its columns of magazines which, besides the few films we saw together, were the only spot of glamour she allowed herself.

Writing *A Dog's Life* in the mid- to late nineteen-fifties I gave a picture of my Aunt Yolande as she appeared to me in her fifties.

The last ten years had brought her to her knees and made her irretrievably old before her time. Like the fine strands of a spider's web, a thousand tiny lines had spread across her face, making her appear, even in her sleep, incredibly harassed. She did not flinch from this truth; she did not even regret the past – but . . . whatever happened she must not make an exhibition of herself. Life went on regardless of misfortunes . . . in an angry voice she began to lecture herself

'Mathilda Farquhar!'
'Yes?'
'This will never do!'
'No.'
'Pull yourself together!'
'Yes.'
'Stop all this nonsense, this instant!'
'I will!'

I can remember my aunt fiercely lecturing herself under her breath in this manner at Norhurst. In my novel the event that brings on this self-tutorial is the death of her dog Smith. But behind this loss rises the memory of another loss years back, that of an Italian boyfriend or lover whom she thinks of in her bedroom that night.

It was difficult to believe that she was the same person as she was now, difficult to believe that any of it had ever happened at all . . . he had been a terrible rogue of course, everyone knew that. Still . . . whatever anyone cared to say about him . . . she often wondered whether she had really had such a lucky break as the family liked to make out. Anyway, he had given her what real happiness she had ever experienced, for however short a time, and no one had been able to take his place afterwards – no, not with all his faults!

It was this page that particularly alarmed my father, I now see, and made him insist that I 'alter the story as far as Yolande is concerned'. I must have picked up some rumour of my aunt's early life, otherwise I would not have chosen an Italian for 'Mathilda'. But only now can I begin to assemble some of the pieces in my aunt's story.

At the end of 1926, when Yolande was aged twenty-four, her

father had sent her some money from the Royal Automobile Club 'for your wedding clothes'. But there was no wedding and the following year he is writing of 'the sorrow you have suffered'. If something went wrong it may have been due to 'the slur cast on the family name' by Fraser's notorious escapade with Agnes May. This episode made all his children ask the question, as Basil put it: 'could we ever hold up our heads again?' But in his novel *The Directors*, he put forward another reason why his sister did not marry.

> Thelma grew into an unbelievably lovely girl and her Mother was determined to salvage the family fortunes by getting her daughter a rich husband. Thelma was paraded round all the smart places but she was never allowed out with anyone on her own. Wherever she went her Mother went too . . . A great many men wanted her, but those whom her Mother considered ineligible were turned away whilst the few who were permitted to pay their addresses soon decided the old lady to be too great an obstacle.

I have no doubt that this is my father's summary of the relationship between Adeline and Yolande. It was far easier for the sons to escape into their other lives. The little hammers of duty boarded Yolande up first at Brocket and finally in Norhurst. 'You – as much as any of us – must know what hell has been made of your aunt's life,' my father wrote to me after reading *A Dog's Life*. 'Your grandmother ruined what chance she had of marrying when she was a young girl.' Certainly it would have been all the more difficult for Yolande to leave her mother after Fraser himself had left. And when he returned early in the nineteen-thirties her wedding clothes had not been bought. 'I have been wronged for years,' Fraser declared from the Royal Automobile Club. But as the years unrolled it was Yolande who seemed most grievously wronged.

The pictures of her in the South of France between 1928 and 1932 show a sunlit smiling face. She looks happy. She is usually with other women also in their late twenties. There are few men.

But there was a man.

When my mother began visiting Brocket in 1934, she saw Adeline playing bridge indoors and Yolande playing tennis in the garden. They would meet on the veranda for some light bickering before the tea ceremony. Yolande had her little Ford, the very one that, later stabled in the garage at Norhurst, I was to use for my private concerts of Tchaikovsky and Beethoven. But at Brocket in the nineteen-thirties Yolande was chiefly buzzing about, my mother noticed, taking Adeline to and from her bridge parties. Yolande was disappointed that Ulla (she pronounced it 'Oh-la') did not play tennis. She was running out of partners. But unlike Norhurst, Brocket did open its doors to visitors, and people 'popped in'. Mostly they were Yolande's friends – Cathie, Cynthia, Freda, Nina and a few others who lived near by. And my mother also met Captain Hazlehurst whom everyone called 'Hazel'. There is a snap of a yacht among my mother's miscellaneous photographs which apparently belonged to Hazlehurst on which my parents and my aunt spent a weekend in the mid-nineteen-thirties. Among Yolande's albums there is no photograph of Hazel himself. But this man, my mother wrote, was the love of Yolande's life.

My father assumed I knew about Hazlehurst, but I never met him and can recall no more than the hushed whisper of his name. Among the cheque stubs, vets' receipts, bank statements, odds and ends my aunt preserved at the end, lay a few small bundles of correspondence. They are mostly letters of condolence on her parents' deaths, letters from building societies and banks, and one or two letters with foreign stamps including a couple from myself posted in the United States. There are also about a dozen letters dating from the nineteen-thirties. These are signed 'H'.

*

And now arises the question of whether I am entitled to read these letters written sixty or more years ago, and use them in this book. For as I write, though in her advanced nineties she can hardly speak or hear, has no memories and does not really know where she is, Yolande is alive.

It is a question with which biographers are naturally familiar, but never in my own writing life has it arisen so acutely. For if I read them am I not trespassing? And if I quote them do I not commit the sin of which my father so angrily accused me? Or is this my chance of atonement?

To other people I know that I appear reticent. This surprises me, since I do not always *feel* reticent or keep my opinions to myself. Have I not been in tears while writing parts of this book – tears of laughter sometimes? Doubtless I have a self-protective manner, the reasons for which are scattered through this narrative. Nevertheless, despite my appearance of reticence, I have gained something of a reputation as the biographer of Lytton Strachey and Augustus John for beating back the frontiers of reticence in other people's lives. So what can I do in this near-autobiographical story? To some extent I am obliged to reflect the silence and repression within my family – a code of privacy shared by most ordinary people of those times – because they do not hand me the codebreaking clues of any correspondence. So what I can reveal emerges more between the lines of my writing.

My father and mother kept no letters from me or anyone else, and my aunt has not kept these few letters for publication. It is merely bad luck that her nephew turns out to be what James Joyce called a 'biografiend'. In a sense she has not deliberately kept this correspondence at all – its incompleteness and the haphazard way in which it is scattered through miscellaneous bits and pieces of paper indicate that these letters are merely 'undestroyed'. For the act of destruction is like a sentence of death, a second death, which we cannot easily bring ourselves to commit on those we have loved. But can others do it for us? Is that an act of mercy or an act of vandalism? And does the passing of time alter the purgatorial state of these papers, raise or lower them from a heartbeat to a text? Then, if I keep them and they are never used what of that? Does their interest gradually leak away? Have I been cowardly? Why should my aunt be any different from the band of semi-public characters who have been dragged in to play parts in my biographies? If there is a principle that entitles me to do this to them, what principle permits me to act differently with her? Remember that, though the contents of these letters may not shock a reader at the end of the twentieth century, their publication would have been considered highly indiscreet only fifty years ago, quite unacceptable to my family, and absolutely unthinkable to my aunt herself. For here, in its muted form, lie moments, private moments, from what is perhaps the most vital part of her life. And if I feel a need for self-protection, so may she.

'No serious biographer working in the twentieth century will have failed to lay down some ethical foundations to his craft,' I wrote in a lecture on biography.

Far from adding a new terror to death, the good biographer gives an opportunity to the dead to contribute to the living world. It is understandable and right that people should seek to protect themselves and others close to them during their lives. We all need our prevarications, evasions, our sentimentalities and silences. We have a need, too, for the privacy out of which our work comes. But I make a distinction between the living and our friends the dead. I believe we pay a compliment to the dead by keeping them in employment to assist the living. For if we have all these necessary prevarications, evasions, sentimentalities and silences as our guide to conduct . . . we will make ourselves unnaturally miserable by imposing impossible standards on ourselves.

The general pattern of my aunt's story is not uncommon. But whenever the chorus of conventional family sentiment bursts forth, she should be able to step forward with others, including perhaps her own aunt Norah Palmer Holroyd and her grandmother Anna Eliza Holroyd, to remind us of what families may inflict on themselves. What happened to Norah and Anna is largely irrecoverable, but an outline of my aunt's predicament may be traced. Now that she can no longer be hurt by me, by her family, by those who knew her, by any of us, surely I may open her letters and use them to help tell her story? But I hear my father's warning: 'Please remember that one day someone may have to write your biography.' I devoutly hope not. Like many others, I do not want a biography of myself written. I have all the familiar objections. Whoever tried would get it wrong. I would prefer to do it myself – and perhaps this is what I am indirectly doing. But then of course I am merely alive, and when dead may think differently. Or I may think and feel nothing. Besides, as the examples of T.S. Eliot, Somerset Maugham, Jean Rhys and many others testify, the dead have never been able to control the living, nor the living the dead. What matters is the spirit in which they communicate, the imaginative link made between us and those who 'though dead, yet speaketh'. At any rate, I feel I must go on and do the best I can.

Hazlehurst's letters are mostly undated but a number of the envelopes exist which have postmarks, so it is possible to arrange the others chronologically by matching writing paper and addresses. The correspondence opens with a dramatic argument. From a letter sent to Brocket on 1 June 1933 from Yacht Frothblower in Cubitts Yacht Basin at Chiswick, it appears that Yolande had recently accused Hazel of 'making use' of her while 'looking for someone else'. It emerges that he has had two previous love affairs about which she knows, and that both women have 'moved on'. But he is convinced that Yolande now has

grown tired of him and is herself about to 'move on'. For she too
has had romantic attachments. What about her near-marriage in
1926? And that was not all.

In one of her photograph albums there is a picture of an
upright gentleman in hunting regalia seated on a white horse, its
ears pointed. He looks about thirty and the caption unusually
identifies him and not the horse. He is 'Major Ogilvie'. The date
is in the late nineteen-twenties, probably 1929. Also in my aunt's
box of papers are three letters she has kept from 'Og' written
from the Whittington Barracks in Lichfield. It appears that they
had known each other only a few weeks, but that he has fallen
in love with her and wants to marry her. However, she is already
engaged or committed to someone else. He apologises for worrying her with his declarations and attentions: they were, he
tells her,

> the result of day dreaming, of sitting in the sun &
> thinking of the impossible & making it seem possible,
> and impossible though it was I hadn't really, in my heart
> of hearts, given up hope . . . I have had enough
> experience of the world to know how intensely
> unwelcome unwanted love letters are, so when I write it
> will be just as a pal. This time, though, I am going to
> transgress & tell you I miss you & want you & love you.

Perhaps because he is to have an operation, Yolande writes affec-
tionately back, sends him at his urgent request three
photographs of herself and altogether, as he gratefully acknowl-
edges, 'makes a fuss of me' by going up to London to see him at
the King Edward VII Hospital for Officers. 'It's funny dear,' he
writes, 'that though I didn't know your name six weeks ago, it
will be your hand I shall be holding when, in a few minutes, they
wheel me out to a great adventure, & it will be your photographs I shall find by the side of my bed when I wake up

again . . . I am so happy that I love you.' After the operation he
writes once more: 'I often look at your photographs & wish you
belonged to me.'

But it was to Hazlehurst, apparently, that she belonged. By
1933, however, they both have doubts about the other's commitment. Hazel has the idealistic notion that women are
naturally of finer clay than men. In any event he felt 'damned
inferior', he admits, to his previous loves, and Yolande is 'very
much more superior' to both of them – which means of course
that he is 'worse off'. Is he trying to 'move on' himself and
giving her the most flattering grounds for doing so? He blows a
lot of froth as he sails round his predicament.

> Suffering as I do from stupid shyness, I must imagine a
> lot of things that are not meant and yet, although I
> know this, I haven't the sense to coordinate this
> feeling. In the almost impossible hope that you won't
> discover too quickly my gross inferiority, you had
> better keep this as evidence against me, and in the
> likely event of my backsliding produce it to stimulate
> me up again.

This convoluted Victorian sentiment leads on to a simple
nineteen-twenties conclusion. 'I suppose the only way to look at
things is to live for the present. The past gone, tomorrow
unborn – to-day is sweet.'

But can Yolande be part of this sweetness? 'I was quite the
proudest man in London to be even seen with you,' Hazel
writes. 'You must know how awfully attractive you are, & how
any person would give anything for the privilege of your presence . . . You are too adorable. I cannot think of even one tiny
flaw in the whole of you. I cannot say more . . . Do believe me.
You are too sweet to me.'

The two of them spent much of that summer together. It was

easier for Yolande to get away now that her father had returned to Brocket, and Hazel could come and stay there too. Their affaire was full of 'naughty things', but Yolande was generally careful to 'restrain' herself, and seems to have made no final commitment to her lover. Though he would frequently profess his love for her, she could never quite bring herself to say 'I love you' however passionately he invited her ('I live for the day'). Did she find such exchanges silly? Was she, like her father, having difficulties in showing her feelings? Or did she shrink from what must inevitably follow such a declaration? For he had spoken of marriage, or at least it was implied in much he said. Of course there would be obstacles. He was not rich ('I must make haste and make enough money for you'), and Adeline would certainly oppose the match, wouldn't she? So they must be careful, very careful, and meanwhile he would cultivate the rest of her family. All this lies in the second surviving letter of the series which he writes from his home in Teddington in the second week of September 1933.

Yolande has gone the previous month to Monte Carlo. She is probably staying with her girlfriend Cathie who has an apartment in the boulevard d'Italie. Hazel, anxiously waiting for news, imagines 'all sorts of things such as you finding someone else'. When a letter from her does come he is elated. 'To me you are just too wonderful, & it is still incomprehensible that you should deign to look at me even much less like me. Darling one . . . I never missed anyone so much and never felt so completely dependent upon one person . . . I never hope to be fonder of anyone for it really hurts, & I'm afraid so very afraid.'

Hazel has been staying again at Brocket and has invited Yolande's family to visit him that weekend at Teddington, some twenty miles east of Maidenhead. It is 'sweet' of him, Yolande writes. But there is more to it than this, he explains. He likes her father and brothers and 'some day it might stand me in good stead if your mother ever commenced to go off the deep end'.

Kenneth and Basil arrive while he is writing this letter – it is twelve pages long and occupies him intermittently all weekend. Adeline does not turn up. Instead she telephones regularly and when she learns that Kenneth has a temperature and is in bed, she creates tremendous scenes, 'crying copiously all day' and telling her friends of the calamity. It is essential that Adeline's nervestorms do not break over Yolande and Hazlehurst themselves, at least not yet. Because of his work, 'I shall not be able to come to France,' he tells her. But he suggests 'sneaking a night' by meeting her at Dover on her way home. 'What do you think?' he asks. 'Even if I met you in London and we went away somewhere. As I am back on the boat I can go anywhere . . . But, darling Yolande, if there is the very tiniest chance of upsetting things then like you [I think] such a move would not be worth considering . . . I am waiting for the marvellous time you promise me when you return . . .'

What happened when she returned, what developed between them secretly, cannot be traced through any subsequent correspondence. They went on seeing each other, but the next letter among my aunt's papers was written from Yacht Llanthony on 16 May 1939 and sent to Norhurst. Yolande is still 'Darling' and he is still 'H'. But inevitably the tone has changed in the intervening six years. The passion has disappeared, though they are emotionally at ease with each other. They are almost like a married couple – only for some reason they aren't married. Since Yolande is in her thirty-eighth year, the possibility of them having children has probably been eliminated. She writes to him about her 'canine troubles' and of Nan's health; he is full of sailing adventures and tells her of an enthralling trip up the Rhine ('we only just made it . . . I wouldn't have missed it for anything. The whole river is full of wrecks & broken ships so you can guess the thrill . . . will go into detail and places visited when I see you').

The remaining nine letters are all written during the war. In

August and September 1939 he writes from Yacht Goddess which is moored at Tilbury Landing Stage as part of the River Emergency Services, and describes the 'complete chaos' of the first air-raid warning during which he is trying to buy milk ('really the war is most inconsiderate'). He tells her he has been ordered to report to Liverpool. 'Here am I the head man perfectly comfortable in possibly the safest place in the land & have to go and leave my comfy bed & home and go to some perishing outlandish heathen hole to do God knows what.' He signs his letter 'As ever, H'. But this is a world away from the man who half a dozen years ago had felt so emotionally dependent on Yolande, and cried out when she was away in France: 'I miss you hellishly & long like the devil to have you back again, Darling, darling, so much.' Yet there is the habit of an attachment, the assumption of an understanding, between them still. He telephones her, is careful to let her know where he is going, hopes 'I can come to you or you to me depending on petrol', and exhorts her to 'Cheer up, be good, & happy.'

The next letter in the series comes in mid-October from the General Hospital at Ormskirk, some fifteen miles north of Liverpool. Hazlehurst is not adjusting well to the war. 'In the black out after an Air Raid Practice I fell into a concrete shelter 10 feet deep on my head,' he explains. Some 'damned fool' had left the door open 'against all orders' and there would have to be a Court of Inquiry. Meanwhile he lies bandaged in bed like a hero, with concussion, cuts to his face, an amazing black-and-red eye, sprained shoulder and thumb and broken tooth. 'I am as beautiful as ever,' and of course he is 'as ever Hazel,' he assures Yolande. He hopes to be coming down to London in a week – to see his dentist.

Over the following eight months Hazlehurst's letters from 'C Camp' and elsewhere near Liverpool show how greatly people's lives have changed since the nineteen-thirties. London itself seems far away and long ago. 'What a long letter!' he exclaims somewhat in dismay at reading Yolande's news from Maidenhead. He does his best to take an interest, but really his own news is much more interesting. The simple, active, open-air life of the army is beginning to suit him. 'I have over 500 men in my company,' he informs her. His only complaint is the cold. 'If you ever knit anything other than jumpers, you might try your hand at a pair of gloves,' he suggests. It is the only opening he allows her, and Yolande immediately responds by sending him 'a lovely dressing-gown & gloves. They are grand, but how naughty you are to spend so much money.' Then he returns to his war-talk about Baldwin, Chamberlain, Churchill and that 'damned clever man Hitler'.

'I have always impressed on everyone I know that we have been taking the [war] too lightly,' he writes. '. . . We are now fighting literally for our lives and everyone must do something.' It is probably this call to duty that persuades Yolande to drive library books to prisoner-of-war camps and then join the telephone exchange in Maidenhead.

For reasons of security, Hazlehurst is not allowed to 'say of course what we are doing'. But he cannot help revealing some of the 'eventful things happening', the hectic hours of work in twelve-hour shifts, and the fact that 'we are all in tents'. He has had a sense of seriousness forced upon him. It is a difficult grafting process and, in moments of reflection, he feels that he has 'rarely if ever been so depressed about things'. The happy world of yachts and picnics and long summer holidays that he and Yolande inhabited has vanished. 'There will be very few parties & fun in London in less than a month,' he writes on 20 May 1940, ten days before the British forces are to evacuate Dunkirk. All the same he is curiously well, and he repeatedly urges Yolande to 'keep fit, & happy and above all don't worry about anything'.

Though he signs off with 'all my love', there is no actual expression of love in these letters. Yet it seems unlikely that he is writing so openly to anyone else. Yolande is a real friend, a confidante, a pal. Realising that he is revealing to her more than he should of his military life, which is now all his life, he asks her to burn what he has sent her. But of course she cannot. This correspondence is all she has of him, and she continues sending him long domestic letters from Norhurst.

By the autumn of 1940 Hazlehurst has been posted with the 14th battalion of the King's Regiment to the Isle of Man (where Ronald Stent had recently been dispatched). He feels cut off from everything. 'No bombs even,' he complains. His duties include escorting the Governor's wife to cocktail parties, raising funds from charity events, and starting an officers' club. 'I want to get abroad & do something in this war,' he writes impatiently, 'and not sit back in England all the time . . . Better to see some real action than listen to a lot of bloody huns going overhead dropping their loads . . . If only I were a bit younger,' he adds, 'I should be in the RAF.' This is the time of the Battle of Britain, the German blitz on London and the intensification of U-boat warfare in the Atlantic. There are rumours that Hitler is planning to invade England. Hazlehurst by then must have been in his late forties. 'Even now the age limit may cease to function & if the worst comes the old brigade can have a go,' he tells Yolande. But apart from the news that he is being made Brigade Major, 'I don't appear to have anything else to say.'

By the summer of 1941 Yolande has some war news of her own. Kenneth has been captured in North Africa by the Italians and taken to a prisoner-of-war camp in northern Italy. From here he escapes, is hidden in the mountains by Italian peasants, but then recaptured and taken to a prisoner-of-war camp in Romania. Basil, in the RAF at Wilmslow, seems to be at war with Ulla; and German planes have again been flying over Maidenhead, dropping a few bombs on their home runs and driving Adeline into hysterics. Hazel is the only person to whom Yolande can confide such things, for he is as it were part of the family, part of herself, and so she is not betraying anyone by

telling him. 'You have had a perfectly bloody time,' he acknowl-
edges. Kenneth, as a prisoner of war, is 'fairly sure of decent
treatment', because 'we hold such a lot of their people, &
reprisals would be easier for us'. As for Basil and Ulla, they
'appear to be behaving up to their usual form. I'm afraid I did
not expect anything else. If Basil can put up with what seems to
be a fairly promiscuous wife, well he is a poor boob. I'm damned
if I would. I would have too much pride to accept her second-
hand from that fat slob Thurnell.'

Thurnell, I now recall, was the name my mother told me never
to mention within the hearing of my father. Hazlehurst's reaction
to her affaire with him must have been the conventional one.
This was the climate of opinion in which my father made his
decision to take me back to Maidenhead and, since she would
not go there herself, leave his twenty-six-year-old adulterous
wife to fend for herself in wartime England.

What Hazlehurst wrote was intended to comfort Yolande.
His own opinion surely supported hers. How well she had
behaved, and how badly Ulla was behaving, in this war crisis.
But the hypothetical reference to his own wife, so impersonally
thrown into the argument, may not have brought Yolande much
comfort after all. Who is to say what was in her mind when
introducing this scandalous family business into their correspondence. But Hazlehurst is preoccupied with Hitler and no
longer feels so intimately involved with Holroyd affairs. 'It is
none of my business,' he writes, 'so we will forget it.' The rest of
his letter is full of news which Yolande could hear any day on
the radio or read in the papers or, if she ever went to such places,
pick up in the pubs. It is the stuff to give the troops (Hitler 'has
got his hands full with Russia . . . the terrific pounding the RAF
are giving the hun cities in the Ruhr must be having its effect',
etc.).

There is one more letter in the series. It is difficult to date, being without an envelope, incomplete (ten from what appear to have been fourteen pages) and scribbled in pencil on the writing paper of the Cheshire Regiment. Hazlehurst has been ill with shingles and 'crops of boils in the most awkward places'. This is due to his not having 'relaxed literally for years' and to 'never [having] had any leave'. When he does get leave, 'I propose to go & have a fish or something to give me a complete change.' Without the 'Yolande darling' on the missing first page and the regular 'All my love' on the last, the letter reads as if it were written to another man.

Hazlehurst did eventually get one of his wishes. After Mussolini fell from power in the summer of 1943, he was sent out to Italy. Less than three years after declaring war on Britain, Italy then declared war on Germany, and Hazlehurst found himself in a friendly country. He must have written a letter to Yolande, but she did not keep it. 'She learnt one morning that her fiancé had married an Italian woman of 20 (he was nearly fifty),' my father indignantly explained.

The consequences of this – Yolande's endless running with the dogs across the fields, her inability to tolerate us as we sat about gulping down our meals, the barricading of the house against visitors, the fiery outbursts at her mother, the putting away of her records in the garage, her retirement into her bedroom – I could see every day at Norhurst. But I could not interpret it and did not try until I came to write *A Dog's Life*. 'Poor Yolande!' my mother exclaimed in her account. My father's reaction was one of outrage. 'She was reduced to unpaid nurse to three old people,' he wrote to me after reading part of my manuscript in 1968. 'Not much need to ask you to remember what sort of life she leads now – you see it often enough.'

What had gone wrong? And why had her brothers done so little apparently to help her? Perhaps that is the question of a single child, and brothers cannot be used in this way. Besides, it is impossible to tell from this packet of letters whether Yolande really loved Hazel or whether he was the only man she really knew and somehow not quite the right man. Whatever the reason for this sad end to their affaire, her mistake, whether from excessive loyalty or a failure of nerve, was to have gone on living with her family. She may well have protected her father from his wife, but he could not protect her from the consequences of living with them both. And the consequences were awful.

# 12

# *Scaitcliffe Revisited*

Scaitcliffe had not changed very much since my father's time there. The school had grown from forty to fifty-five boys between the two world wars, and one of the classrooms had been enlarged. A squash court and rugby fives court which had been built were 'in constant use' the prospectus assured parents. An extra playing field had been bought from a farmer, extending the grounds to some twenty acres. Otherwise the red-brick, late-Victorian pile stood with its chapel in Crown land as before. My father would also have been able to recognise some of the names – Riley-Smith, Cornwall-Jones – of boys whose families, like himself, were continuing to send their sons to Scaitcliffe. So he was doing the customary thing. Yet after reading the account he wrote towards the end of his life of the hell he endured there, I cannot help being surprised. Why did he do it? One answer is that Scaitcliffe was the only preparatory school he knew, and there was little opportunity during those war years of getting to know other schools. But I don't think that he would have wanted to act differently whatever the circumstances. Though he spoke to me kindly about homesickness, I had no idea he had been miserable himself at Scaitcliffe. Quite the contrary. The only clue lay in a book he gave me, F. Anstey's *Vice Versa* (which I later saw filmed by Peter Ustinov as *A Lesson to Fathers*). In this story the father, Mr Bultitude, who is much given to praising his time at school as the happiest days of his life, is magically obliged to change places with his son and re-experience the tortures of his boarding school. I enjoyed this novel, but I did not pick up the signal my father was sending me.

He was an optimist, my father. He wanted to believe that things were getting better and all was for the best. He had suffered because of his brother, but I had no big brother overshadowing me. Besides, it was only when he was approaching the fragility of his second childhood that the miseries of these early years came back to him. In his late thirties, during these war years, the ups and downs of school life did not seem such a big business.

Yet my father was eager for me to do well at school. He had never really come to terms with missing so much through illness when a boy. Success had been blazing away somewhere else while he languished in Switzerland. When had he ever been applauded or thumped admiringly on the back? He won no silver cups, wore no coloured badges. He breasted no tapes ahead of others, saved no penalties, never scored a century. Everything he had missed now seemed to return and take hold of his imagination. I was to be his second chance, play another innings for him, take the field as his substitute. I ran, I jumped, batted, bowled and kicked for him – and looking through the school records I find I represented him not badly. At the age of twelve I made the winning long and high jumps (13ft 2in and 4ft 4in); I won the Senior Challenge Cup and a cup for fielding; I became vice-captain of the football and the cricket teams.

By far the oddest of my accomplishments was as opening batsman for the cricket eleven. The family money had dwindled so drastically by then that my father and grandfather could no longer afford to buy all the equipment I needed. So they were delighted when I came in from the garage at Norhurst one day carrying my Uncle Kenneth's bat and pads. He had put them to good use at Cambridge in the nineteen-twenties, but would not be needing them now, we all agreed, in his Romanian prisoner-of-war camp. So I could have them. We would write and tell him they were in use again, and he would be pleased. Many years later I wrote an essay called 'Not Cricket' in praise of this bat and pads.

> The pads were deeply yellow and reached almost to my shoulders. I peeped out from them unafraid. The bat was a mature instrument, well-bound and fully-seasoned, giving out a deep note when struck, like a groan. I admired that bat – but I could not lift it. I was ten or twelve; the bat was more than a quarter-of-a-century old . . . I would drag it to the crease and then, as it were, leave it there. As I took guard there occurred a total eclipse of the stumps. The bowler had not even a bail to aim at . . . We stood there, my uncle's bat and I, keeping our end up, while runs flowed and wickets fell at the other end. I had a good eye and would watch the balls swinging my way with great keenness, making lightning decisions as to what shots I could play. But I never played them except in my imagination.

The Scaitcliffe School Notes record that, like my grandfather at Uppingham, 'Holroyd was the soundest and most correct [batsman], but a slow scorer.' That was a polite understatement. Occasionally, over the seasons, a ball would glance off the edge of my uncle's bat and flutter through the slips bringing me a run.

But it had to go almost to the boundary to gain me time to reach the other end in those pads. What the score sheets do not reveal is that, despite my meagre totals, and though going in first, I was often out last doing something desperate with the bat, handling it as if it were a Scottish caber. I was the nightwatchman who watched the day, and my perfect total was nought not out. If I was not popular with the other side, I was scarcely a hero with my own. My batting partners were obliged to score most of their runs in boundaries, and those lower in the batting order seldom got much of an innings. Once, when stranded between wickets with my vast anchor of a bat, I was run out, I could not tell which team uttered the loudest cheer.

Nought not out summed up my achievements at this age. There seemed to hang about me an undefined air of promise that prevented me from doing anything at all. I seldom spoke first and never took an initiative. To attract attention, it seemed to me, was to ask for trouble. I strove for invisibility. What I liked most, because I had never experienced it before, was 'joining in' whatever was going on. I liked the Sunday walks in our blue suits through beechnuts, conkers and sweet chestnuts (which we were allowed to take back and toast for tea) to the 'Copper Horse', the equestrian statue of George III that looked towards Windsor Castle down an avenue of trees three miles in length called 'the Long Walk'. Sometimes we walked to the Duke of Cumberland's Obelisk at Smith's Lawn, heads bent, on the alert for pieces of shrapnel. I loved also the epic games of 'Convoy' in the wilder reaches of Windsor Great Park, hiding in the heather or behind trees, then veering off between 'destroyers', or 'submarines', 'minesweepers' and 'battleships' as we risked finding out who was what and then tried to remember as we raced for headquarters. On our way back, walking in crocodile past the flaking white façade of Fort Belvedere, we would glance around for items of the Crown Jewels which Edward VIII had thrown over the wall and into the park, we believed, when told he had to abdicate. I remember too the excitement of climbing into one of the massive hearse-like Daimlers that took our teams to play matches against other schools: Sunningdale and St Pirens; Heatherdown and Earlywood, each with their tribal rallying from the edge of the playing fields. I even enjoyed lining up with all the others for Nurse Minima to spoon us our 'Virol' or 'Radio Malt' each morning; also lifting up my voice in the chapel and losing part of myself in the collective singing: Decani versus Cantoris.

My moments of happiness often came from these conspiracies of self-forgetfulness. I also made at Scaitcliffe my first two friendships. One was with a boy called John Mein with whom I often paired off during our Sunday walks. One Sunday afternoon he came back with me to Norhurst and I showed him the walking-stick gun with which I had almost shot my grandmother. As a precaution, it had been hidden on the top of a tall dresser in the dining-room, but unfortunately my grandfather had not unloaded it, and we unintentionally shot a cartridge past the parrot and into the ceiling. No one found out, and after the shock we had to hurry into the garden and burst into laughter. What we laughed about at other times I no longer know, but we were always laughing and the joy of that laughter I remember vividly. Sometimes we laughed ourselves into sheer helplessness, '*I'll give you such a smite, Holroyd!*' one of the masters cried out in despair after John Mein and I had spread our staggering laughter through the complete cast of the school play, a historical drama with us attired as General Wolfe and the Marquis de Montcalm at Quebec. It was a passion, this laughter, that released me from innumerable apprehensions. At another time when I went to stay at his mother's house in Sussex, we almost drowned ourselves in a boat so uncontrollable was our condition. John Mein remembers taking me ferreting that week and 'you didn't like me wringing the rabbits' necks – but you always were a tender soul!' I have no memory of this, though I recognise my squeamishness. For me John Mein was a poet of the ludicrous and an imaginative storyteller, who lost his shyness in comedy and stories, and taught me how to do the same.

Another wonderful storyteller was my friend Christopher Capron. He would fill Wellington dormitory after lights-out with glowing tales of adventure and mystery. I could never have enough of these stories. 'What happened next?' I would demand, and he would give another spin to the plot. One by one the other boys, Bowman (the clever one who was bullied), Drummond (who played the piano), Molins (who was always being beaten), Palumbo (who was our sports star) and Stirling (who had a secret society with a language no one understood) fell asleep. But I was always awake at the end, clamouring for more.

I knew John Mein and Christopher Capron only four years of my life, but I count them both as lifelong friends, one the Muse of Comedy, the other a Keeper of Stories, because their liberating influences have lasted all my life.

Scaitcliffe was probably no worse than other preparatory schools of the time, and in one respect it was certainly better. In the grounds, between the playing fields, lay an excellent kitchen garden from which, for much of the year, we had fresh fruit and vegetables to add to our war diet of dried eggs and baked beans, our porridge and chocolate tart. Other schools loved coming to play us at cricket and football because they could wolf down such scrumptious teas. This was largely due to Mildred Vickers, a believer in milk and, fortunately, in cream. She studied our diet sheets, and prescribed Haliborange to supplement our rations.

Ronald Vickers, the formidable headmaster of my father's time, had died eighteen months before I arrived. In the attic at the top of a pitch-pine staircase lay the first Mrs Vickers. Or so we believed. Mr Vickers was now up there too, of course, encased in lead, awaiting arrival of his second beloved wife. After lights-out we dared one another to climb the stairs to this

attic and look through the keyhole. Chetwynd minor said that
when he did so the handle of the door had turned and a voice
whispered 'Come in!'

Ronald Vickers's twin sons, whom my father had seen when
a boy being wheeled across the lawn in their double-pram, were
abroad fighting in the war, and the acting headmaster was Denis
Owen.

Denis Owen was a remarkable man. As a teenager, he had
won an exhibition to Oxford but was unable to go there because
his family had no money. In 1927 he had been recruited by
Ronald Vickers to take the place of Edgar Ransome, that twenty-
stone 'coarse old man' my father had so hated. All the distinction
of the school during my time there derived from Denis Owen. His
career was spent teaching the sons of well-off families who did go
on to university. He was a small, wiry, tough character with a
hooked nose, dark hair, a grim expression and demonic energy.
He coached us brilliantly at cricket and football; he ran a debat-
ing society, played the organ in chapel and gave the sermons,
took shooting lessons, taught Latin, French and English, worked
himself and us, indoors and outdoors, round the clock. Though
boys from other schools envied us our delicious teas, they were
glad not to have our strict and strenuous regime. We were woken
at seven o'clock by the clashing of a bell handled by one of the
gardeners, and after washing at the bowls of decanted water in
the dormitories and hurriedly pulling on our grey shirts and
shorts, our ties and sweaters, we proceeded in line to our first
service in the chapel where the biblical figure of Denis Owen
was already at work on the organ. Then, following a ten-minute
scripture lesson, we went in to breakfast. The rest of the day was
crowded with Latin gender rhymes, fielding practice, multiplication tables, gym, English grammar and spelling, cross-country
runs, the recital of dates in history, and appalling plunges into the
open-air swimming-pool (an uninviting arrangement of concrete
and corrugated iron in which we nakedly splashed, watched by

the keen eye of Mr Bailey who also took us for drill). Most of the teaching was unmemorable, but Miss Stanton's hesitant French lessons, and the spitting and shaking of Mr Perry's mathematics reinforced by something known as 'the Perry Punch' (a clenched fist, one finger angled, delivered to a painful spot on the upper arm) stay in my mind as being peculiarly terrible. Mr Perry was an irritable old man, stinking of tobacco, whose large yellowing moustache concealed a bullet hole from the First World War which was, in our opinion, his one distinction. Worst of all were the piano lessons in a tiny room called 'the sardine tin'. When I struck a wrong note I was immediately stopped, my finger taken and placed on the correct note, and then forced up and down on it, again and again, jarring the sound through my body. I gave up piano lessons, saving my father three guineas a term, but have regretted it for the rest of my life. Perhaps the war was responsible for such bad teaching. Perhaps it was the same everywhere.

But Denis Owen commanded our respect if not our affection. I think we all recognised that he was somehow special, though we also thought he was extremely frightening. 'He certainly petrified me,' John Mein remembered. The beat of his footsteps through the corridors of the school, especially at night, started a wave of pounding fear ahead of him, and we would hold our breath until the sound receded. Maybe I feared him more than most, for I was ridiculously sensitive. I can still blush when I remember the eruption of laughter in class when I pronounced surgery as sugary, called a Quaker a Quacker, came out even more disastrously with an 'earthquack', and gave the Thames two phonetic syllables. Mr Owen appeared unaware of my sensitivity, however, until awareness was forced on him by a sensational episode.

One morning when the bell clanged outside and we all got out of our beds, I noticed across the lower sheet a large cherry-coloured stain. Nurse Minima noticed it too and I was closely questioned. I answered that I did not know what it was and felt

quite as baffled as she did. That evening I was summoned to
Denis Owen's study and after waiting nervously in the passage,
that same passage in which my father had sometimes waited
thirty years earlier, was severely questioned again about the red
area on my sheet. At first I had thought it must be blood, but I
had no wound or nose-bleed. It was inexplicable. My ignorance
must have been transparent, and perhaps Denis Owen suspected
that I had been the victim of a practical joke by the other boys in
the dormitory. In any event I was not beaten that night. Instead
I was told that, whatever the stain had been, it must never reappear. I thoroughly agreed and returned upstairs. But a week or
two later it did reappear, bright cherry-red across the sheet – and
this time I knew what it was. In the early hours of the morning
I had half-woken, found that I had wet my bed and, still half-
asleep, put my red dressing-gown underneath me before going
back to sleep.

Nurse Minima sent me back that evening to the headmaster's
study and Denis Owen, who was busy, told me that I must come
to him next day with a convincing explanation. This was more
difficult than it sounded, not only because I felt the explanation
to be unspeakably humiliating, but also because Denis Owen
was so awfully unapproachable. Between the formal lessons,
the organ-playing and sermons, he appeared to inhabit
Olympus. I saw him once that day striding across a distant field
with that grim expression on his face, and I ran some way after
him but did not get near. The thought of interrupting his
progress with my dreadful story was simply impossible.

That evening I was again summoned down to wait in the passage outside his study. Then he called me in, told me it was too
late now for explanations, bent me over a chair in my pyjamas
and began beating me. However, I was by this time in an
extreme state of nerves and, at the first stroke, releasing all my
pent-up emotion, let out a vast cry. It was as much a shout as a
cry, mingling protest and pain in a great emotional eruption. The

sound, I was later told, travelled upstairs and into rooms throughout the school. No one knew what it was, but everything came to a stop. Nothing so loud and unexpected had happened since the famous night when a public house nearby called The Bells of Ousley had been blown up by German bombers. Even Denis Owen appeared shaken. He told me to go back up to the dormitory, and at the end of term wrote a devastating report to my father, questioning him as to whether I was really fit for the rough-and-tumble of a boarding school. It was, I now think, an opportunity for my father to tell me about his own 'absolute hell' at Scaitcliffe, but I do not recall that he did so. He was worried by the practical difficulties of having to remove me, as he had been removed for different reasons. So I went back all the more determined to develop my skills of avoiding attention.

My last year at Scaitcliffe was the best. I did not actually like going there after the holidays, but then I did not like going back to Norhurst at the end of term. I did not know what I liked or where I was going: whether to Maidenhead with my aunt and grandparents; or to various places in France with my father; or to London with my mother, and then across the North Sea to meet my other grandmother in Stockholm and roomfuls of my incomprehensible Swedish cousins in Borås and Göteburg.

I needed everything to be simple. But by the end of the war my parents' lives were growing more complicated, and these complexities began infiltrating my own life.

# 13

# Three Weddings
# and a Funeral

My mother wrote that she was 'without a penny' at her board-ing house in Cresswell Gardens, and that there were 'days when I only had a glass of milk'. She lived largely on what Kaja was able to send her from Stockholm via the Swedish Consulate. Occasionally she would come down by train to Scaitcliffe, and sometimes also to Maidenhead 'where you were left for me to see for a few hours. We always had tearful partings – you wanted to come back with me. I was desperate & believe that you were too.'

Everything began to change after my father left the Royal Air Force. In the first week of April 1946 he attended a medical board which found that he was still suffering from rheumatoid polyarthritis. His disability was rated at forty percent and, 'with regret', he was declared unfit for further service. He had been billeted in Paris for eighteen months 'chez Madame Dimier' in the rue Sergent Hoff, a small street near the Arc de Triomphe, and after his discharge he continued living there. It was a solid, spacious apartment block built in 1912 and decorated on its balconies by sandstone flambeaux containing quivers and arrows, also pineapples and lions and swags of dependant fruit and flowers. Above the large portal with its art nouveau decorations was fixed the head of Silenus framed with grapes and vine-leaves. Inside were marble floors, and a slow and stately lift up the five floors. I remember visiting my father there during my holidays and being astonished by Madame Dimier's ability to pour forth rapid continuous loud incomprehensible French without ever taking breath. It was an artillery of sound that killed off all other speech and covered everything we did, or thought, or saw, or imagined. I wondered how my father, no mean speaker under ordinary circumstances himself, could endure such a perpetual battering of noise. And then I suddenly realised that he had fallen in love with Maman's voluptuous daughter, Marie-Louise, or Marlou as everyone called her.

Marlou was the most glamorous woman I had met. She was always elegantly dressed, had gorgeous raven hair that was swept back but kept falling forwards, rather pouting lips, and large expressive eyes with hooded lids that fascinated me. Her sultry looks made the climate around her seem warm and relaxing. I thought her the height of sophistication. I liked her too, but felt shy after my father took me to one side and asked me to give her a kiss each night because she was unable to have children of her own. This revelation led to a brief man-to-man talk about the 'facts of life' which left me rather unconvinced by the unlikeliness of it all, and wondering whether I had misunderstood. I doubt if, in my nervousness, I was as affectionate to Marlou when she came to say goodnight as I should have been. She took me to various fashion shows and praised my taste; and she gave me a camera with which I took a spectacular shot of the Eiffel Tower, making it appear like the leaning tower of Pisa.

Marlou's full name was Marie-Louise Deschamps-Eymé. She

was in publishing, her business partner being Marcel Brandin, 'a cool, slim, bitterly disillusioned ex-Resistance fighter', as the novelist Winston Graham described him, 'who saw France returning to its old corrupt ways.' It was in their publishing company, Editions Begh, that my father bought a directorship, using the invalidity money he had been granted by the RAF. He also brought with him an idea, which was to corner the market in translations of books that were being, or stood a good chance of being, made into films. Winston Graham, whose Poldark novels were later to be such a success on television, was one of his early authors; another was the well-respected, now-forgotten novelist Claude Houghton (whose 'novelisation' of Jerome K. Jerome's play *The Passing of the Third Floor Back* was also filmed). Love and money were to be the ingredients of their success, but it was love and money that undid them.

Marlou was known to be the mistress of a millionaire newspaper owner on whose financial support Editions Begh largely depended. Nevertheless, my father proposed to marry her – once he had divorced my mother. In the summer of 1946 he hired a London detective who soon came up with the evidence he needed. The decree nisi cites Rowland Hill as co-respondent. It is not a name that appears in either of my parents' accounts or that I ever heard them mention. In the London telephone directory of 1946 there is one Rowland Hill. He is living in the Marylebone Road, but disappears at the time of the divorce.

This divorce legally freed both my parents for fresh chapters in their lives. Or so they believed. In fact, probably because my father was in Paris, they forgot to take the formal step required to make their decree absolute. The result was that, though they never knew this, they actually remained married to each other, and all their later marriages were invalid. Fortunately perhaps they did not have children by these four subsequent marriages, though from time to time I was presented with a new stepbrother or stepsister for the holidays.

Late in 1946 my mother, still aged only thirty, moved into a nice small flat on the eighth floor of Sloane Avenue Mansions, near the King's Road in Chelsea. I often stayed with her there before and after our journeys to Sweden. How I hated those awful bucketing voyages across the North Sea! We would start out from Tilbury in one of the regular Swedish boats, the *Suecia*, *Saga* or *Patricia*, creaking and groaning, swaying and heaving – and I was soon down in the cabin groaning and heaving with sympathetic sea-sickness. But my mother was not ill. She was popular on board, never missing the *smörgåsbord*, or the music playing and the sun shining, and the company of strangers. Occasionally I would crawl up on deck and see her talking to some admirer and exchanging addresses. I remember only one of these gentlemen, a Mr Smith, who wore his watch with its face on the inside of his wrist. I was so struck with the novelty of this that I turned my own watch round, and have worn it so ever since. Later, 'Mr Smith on the boat' became a generic term, and I would tease my mother about this ever-recurring gallant on her travels round the world.

It was unusual during those years immediately following the Second World War for people to go abroad, and for a time I became a person of exotic interest to other boys. I would return to school like a mariner disembarking from some exciting piratical expedition, with strange glowing booty: a Lapland knife in its multicoloured leather-and-fur sheath; a brilliantly exciting board game of ice-hockey; a vast marzipan pig with chocolate features; a magically tilting wooden maze over which, like a minefield, you could steer a silver ball. Such treasures made me appear like a magician in those drab years and granted me an illusory popularity. 'Can we borrow your ice-hockey, Holroyd?' I can hear their voices still. I always said yes and was proud when my best friend 'Cuffy' Capron made an astonishing score on the tilting maze in the school sanatorium.

This was the best feature of my travels overseas: the popular return. For though I loved my mother and could imagine no worse calamity than her death, I never found a way of life that fitted her style and rhythm of living. The fact is *she was always lying down* when I wanted to be bounding around. Dawn, it seemed to me, was the right time for leaping up. But left to herself my mother would not get out of bed till nine or ten o'clock. It was an agony lying in bed and waiting for her to wake. And when she did get up she almost immediately *lay down again* to sunbathe. The least glimmer of the sun and she would *lie down*. Is there anything more tedious than sunbathing? In my view there was not. But my mother loved nothing better unless it was, after the sun had gone down, to dance.

My mother's dancing was not boring: it was excruciatingly embarrassing. She knew no shame. She would sing the tunes, kick up her heels, smile stupidly, drink all sorts of coloured drinks, make jokes in five or six languages. And she would dance. She could not be stopped. It was not beyond her to grab a waiter and propel him laughing round a restaurant. I saw her dance on tables too. I would close my eyes and long to disappear. It was then that I first determined to master the secret art of disappearing. But the penalty you pay for this vanishing trick is that your past vanishes with you. Now, as I bring those scenes back, I curse the terrible self-consciousness I felt that hardened into an inhibition preventing me from speaking the languages my mother spoke, and a paralysis that all my life has stopped me dancing, though I love to watch other people dance – indeed it is one of my vicarious passions. I rejoice now in the memory of my mother whirling about those floors and tables, but I could not possibly join in. All is in retrospect for me.

When she was surrounded by her family in Sweden, my mother was obliged to behave more formally. I was reminded of our large family gatherings at Easter or Christmas or on St Lucia's Day when I saw Ingmar Bergman's film *Fanny and Alexander* in the mid-nineteen-eighties. We preserved something

of the same strict protocol of hospitality, the correct toasts and
then the growing merriment and finally a soaring into surreal
entertainment. It was all fantastical to me, for though everyone
addressed me in English, they spoke fast incomprehensible
Swedish among themselves. And then, though they were all
introduced to me, my mind had somehow wandered and I did
not know who most of them were anymore.

It was a relief to get back to London, even back to school
sometimes. Coming up from Scaitcliffe to my mother's flat at
Sloane Avenue Mansions, I would crowd my uncle's bat and
pads into the hall, and eat up huge plates of bangers, beans and
mash, followed by trifle and tinned cream – my mother knew
what schoolboys liked. I did not realise that her 'cabin in the
sky', as we called it, was rented for her by a man named
Edouard Fainstain, nor that my mother was his mistress. She
took me to meet 'Edy' and, what was most important, she borrowed his car, a sparkling blue Packard with an open 'dicky' or
jump seat at the back in which I travelled dramatically in the sun
and the wind. With this wonderful machine she would whizz
down to Scaitcliffe, a blonde bombshell in a blue racing car,
astonishing the other boys whose own mothers appeared so
much older and dowdier. 'You were notorious, pitied and
envied, because your parents were divorced,' my friend
Christopher Capron remembered. I was the only boy at
Scaitcliffe with divorced parents and after my mother began
driving down on Sundays, I gained a certain status – Christopher
Capron spoke of the 'rather daring wickedness' surrounding
me. Once or twice I invited Christopher Capron or John Mein
out to lunch with my mother at a rather grand hotel on
Englefield Green. But she found it difficult to say anything that
interested us, and we wandered around the gardens rather
bored. Her notoriety was more potent from a distance. My great
fear was that she might bring down Kaja on one of her visits to
England. Occasionally she did this, causing me anguish over

lunch when my grandmother examined the menu through an exquisite pair of eye-glasses held prominently by a single handle – 'my *lorgnette*' she called them. Another time, which was almost worse, she glared through an imposing monocle, looking like an aristocratic pirate. The embarrassment in case another boy, Bowman or Drummond, Palumbo or Stirling, should see this exhibition of adult eccentricity was agonising.

In 1948 Edy Fainstain was divorced from his wife Ida and on 25 February 1949, at the Kensington Register Office, he married my mother. 'Then things were O.K.,' she briefly noted in her account. She moved into a splendid maisonette on the top two floors of 24 Wetherby Gardens, a house once occupied by Viscount Allenby and round the corner from Drayton Gardens where I had spent my first couple of years. I was given a bedroom of my own and introduced to the first of my stepsisters.

Edy Fainstain was a Hungarian Jew whose father had been a farmer. For their honeymoon he took Ulla to Stockholm and, with his strong sense of family, was shocked to discover that she scarcely knew her father. He insisted that Kaja invite Karl to her apartment, and she absolutely refused. But nevertheless he still insisted, and so it went on over the honeymoon, this rally of obstinate insistence and absolute refusal until, to her own surprise, Kaja found herself conceding. She knew that, at some level of respectability, Edy was behaving correctly. And it would look so bad if, in however dignified a fashion, she went on refusing. Her own family liked Karl, or Kalle as they still called him. They thought him 'charming and colourful', a man of 'humour and humanity'. Did they blame her for his lack of promotion in the army? Everyone had expected him to be made a general, but his inability to impose harsh discipline was said to have been held against him. He had behaved better to his men, Kaja sometimes thought, than to her. He had not grown aggressively drunk with them. She knew that some of her family still believed that the marriage had been broken up by her own persistent flirting with men of higher rank. Of course it was absurd – was he not a flirt also? – but that is what they thought. It must have been difficult for her to telephone this man who, she had told Ulla, had made her life so awful during the late nineteen-twenties and early thirties with his demands for money, his venereal disease, his threats of violence. But perhaps she exaggerated his vices. Neither she nor my mother had seen him for over fifteen years, though he was living not far away with his second wife Marianne. But Kaja spoke to him, and he accepted an invitation to a cup of coffee at her apartment in Artillerigatan. Edy then went back to his hotel so that Karl could spend some time alone with his daughter. 'Pappa Kalle arrived – pale – drawn – nervous – with a bunch of red carnations,' my mother wrote. 'A very awkward hour – Kaja made it so. I felt sorry, but also quite a stranger after so many years. Kaja never sat still & kept looking at the clock & bringing up awkward moments in the past. I did my best & I knew he knew that. That was the last time I saw my father.' He was to die less than three years later aged sixty-five, at Växjö, on 14 December 1952. 'This chilly December day when Karl Hall's life ended seems very far from the idyllic warrior's life in the happy 1920s,' wrote the obituary writer in one of the Swedish newspapers.

> Now when we are all middle-aged, the officers and men and the young ladies of the ball, we treasure the memory of this chivalrous heartbreaker, Captain Hall . . . Yet in this moment of farewell one doesn't chiefly remember the carefree Kalle Hall from the balls and evenings of song, but the silhouette of Major Karl Knutsson Hall in the saddle after the company's hard day-long marches or night manoeuvres . . . The tall horseman has passed the last post on his journey.

His brothers and sisters and his widow went to the funeral at

Växjö, and so did Ulla. But Kaja did not go. There was no mention of her among the mourners, or in the obituaries. From this time onwards she reinstated her own family name, calling herself Kaja Jagenburg Hall. Her husband had already been as good as dead for many years, and such was the annihilating force of her feeling that my mother sometimes echoed it. That was probably why, in her account, she had written that her father had died in 1945. It surprises me now that he was alive while I went on my trips to Sweden, and that I never met him. But I was not interested then in the past.

My new stepfather must have been a relief to my mother after her sequence of inadequate Englishmen. Edy was forty-five at the time of their marriage, some thirteen years older than his wife. He was the sort of person men instinctively distrust and women like. But I liked him, as all young people did. He gave the impression of having lived a generous life, not all of it respectable. On the marriage certificate, as his 'rank or profession' he put 'Company Director', the profession that had by then supplanted the rank of 'Gentleman' on such documents. He was a director, I understood, of several property companies; the owner, or one of the owners, of 'The Brief Encounter', a smart café-restaurant opposite Harrods, and an expensive furniture shop round the corner in Beauchamp Place. It was here my mother met 'a charming man' to whom she sold a chaise-longue. He was a Mr Haig, soon to become notorious for a series of acid-bath murders. But that, as Kipling would say, is another story. Or might have been.

Edy had entertaining cosmopolitan friends: a white Russian; a much-photographed model; a radio scriptwriter; an actor. Jon Pertwee, a future Dr Who, came and sang to a small guitar, greatly irritating me. Was this the sort of performance you had to put on to get adults' attention? Was this what my mother admired? I despised his pattering jokes, his insistent strumming, and refused to smile or even listen, knowing I could never do such tricks myself. Edy belonged to a far more glittering world than any she had known in Beckenham, Maidenhead or Wilmslow. It was a world she thought she had been entering when she married my father – and very near his Basil Street showrooms and the hotel where they had spent their honeymoon. Among Edy's scattered properties was a villa called 'L'Oiseau Bleu' near the village of La Turbie, just above the Grande Corniche overlooking Monte Carlo. The world was opening up for my mother.

But it was beginning to close in for my father. He had married Marlou in 1948, having talked her and everyone else into believing that his ideas would liven up their publishing house in Paris. The ideas were good enough, but they needed money to implement them. 'Editions Begh went down the drain when the millionaire withdrew his financial help,' Winston Graham later wrote. 'If Marlou deserted him for your father, perhaps this is the reason.' Probably it was. By the beginning of the nineteen-fifties my father returned to England; Marlou eventually got a job with another publishers, Les Editions Mondiales, in the rue des Italiens; and their partner, the cool slim Marcel Brandin, accepted an offer from André Malraux to become his *chef de cabinet*.

There was one more family marriage in these years. My Uncle Kenneth, having escaped from his prisoner-of-war camp in Romania, had been captured once more and ended the war in a German prisoner-of-war camp. We saw him at Maidenhead again in 1945, terribly thin and ghostlike. But he had plenty of stories for us – stories of hiding in the Dolomites with Italian peasants; stories of living on a diet of turnips in appalling conditions; stories of death and friendship; stories of humane or inhumane commandants and guards – and the awful retribution afterwards; stories also of the ingenious methods he had picked up for passing time (he had even learnt, my grandmother was delighted to hear, how to play bridge).

We listened to these stories with fascination at first and then, despite our valiant intentions, with overwhelming boredom. He was so nice, so quiet, so achingly dull. We were all experts in tedium and recognised a master. He took an infinitude of time to tell his stories and he told them in an unwavering monotone. Perhaps it didn't matter. We were all pleased to see him. But we felt that, after all he had endured, we really should keep our eyes intent, our heads set at intelligent angles, our smiles and frowns coming and going. Doing all this I almost fell off my chair, so overcome was I with drowsiness. The others were no better. My grandfather could hear so little, my grandmother never listened, my aunt could not keep still, Old Nan gave no sign of anything as these ghastly tales of war slowly unfolded before her, and my father, seething with impatience on his visits to us, tried unsuccessfully to insert some RAF anecdotes. As for myself I was mainly anxious to hold on to my uncle's bat and pads for my last cricket season at Scaitcliffe. Poor Kenneth!

My father's marriage to Marlou caused no surprise at Norhurst. He was known to be hopeless over women. First a Swede, now a French woman – my grandparents almost laughed out loud, and my aunt nearly joined in. But when Kenneth married, the same year as Basil, they fell back into tortuous explanations involving his long imprisonment (wedlock being in their experience another form of imprisonment). After all, as my grandmother reminded us, Kenneth was only in his mid-forties, 'no age at all for a man'. The infinite perambulations of his speech had not prepared us for such precipitate action. We were all thoroughly shocked, and went about the house tilting our heads, clucking our tongues and raising our eyebrows to the ceiling. In the family saga, Kenneth had seemed cast for a similar destiny to Yolande. Like her, he was on the verge of matrimony in the nineteen-thirties: and then it all went wrong. He was one of the admirers of 'Brownie' Hollway, the beautiful daughter of a distinguished Rajmai Tea director – indeed he appeared to be engaged to her. But when he introduced her to one of his younger aristocratic friends, she suddenly ran off with him and, at the end of 1939, became the Marchioness of Tavistock. That may have been one reason Kenneth was so keen to get abroad quickly in the war.

After he returned, having survived so much illness and danger, he found that Brownie Tavistock had recently died. And it seemed to us watching him, so frail and spectral, that his adventures must now be at an end.

He shared a London apartment at Nell Gwynn House with two ex-prisoner-of-war friends, one of whom got him a job in the Anglo-Iranian Oil Company. There was a strong bond between these ex-prisoners, quite a few of whom were to die within a year of one another from the same cause (cancer of the pancreas) brought on by their prison diet. Their reunions became a way of recovering the years they had missed. At their parties it was almost possible to believe that there had been no war and everything was continuing without interruption from the nineteen-thirties. Time itself was cheated and all wounds healed.

During one weekend tennis party at a house on West Heath in Hampstead, Kenneth met a woman in her early thirties called Sheilah Sayers. She was the widow of devil-may-care 'Mike' Sayers, a spectacularly good-looking and popular Irish sportsman and army officer who had been killed in an air crash at the end of 1943. When she met Kenneth three years later, Sheilah was living in St John's Wood with her two young sons. Mike Sayers had not been a rich man, but Sheilah was an heiress – one of the three daughters of William Lawrence Stephenson, founder and first chairman of Woolworth.

She lived pretty grandly in those post-war years with a resident cook, a maid and governess, a gardener, daily cleaning woman and half a boilerman whom she shared with the musician Sir Thomas Beecham. But what some of her suitors did not know was that her millionaire father disapproved of inherited wealth and had taken no steps to avoid the full rigour of death duties (then set at eighty percent).

Though she was beginning to put on weight, Sheilah was still a good-looking woman and it soon became obvious that Kenneth adored her. He seemed quite unlike the regular pack of admirers who escorted her to theatres and cocktail parties. He was not keen to spend her money – indeed he appeared embarrassed by their financial incompatibility. His gentleness too impressed her as romantic, and her two boys almost heroworshipped him. But what really touched her was his need of her. Without her love, it appeared, he had no future.

We all went up for the wedding in September 1947 and there is a picture of us standing in a group before the Marylebone Registry Office. I am at one end of the front row wearing my light suit and dark shoes, gawky, smiling faintly but not knowing what to do with my arms. Also in the front row are my new step-cousins, Christopher (who has forgotten that he is being photographed) aged nine, and Michael (who is giggling) aged seven. Old Nan, whom they call 'Big Nan', looms hugely between us in her coat. In the back row my father, temporarily wifeless, is wearing his Old Etonian tie. Further along are Adeline, in a tall improbable hat, and Fraser, the very image of a storybook grandfather. The rest of the group is made up of Sheilah's family whom we don't know. At the centre are Kenneth, whom Sheilah's family all call 'Larry', looking handsome and serious; and Sheilah herself, a little wary in her brilliant silk dress.

But there is one figure missing. Yolande is not there. She was of course invited and I feel sure she went. But she has missed the critical moment, as she often did, as if it were another meal to be avoided, as if there were a dog to be exercised, as if the implications of it all were too painful.

At the far right of the wedding group stands Bill Stephenson, an active-looking man who is glancing across at the rest of us. He has just given his new son-in-law a cheque for £100,000 (roughly equivalent to two million pounds at the end of the century) to ensure that he will be financially independent of his wife.

Kenneth was to use this money in two different ways. After the birth of his daughter Vicky in 1950, he left Anglo-Iranian Oil and bought a 300-acre farm in Sussex, hoping to combine a healthy life for the children with a modest profit-making enterprise. But this romantic notion never really worked. The children loved the farm, but after the boys left it became more of a 'gentleman's estate', like a comfortable prison camp, where Sheilah grew fat and idle and shut herself off from visitors.

Kenneth used some of his capital to rescue Fraser who had been obliged to raise a double mortgage on Norhurst to pay my school fees. Kenneth paid off these mortgages, bought the freehold of the house for £2,750 and then handed Norhurst back to his father. He also bought back all Fraser's shareholding in the Rajmai Tea Company, invested in it himself and became a director.

So for a brief period it seemed possible to believe that the family fortunes were restored. At any rate my father felt optimistic enough to send me on to Eton.

# 14

## *E t o n*

I left Scaitcliffe at the end of the summer term in 1948 – in fact
I left two weeks early. My father wanted us to travel together to
the South of France for a holiday with Marlou. I resented this
premature leaving bitterly, being unable to say a proper good-
bye to my friends Christopher Capron and John Mein. My
father, perhaps sensing this, presented John Mein with a wonderful French banknote. 'I miss Holroyd very much,' Mein
wrote to his mother the next Sunday. I was almost in tears as I
handed over a book on the Arab Legion as my farewell gift in
the headmaster's study – that same study from where I had
briefly brought the whole school to a halt with my howl of
unhappiness.

About a year or eighteen months after I went to Eton, my
father found he could no longer afford my school fees. He had
almost bankrupted his own father who was gradually being
raised to the surface and floated again by Kenneth. But this was

a vessel without treasure and there was precious little more help to be salvaged from Norhurst.

In his novel *The Directors*, the character based on my grandfather, head of a business company (i.e. family), is accidentally killed through the inept financial machinations of a junior director. There is no doubt that my father felt uneasy over borrowing money from Fraser. But the very last thing he wanted was to remove me from Eton, as he himself had been removed. I must complete what he had begun. So he turned to my mother and her husband, Edy Fainstain. It cannot have been easy for him. 'Edy paid half your Eton fees,' my mother wrote. 'Edy loved kids so he gladly stepped in so that you could finish your education.' There is no mention of Edy's assistance in my father's account.

I soon noticed around this time that Edy was beginning to question me about the nuances of cricket. Were leg-breaks as painful as they sounded? Could you get far with long-hops? Were yorkers invented in Yorkshire? His middle-European accent combined with much gurgling laughter did not unsettle me as Kaja's *lorgnette* had done, and I did my best to respond to these overtures of friendship. But my answers were often lacklustre. I think we liked each other, but we belonged to different cultures and talking together was rather like walking uphill. We were soon out of breath, having run out of things to say.

To prepare me for my first summer at Eton my father had asked the greengrocer in Maidenhead High Street to give me a few nets while he himself made one of his last forays to sort things out in Paris. In the corner of a large field one evening, this greengrocer sent down a vicious outswinger that clipped the edge of my uncle's bat. Sparks seemed to fly in the dusk. He bowled again and I saw the bat, like an old ship in a tempest, begin to break up. There was nothing I could do – there never had been. By the end of my net practice my wicket was intact, but my uncle's bat lay splintered and demolished. The pads too were sprouting strange yellow and grey matter. On the way back to Norhurst, I heaved the wreckage on to a rubbish dump. It was the end.

My reputation as a chap who might force a draw from an impossible position had travelled to Eton before me, and I was immediately placed in the top game. What happened I have described in 'Not Cricket'.

Approaching the crease in my gleaming new gear I seemed to be walking on air. Where was my ballast, my anchor? . . . My new bat wouldn't keep still. It sent the first ball I received for an astonishing four through the covers. I felt like apologising. After all I had done no more than contemplate a cover drive: the bat had done the rest. To the second ball it offered a leg-glance, and I walked off the field while the wicket-keeper righted my leg stump.

This was disappointing for my father. He had done his bit in the war and, when acting wing-commander, had worn a series of gleaming blue stripes up the arms and across the shoulders of his uniform and around his hat. Now he was a civilian again, he looked forward to reflected glory from my Etonian accomplishments. In his generous imagination, he saw me scoring for the Oppidans at the Wall Game, captaining the Field Game, distinguishing myself against Harrow at Lord's. I performed none of these noble deeds and there was very dim glory for him to bask in. I doubt whether my stepfather understood the enormity of my failure. Boys went to Eton in the hope of being capped with amazing colours, quartered or striped, and walking the streets under a halo of athletic glamour, shimmering with their cream blazers trimmed with blue, their high collars with butterfly ties, their exotic flowered waistcoats. They didn't go, for heaven's sake, to learn algebra, but to shine in this fancy-dress parade. However, I pretty well gave up cricket, never rowed, played almost no tennis (largely because I couldn't find the tennis courts), and never saw, let alone took part in, the famous Eton Wall Game. And I was no good at algebra either. Was I there at all? I sometimes wonder.

One of the troubles was my housemaster, R.J.N. Parr. There was really rather a lot of him, some sixteen stones approximately, all of it signifying very little. He was a portly, well-waistcoated and bespectacled man, and had a very red face. Everyone called him Purple Parr. He was rumoured to be some relative of Catherine Parr, Henry VIII's last wife, and was himself married to a very thin widowed lady from Ireland, Mrs Murphy, whose meagre glamour we occasionally glimpsed, but who took no interest in the house or its boys. Purple Parr, so far as we could discern, took only a remote interest in us. For a man of his bulk, he spoke in a curiously soft voice muffled by continuous catarrh. In the evenings, like some amphibious monster, he would glide quietly along the perspiring corridors, occasionally stopping, entering a room at random and lugubriously passing the time of day. These sudden appearances, their pointlessness, and the nasal snuffling that would sometimes erupt into hooting volleys of sneezes, were mildly disconcerting. By trade he was a mathematician, but he also took us for Latin in pupil room – a sort of homework. As a teacher he was uninspiring, as a housemaster damp and undynamic. His main interest appeared to be 'real tennis' as opposed to what he called 'lawners' – the sort of stuff they played at Wimbledon. He would sometimes introduce this or that arcane aspect of real tennis – the origin of the 'Dedans' or the significance of the 'Tambour' – as a means of initiating an informal conversation. He was, it now occurs to me, a shy man and probably insecure. He appeared more at ease with furniture than boys – indeed he loved good furniture. His long letters to our parents showed that he noticed far more than we realised, distanced as we were from him by his unsympathetic qualities of pedantry and snobbishness.

We felt more comfortable with 'm'dame', the house matron Miss Grieve, a cheerful woman with dumpy legs, who spent her summer holidays on the Isle of Wight. I only once saw her seriously rattled. At lunch one day I heard myself uttering the words: 'the caper sauce is capering, m'am'. The meaning of this remark, beyond its experimental play on word-sounds, I cannot now decipher, nor I suspect could anyone else at the time. But, caught unawares, and feeling that they must contain some impenetrable impoliteness, possibly even a profound obscenity (the food was certainly not good), Miss Grieve reported me for insolence.

Purple Parr was a comparatively new housemaster and had inherited his house in its vintage years. When I arrived in the autumn of 1948 it still possessed a tremendous reputation. The dining-room glittered with the trophies it had won on the river. At the centre of this display stood the magnificent Aquatic Cup itself, a proud mass of silver. But over my first year, as we were bumped or bravely beaten in one race, then another, these cups, shields, medals, honours were removed until we were left with nothing at all. We entered the nineteen-fifties, by popular consent, as the worst house in the school. This is no empty boast. I write with authority. For two years, despite playing no games, I was the Captain of Games; and in my last half, despite an indifferent academic record, I was also Captain of the House.

Carlton, Holroyd, MacLeod, Philipps, Valentine: those were the new boys in September 1948. Our parents came with us the first afternoon, and were given tea and cake by Purple Parr in the drawing-room which, on the other side of a green-baize door, was to be a world away from our ordinary life at Eton. They shook hands, these adults, joked and laughed, then slipped guiltily away. It was as we were standing around indecisively afterwards that someone said something to me. I jumped back, not being used to such attention (indeed having gone a long way in the last year or so to avoid it), then saw it was Philipps who had spoken to me. He still had some cake in his hand and was asking me about my uncle's bat. I recognised him. He was a large crouching sort of boy, with a round face, hawk-like nose, hanging arms and intent brown eyes. Through his feet most of my sparse totals had trickled on the occasions when Scaitcliffe played Sunningdale. I had seen him with cake in his hand before, at our tea intervals, and I remembered his alert yet curiously blank expression. He appeared to miss nothing, while taking no part in anything. I told him about my uncle's bat and he immediately understood. During a walkabout round the school on which Purple Parr led us early that evening, we got talking and I learnt that his parents, like mine, were divorced. Over the next five years Griffy Philipps became my special friend.

He called me 'Hagga', an odd name that caught on in the house to the extent of Purple Parr sometimes using it when he had drunk too much in the evenings. 'Dear Hagga,' Griffy writes to me, attempting after an interval of forty-five years to explain the derivation of this name. 'At the time you always looked, and indeed probably still do, though for other reasons, quite haggard. Also at that time I was reading the works of H. Rider Haggard (*She* etc.). Hence the name Hagga.'

Griffy came to believe that the catastrophic fall in our house 'from majesty to disrepair', combined with the unsupportive, discouraging nature of Parr himself, affected us all. Can there really, I asked myself, have been long-term consequences? Were we in any way exceptional, Carlton, Holroyd, MacLeod, Philipps, Valentine? One of us became an alcoholic, killed two people in a car crash, and died himself; one of us went to prison; one of us, perhaps the most fortunate, was removed prematurely from the house; one of us was informed in his last school report that he would never achieve anything worthwhile; one of us was striving to become invisible. I reckoned we were an average intake.

Having come from 'broken homes' and finding ourselves now

in a broken-down house probably did have some effect on Griffy and myself. 'I opted for a quiet life and studied *Wisden*,' Griffy wrote to me. He hardly does himself justice. He was the very spirit of *Wisden*, that bible of cricket, and the greatest scholar of the game I have met or could imagine. His command of bowling analyses, stretching over continents and back years, was breath-taking. Batting, too, in this respect, was no difficulty to him. I would have backed him in any quiz, and he was never dull. When he quoted statistics, they danced and sang for him. He spoke with a quiet passion and authority that touched even oars-men and tennis players.

But no one bothered to encourage him as, over a short period, they tried to help me. Though Griffy knew everything about cricket, no cricketers knew about Griffy. Our Captain of Games in 1949 was Peregrine Pollen, a tall chap who looked like the Knight of the Sorrowful Countenance, and who later became a top man at Sotheby's. He wanted me to recover my cricketing status by turning into an experimental spin bowler. Under his tuition at the nets I invented a new recipe for the googly which seemed less risky for the umpire. My bowling was acknowledged to be unusual, but no legend adhered to it as it had to my uncle's bat. While I operated at those nets with this mournful, kindly Don Quixote, Griffy, it now shames me to remember, volunteered to come along and field the balls that were slouted over my head. Fielding was all he ever did.

I made Griffy the hero of my essay 'Not Cricket'. The top game at Eton was played with frightful earnestness, but all the other games were circuses of misrule. I felt happy neither with the solemnity of the one nor the lawlessness of the others. Having no river-ambitions (I could barely float), I descended into what was contemptuously called a 'slack-bob'. But Griffy never gave up. He would be dispatched to obscure pitches on the edge of the school territory, yet his keenness and devotion to the game were never extinguished by the drudgery of his experiences. In the evenings I would come across him oiling his bat and turning over his arm against the day when he would be invited to bat or bowl. That day never really came. One of the consequences of his parents being divorced, I understood, was that he didn't own a pair of cricket boots. But this didn't matter in the games he played. Nothing mattered. 'They were less cricket matches than exhibitions of anarchy,' I wrote in 'Not Cricket'.

> No one bothered if you turned up or didn't. Philipps always turned up early. Sometimes he had to wait almost an hour before enough people ambled along to make up a couple of scratch teams . . .
>     Philipps took his role as spectator to the centre of the field. He knew more than anyone there and he remained there, year after year, waiting to use his knowledge. I would see him in the summer afternoons setting off to the fields like clockwork . . . Possibly because of his divorced parents, he never got a new bat or pads or anything else during his five years at Eton. In a sense they weren't needed. Everything looked new: but smaller. By his last year all this miniature paraphernalia with which he stood waiting to try his luck looked Lilliputian.

While Griffy Philipps lay at anchor in the mainstream of Etonian sport, I was carried off into an odd tributary. Avoiding the conventionalities of team games, I would make my solitary way down a long avenue of fives courts with their stone 'pepper-pots' to a cluster of huts grouped in a shallow valley, like a primitive African village. These were our squash courts. Squash, unlike rackets and fives, was not a fashionable game in the late nineteen-forties. It gets no mention in a well-known book on the school called *Eton Medley* that was published in 1948, not even in 'Sport', the longest chapter in the volume. But this obscurity appealed to me. After a winter storm no one could feel quite confident that these hutches would still be standing. Usually they were for the most part, and I devised ingenious games of water-squash among the copious puddles.

Dominating this village were two superior courts. When their lights were turned on (a complicated business involving numerous keys and switches) they glowed like magic places. To see the illustrious senior players, you climbed up a wooden staircase and stood on a platform in the freezing weather viewing them through a wire mesh from above – like opera-goers standing in the gods. I venerated the Keeper of Squash, Ian de Sales la Terrière, whose exotic name seemed to add lustre to his elegant play.

Ian de Sales la Terrière, who later played for England, was influenced by the great Egyptian player, Open champion of the world, M.A. Karim. In fact, we all were. Karim wore long, cream-white flannels and he gave this sweaty, thundering, claustrophobic game a quiet and classic beauty. While others laboured, gasped, pounded around the court, Karim stretched and stroked the ball this way and that. He had what all legendary figures must have: he had mystery. His style masked his intentions so cunningly that, however hard you studied him, you could never tell whether it was a lob or a drive, a deft reverse-angle or a tender drop-shot that was coming. We were like children watching a magnificent conjuror.

I modelled my style of play on Karim, though not being very strong, I was obliged to hold the racket very high up its handle, and was much criticised for this eccentricity by the master in charge of squash, Dr Lefevre. Nevertheless, despite my handicap, I thrived. Players with the smartest of Etonian names, Colin Ingleby-Mackenzie, Richard Williams-Ellis, eventually fell before my blade. Though I made a speciality of losing very brilliantly, I went on to win the public schools under-fifteen cup, and then in 1951 the British Open Junior Championship for under-sixteen-year-olds.

This was not of course a triumph on the playing fields of Eton where the Duke of Wellington was reputed to have said the Battle of Waterloo had been won (and where, according to George Orwell, the opening battles of all subsequent wars were lost), but it was something my father could enjoy. He liked telling me of a famous Egyptian player of his day called the Amr Bey, Open champion in the nineteen-thirties. His deadly lob, so altitudinous, so accurate, was unreturnable, my father boasted. He was of course speaking up for his generation, but it sounded as if he were playing the shot himself, and I was sceptical. Karim, I told him, was in a different sphere. He made even the finals of the world championship, I explained, look like exhibition matches. I used to go and watch him play at the celebrated Bruce Court at the Lansdowne Club off Berkeley Square, where all the major championships were held in those days. His victories rose above national pride. I felt delighted that squash possessed such a miraculous player and would come away from his matches exhilarated as from a ballet at Covent Garden or a concert in the new Festival Hall.

In 1951 a rumour began buzzing round the squash world of a remarkable new player from Pakistan named Hashim Khan. I was in the gallery of the Bruce Court when Hashim met Karim in the final of the Open that year. In his dazzling flannels, Karim glided and stroked the ball everywhere, and Hashim ran hectically after it. Often he ran in the wrong direction. But it didn't matter since he seemed able to change direction in mid-air. It was obvious to me that no one could go on running like that and not collapse. I felt sorry for Hashim. What happened however was that Karim collapsed – not physically, but morally. What was the purpose of out-thinking, out-manoeuvring your opponent if he still won the point? The game was reduced to a simple test of speed and stamina. Hashim won the match 9–5, 9–0, 9–0.

The impossible had happened. I could hardly credit it. But perhaps it was a freak of history. Next year the two of them met

again in the final to decide the future of squash rackets. I saw the
first game proceed very much as in the previous year. But in the
second game Karim made the supreme effort and they reached
seven all. I had never known anyone run as Hashim ran. He
dived and swerved and hurled himself around this way and that,
always smiling cheerfully, and sometimes when he was completely outplayed breaking into laughter. Karim played with
agonising beauty. The wonder of his stroke-play was beyond
anything I could conceive. There was such wit and grace, eloquence, ingenuity in those strokes. I cannot explain the
happiness they gave me. They made squash an aesthetic pleasure
where thought and movement were one. There were gasps from
the gallery at the mesmeric combination of these rallies, first
the delicate potency of Karim's play, then the impossible
retrievals of Hashim. I can see again Karim's dazzling figure
moving so easily about the court, embodying something vital to
me. But he lost 9–5, 9–7, 9–0, gave a small bow as he left the
Bruce Court, and never returned.

It was the end of squash for me. The game was changing and
so was I. As I became less competitive and more of a joker, I
switched to the unserious (though rather dangerous) game of
doubles and actually helped to win the Public School Doubles
and then, partnered by a future amateur champion, Nigel
Broomfield, the Palmer Cup, a doubles competition for under-
twenty-one-year-olds. This may not wholly have satisfied my
father, but for eighteen months, as Keeper of Squash at Eton, I
was able to join the margin of that Vanity Fair up and down the
High Street wearing a dark blue cap with crossed rackets
stitched in gold at the front, which mystified the 'lower boys'.
Yet the glamour of this position, which appeared so bright when
Ian de Sales la Terrière occupied it while I was still a junior boy
myself, seemed curiously to dissolve like a mirage once I reached
it. I had however scored a satisfying technical victory over Dr
Lefevre. The new Open champion, Hashim Khan, held his

racket as far up the handle as I did. I had wandered briefly into fashion.

No sooner had I achieved this particle of glory than, it seemed to me, my father turned his mind to graver matters. I think it must have been shortly after he appealed to my Hungarian-born stepfather for half my school fees that his character appeared to change. 'We need to have a serious talk, Michael,' he said to me gravely one day at Norhurst. I braced myself, as we entered the gloomy morning-room with its lurking telephone, for what I assumed would be another attempt to explain the facts of life to me. But on this occasion it was the economic facts of life my father wanted to explain. The family fortune, such as it was, had gone down the drain, he told me, and I could expect an inheritance of serious debts. It was essential therefore that I wasn't a damn fool. I mustn't fritter away my chances. I must use my education to prepare myself for a modern business life. Being out of work himself, he had been thumbing through advertisements for jobs in the newspapers and seen how huge the demand was for plasma-physicists, chemical engineers, radiologists and other scientific people. He wished to God his own father had spoken to him as he was now speaking to me. I would thank him later – not that he wanted thanks, not that he had ever received thanks for anything. No. Never mind that: it was probably too late for him. But it was not too late for me to become a plasma-physicist or whatever. I must specialise in the sciences if I knew what was good for me.

This was a bleak prospect. My instinct recoiled from all my father was saying, but I had no arguments to marshal against what appeared to be his formidable common sense. To my mind school was something you got through as agreeably as possible. My father, in his concern for me, made adult life sound so appallingly grim that I averted my mind from it. I had little sense of school being a factory which trained you for some profession, or of exams being used for money-making – and nor, I believe, had many of the masters. Of course I knew that I would have to begin a career sometime, but that belonged to another chapter in my life, and who could tell how that would eventually be drafted? My father despaired at the impracticality of my attitude, and I lamented over the impracticality of his anxious planning. But though I trusted to my instinct to direct me in due course, I agreed to my father's schemes because I could offer no plausible alternatives. Besides, I knew that once I had agreed I would hear fewer cautionary tales from the business world.

So I returned to Eton and, from the age of fifteen or sixteen, specialised in arithmetic, biology, botany, chemistry, geometry and physics – with a little astronomy thrown in at night. Over the next two years, my days became filled with a maze of logarithmic tables, geometric angles, and a blackboard covered with algebraic signs and letters that needed to be solved. I can remember vividly the dead frog, saturated in evil-smelling formaldehyde and crucified on a wooden block, at which I picked with my scalpel each week, identifying bits and pieces of its body. From among the bunsen burners with their firm blue and orange flames, and between the array of retorts, flasks and pipettes with their coloured powders, liquids, gases, I can see the exasperated face of our Czechoslovak teacher appear, like a pantomime demon, as he tried to beat back our happy ignorance with eruptions of barely intelligible English. Occasionally, too, a few of us would climb to the top of a remote school building after dark to gaze blankly at some blob of light in the sky and solemnly utter its Latinate name. I believed that I had some interest in astronomy, but it lay in the lure of the unknown, the mysteries of time, the question of our origins and the problem of our destination, rather than this recital of named stars. In short, I was a poor science pupil. But then my teachers were poor.

The Head Master when I arrived was Claude Elliott. 'Elliott did not neglect education matters,' writes the most recent historian of Eton, Tim Card. This was fortunate in a schoolmaster.

He was later knighted for 'services to education', though 'few headmasters have been more determinedly not educationalists'. He was perceived by us to be a kindly and cautious man, rather deaf, somewhat dull, and known by some of the masters as 'Muttonhead'. His influence on the school was far less marked than that of the most outstanding housemaster Oliver Van Oss, an energetic man with some interest in the arts, who bustled about the streets catching our attention, but who failed to catch the attention of the Fellows in his bid to become Head Master himself.

At the beginning of my second year, Claude Elliott was appointed Provost of Eton and a new Head Master arrived. This was the historian and social scientist Robert Birley who was reputed to be a blazing socialist and nicknamed 'Red Robert'. Some of the masters felt apprehensive over this new Head Master. When ripples of their fear reached us, we began whispering among ourselves how he would make early school half-an-hour earlier. The fact that he was coming from Germany (the Labour government having appointed him educational adviser to the military governor in the British Zone) seemed to make him a hostile figure. In fact, he turned out to be a liberal-minded Conservative voter whose red politics were later attributed to a portrait of Johannes Brahms in his office having been mistaken for Karl Marx.

With his white hair and stooping gait, I thought of Robert Birley as an elderly man and am shocked now to discover that he was only forty-six when he came to Eton. I occasionally heard him lecture and realised he was an inspired teacher. But the general quality of teaching at the school, in so far as I experienced it, was fairly lamentable. Worst of all was 'Bloody Bill' (H.K. Marsden), a tall, bent, grim-visaged, churlish, prying mathematics master with a relish for power and a devotion to the theory and practice of corporal punishment. He terrorised generations of boys and was disliked by everyone except a few favourites. But some Old Etonians, having survived the tyranny, later found themselves congratulating him on that fact.

More amiable, though hopeless as a teacher, was 'Hojo' (William Hope-Jones), another mathematics master who had spent almost all his life at Eton. In 1902 he had appeared with Maynard Keynes in a school performance of *Much Ado About Nothing*. After three or four years at university, he then came back to Eton as a master. By the time I arrived in his class he had been teaching there for over forty years and grown into one of those gnarled 'characters' around whom cluster stories that vastly amuse people without much sense of humour. In Tim Card's chapter 'Eton between the Wars', he appears as a celebrated oddity who won boys' hearts by his eccentricity and goodness. 'Was there a more imaginative teacher of Mathematics in his day?' the author asks, '. . . many boys who were not natural mathematicians were glad to be up to Hojo.' But I am not one of them. He was in his mid-sixties by the time he taught me and seemed almost out of control – of his subject and of us. Perhaps, poor man, he was ill. In any event, Eton was no longer between the wars and, though he hung on, Hojo's day was past.

Among the other masters was Tom Brocklebank whose 'difficulties' we attributed to his once having become stuck near the summit of Everest; 'Leggy' Lambert, the Lower Master (later Vice Provost), who used his desk as a kennel during thunderstorms; and Babington Smith who marked our papers out of ten thousand instead of ten.

But there was one teacher I admired. Sydney Watson, our precentor and musical director, was afflicted with such an insistent stutter that some people who heard him utter his full name in public believed he had a knighthood. But his passion and zest, his sheer skill as a choral conductor, turned this terrible hesitation into eloquence. He was known to us as 'Daddy Watson' and, as he led us through the complexities of Haydn's *Creation*, Bach's *St John Passion* and Handel's *Messiah*, through songs by

Brahms and Vaughan Williams, Stanford and Parry, making the rough places plain, it seemed indeed as if he were our father and we, of the Eton College Musical Society, his family. The ECMS was the only society I joined, the one 'team' I played for. We sang in the evenings at a schoolroom in the Eton Wick Road. It had steeply-banked rows of desks up which Daddy Watson would leap and round which he strode, encouraging us, correcting us, explaining, expounding, exemplifying, sometimes tapping his baton to prevent us going off the rails, then urging us on again. I did not read music but, holding the sheets in front of me, I could see roughly where the notes went, could pick up a tune, follow a narrative; and so for some four years as treble, alto, tenor, bass, I belted it out, giving my best, feeling my best.

On Sunday afternoons, I used to sneak off to the Music Schools with Michael MacLeod. We weren't really allowed into this building, not being proper music students, but no one minded us occupying a room with a piano if no one else needed it. Over some weeks, we 'composed' a piano duet that, beginning with a pastiche of chopsticks, went on for almost eight minutes. We were proud of this marathon, but having nothing more in our musical vocabulary to add, wisely forgot about it when we returned from our holidays. But my recollection of it now, when so much else is forgotten, marks it as an emergence from my musical beginnings in the garage at Norhurst. Certainly Daddy Watson gave me a wider liking for music, and after fifty years or so I can still summon up a few of the songs we sang, and startle friends with an odd line or two.

I had been at Eton for two or three years when one night, sometime after midnight, Purple Parr opened the door of my room as I lay sleeping and told me to come to his drawing-room. As I put on my slippers and dressing-gown I remember wondering whether one of my parents had died. But when, a few minutes later, I stood before him, Parr began asking me in a solemn voice a series of innocuous, almost meaningless questions. Who were my friends? Did I have friends in other houses? When did they come and see me? Or did I go to their houses? And so on. After half-an-hour of this surreal interrogation, he told me I might return to my room. When I woke next morning, I thought perhaps it had been a dream. But I soon found that a number of other boys had been taken from their beds and similarly questioned. What was happening, we concluded, was a homosexual inquisition or purge.

Was there homosexuality at Eton? Well, of course there was. Romantic passion and amorous speculation hung in the valley atmosphere of the place, and seeped into our imaginations. With almost 1,400 teenage boys closeted together in some twenty-five houses, how could there not have been infatuations and intrigues, spiced with exciting rumours over who was 'gone on' whom? Boys exchanged signed photographs of one another as marks of favour, and would send each other complex paper knots containing confidential messages which were delivered from house to house by fags scampering through the streets. These running figures seemed to match the palpitating hearts, the breathless tension and suspense, of the correspondents. Our hours were steeped in vague delicious daydreams and pleasurable scuffles on the floor in the evenings that might turn at night into masturbatory fantasies. To all our emotions there was a rhythm that seemed to change with the changing seasons. In the schoolrooms we read poetry that, though filtered through sanctioned translations from dead languages, told of exquisite friendships and carried erotic signals from the past. But we were very much alive and curious as to how we might translate these sentimental stories into present-day adventures. Surely this, in addition to the taking down of Latin Unseen and the recital of gender rhymes, was part of our education? We wanted to live our literature for, as Cyril Connolly wrote in *Enemies of Promise*, 'a schoolboy is a novelist too busy to write'.

In the scandalous twentieth-century novels of public school

life, from Alec Waugh's *The Loom of Youth* (1917) to Simon
Raven's *Fielding Gray* (1967), there is a potent homosexual
ingredient, sometimes disguised, often unenacted, that is nevertheless sensationalised by athletic brilliance, or exploited by the
system of fagging and the habit of boys legitimately beating
younger boys (the very rare beatings by housemasters were inter-
estingly called 'screwings' at Eton). There were, of course, tides
of fashion in homosexuality (we never used the words gay and
lesbian then), and to the general reader one period may seem saturated with it, another quite arid. But we rely on accounts which
have been written either by some of nature's celibates or by
those who were very sexually aware. In earlier days, when some
unmarried housemasters would bestow long kisses on tolerant
boys in their rooms after lock-up, a general unawareness of sex
may have made emotional life simpler. 'Women did not play a
large part on the Eton scene,' concedes Tim Card in his survey of
Eton from 1860 to 1990.

> . . . It would seem that sex may have caused increased
> problems between the Wars . . . Most Housemasters were
> constantly on guard against any physical sexual
> activity . . . Boys were left in little doubt that they would
> be sacked . . . The adult world was still officially very
> hostile to homosexuality, but among the boys it was
> recognised that romantic friendships were natural.

Purple Parr sent my father a letter warning him that I should
be careful of the company I kept. He must have written to a
number of parents about this lurking peril of 'keeping company'. Evidently something dramatic had happened and a hunt
was on – I think one boy may have been sacked. This was something that must have taken place every few years. But my father
was astonished. He braced himself to do his duty and informed
me that homosexuality was 'worse than . . .' Here he paused,

trying to be fair, yet still dramatic. '. . . Worse than burglary.' I would like to think that he coined the phrase 'buggery is worse than burglary', but I cannot honestly say he did. It was all made more difficult for him by having to voice his dismay down the telephone while I was staying with my mother in London. I remember him whispering that during his time there had been 'only one queer at Eton' and he was pretty odd – no one had liked him. My father was whispering because he did not want my stepfather to hear of this scandal, and his whisper made everything sound additionally dark and dreadful. In Norhurst style, he continued lowering his voice on the telephone until it grew hard to pick up his plunging syllables. What he had to say, as it became more buried, also became more infernal. He had instructed my mother not to breathe a word of this affair to her husband, but in order to bring home to me the gravity of it all, he also instructed her not to take me to the cinema while I was in London. My mother, however, was unable to take Parr's letter quite so seriously. For about thirty seconds or so she attempted to show concern, then we went off to see a film together (with me swearing never to breathe a word of this to my father).

We were all in a muddle because no one had decided how much sex-life should be allowed between boys of fourteen to eighteen (many of whom without sisters knew no girls at all). In fact nothing had really changed at Eton in the thirty years since Cyril Connolly was there. In 1920 he had found himself among those boys who were floundering through on 'surreptitious experiments' that were suspected by the masters and would have led to his expulsion if they had been actually discovered. Eton, he came to believe, encouraged 'continence officially and homosexuality by implication'. This tantalising suspension of the emotions, with all its intensity and irresolution, fixed many public schoolboys in perpetual adolescence.

Nothing had changed: but much was about to change. Things simply could not go on like this. Those of us who left Eton in or around 1953 were impatient for the better life that was to begin ten years later 'between the end of the Chatterley ban/And the Beatles' first L.P.'. Though this change came a bit late for us, our impatience was, I like to think, a necessary preparation for this change, a hammering at the door.

Though midnight interrogations and solemn letters were high points of anxiety, my main anxiety over the first three years at Eton was figuring out how the place worked. The streets were busy with boys hurrying from one place to another as if they instinctively understood the choreography of the system. Perhaps I too looked like this as I walked along. But I had great difficulty finding out, keeping up, arriving at; and for years afterwards I was afflicted with exhausting nightmares of following people and losing them, of failing to reach some destination and never discovering what it had been. When Purple Parr, making his amphibious progress through the damp corridors, glided into my room one evening to describe his shame at having a Captain of Games who apparently played no games, I was sympathetic but could not bring myself to explain that I did not quite know how these games were arranged, or even sometimes where they were played. No wonder, as Griffy Philipps observed, I looked haggard.

But in my last year I found there were some blissful advantages to this ignorance. For if I was not quite all there, as it were, perhaps I would not be noticed; and if no one noticed me, then I was free to do as I liked; and if I did what I liked surely my anxieties would evaporate. And they did. There were penalties to be paid for this style. If you affected a forgetful air, you soon found yourself forgetting things you would have preferred to remember. But as a way of avoiding trouble it seemed to suit me well enough, though it meant I avoided other things too.

At the beginning of one half in my last year a boy I had known at Scaitcliffe, Nicky Winter, came to see me. He told me that he had suggested my name for 'Pop', the élite Eton society to which my Uncle Kenneth had belonged. No one, he was able to report, had a word to say against me. In fact, no one had anything to say at all. Between legendary appearances on the squash court, I seemed to disappear and was unknown. However, if I would put myself about a bit, Nicky Winter said, and make some effort, he might perhaps get me in at the next election. It was a kind gesture and I was tempted to do something about it. But I found that I was unable to do anything. It was as if I were already programmed for invisibility and could not reverse the process.

There were to be other symptoms of this process, such as the vanishing of blatant facts and events. I have no idea where I was when President Kennedy was assassinated or Queen Elizabeth crowned; I do not remember my army number; I do not know what examinations I passed or failed at school. Of course I could find out about the exams, but perhaps the truth is better conveyed by not doing so. For I have never been questioned about my qualifications and nothing in my career has depended on them. I do remember that I had the choice of going up to either Oxford or Cambridge (though I cannot recall to which colleges), and that this was partly based on interviews.

My one anxiety during this last year at Eton was how to escape my father's generous plans for me. I simply did not want to be a plasma-physicist. During the holidays, I had continued my intermittent and alternative education at Maidenhead Public Library and become convinced that I was more at home in the arts. One evening at Norhurst I tackled my father, blurting out that I could not go up to university and read science – I really had no talent for it. He gave a long sigh and entered the battle. We argued quite violently into the early morning, and my father, by brute force of speech, appeared to demolish my carefully-prepared position – though I continued to defend it with desperate obstinacy.

Much of what my father said was true. Many people had

made sacrifices to send me to Eton, he reminded me, and now I was proposing to throw it all away. Very well. He could not stop me. But perhaps I would be kind enough to inform him what I was going to do – other than live off other people all my life. There was, of course, one practical alternative open to me, and it was an index of my thoughtlessness that I had not mentioned it. He was referring to the Rajmai Tea Company. This was a fine business, he would not deny that. But if I wanted to go in that direction it would mean my travelling out to Assam and starting at the foot of the ladder. Did I have the guts for this? Did I have any guts at all? If I had he would do everything in his power to help me. He would have a word with my grandfather in the morning and set the wheels in motion. I was lucky. Not every boy had a second chance like this. I had only to say the word. When I mentioned that I had been tentatively thinking of taking up writing, my father sat back and laughed. It was not a happy sound. No one, he assured me, would prevent me writing. How could they? My evenings and weekends on the tea plantations of Assam would be my own, just as my school holidays had been. Perhaps I already had some masterpiece in my pocket. He would very much like to read it. He really would. Meanwhile we had better come down from 'Cloud Cuckoo Land'.

I hardly slept that night and felt wretched in the morning. But my father, who had been so triumphant in the night, also looked drained. His tone was now altogether different. He told me that he had hit on a solution to the problem. If I could argue so persistently why shouldn't I take up a profession that paid me to argue? He meant the law. Many of the Holroyds had been lawyers, so perhaps their genes were shaping my destiny. I had probably left it too late to read law at university, but I could become articled to a firm of solicitors. He knew some solicitors in Windsor and would make inquiries if that was what I wanted. The relief between us was palpable, and I welcomed his suggestion gratefully. It would mean postponement of my National

Service, but that was no disincentive. I had little desire to go to university because I had little notion of what life there might be like. In any event, it seemed beyond my range. What would I do there? I was not attracted to the idea of reading Classics; I had never heard of the humanities; and besides my father would certainly not have paid anything to see me waste my time on such subjects. Later, it seemed to me, I had been shut out of Eden and that everyone at university was clever and in love, and the sun always shone there. Later still, I reacted from this sentiment and congratulated myself on the advantages of having so little to unlearn. Now, I see the advantages and disadvantages as more evenly spread.

There was a strange postscript to our night of argument and morning of reconciliation. For, although my father had dominated the agenda, one of its eventual consequences was to be our collaboration on a history of the world in verse – which really was entering 'Cloud Cuckoo Land'.

For the last few months of my time at Eton I left my dead frog in its formaldehyde haze and the bunsen burners with their orange and blue flames, left my logarithmic tables and blackboard algebra. But what was to replace them? I asked Purple Parr whether I could study English Literature. There were not many boys who did this at Eton and Parr, not liking to take the risk, shook his head. It would hardly be appropriate, he thought. I had heard there was a subject called Psychology and I asked him about my chances there, which gave him the opportunity of explaining that I didn't have the brain for it. Eventually it was decided that I should start Spanish (and resume French) in my last half. From this new language I retain just one phrase, 'Que lástima!', which sums it up.

But it was during this last half that I came across a genuine intuitive teacher among the masters. This was Peter Spanoghe, a name that does not appear in the volumes I have read about Eton. He was not one of those caricatures, like 'Bloody Bill' and

'Hojo', garnished with stale school jokes. There is no obituary of him in the *Eton Chronicle*, and none of the Head Master's files of that time survive. Nothing exists about him beyond a note that he arrived in 1934 and taught German and French. Yet he was a remarkable man. He lived in Willowbrook, was married to a beautiful woman in a wheelchair, was himself partly disabled and walked with a pronounced limp. He was nevertheless one of the most active people in the school. He taught me French – and suddenly I was top of the form. Spanoghe knew no boundaries and we moved easily between French and English literature, from the past into the present and back again. Before this, French had been taught to me as a dead language; English was presented as a set of grammatical rules and obstacles; history a procession of dates and battles, kings and treatises. Spanoghe changed all that. He was quick-witted and made it all fun, made it easy. Somehow he engaged me in the subject so that my feelings were involved, I came alive and no longer felt slow. This was the magic of teaching, and no sooner had I glimpsed it than it was time for me to leave.

I left Eton at the end of 1953, and Peter Spanoghe himself was to leave a year later. I heard a rumour that he was involved in an affair with some girl and I was told that Pamela Spanoghe was divorcing him. Eton was still ludicrously sensitive about such matters (only ten years before, the Provost had informed a housemaster who married the innocent party in a divorce case, and whom he had met only after the divorce, that he was a habitual adulterer). I caught sight of Spanoghe one more time, at a delicatessen in Chelsea during the mid-fifties, but was stupidly too shy to go up and thank him. He must be long dead now. Looking through the telephone book, however, I see there is a P. Spanoghe listed as living in Chelsea still, and suddenly it becomes a matter of urgency to contact him. I telephone: but there is no answer. Then I write. But I am too late. He died a few months earlier, his widow tells me, and so I have missed him again.

What I would have thanked him for, besides his teaching, was a letter he wrote to Purple Parr which was forwarded to my father. Though he lost it, he was impressed by the notion that I was rather a promising tortoise. It also had some influence on Parr himself, 'I agree very much with Spanoghe's letter,' he wrote to my father.

> Michael has indeed a critical mind and its full value will probably not be appreciated for a long time. Indeed, it is in some ways a handicap at the moment. He is still very much an observer of life, even though he cannot detach himself completely. He sees more sides to a question than most schoolboys and is slow in decision because he genuinely wants to be right rather than merely expedient . . . He is neither a disciplinarian nor a rebel, and much of his work as Captain of the House must have seemed to him not right or wrong, but merely petty . . . He is not nearly (thank goodness!) at his peak yet: his honesty, determination, shrewdness and sensibility will come into their own when he has become, as inevitably he must, a little coarser-grained.

Parr's previous reports had emphasised rather less appealing aspects of what he called my 'doubtful temperament'; my nervousness, indecision and egocentricity. He thought, though I cannot recognise this in myself, that I was swayed by superstition ('he lacks robustness against omens!'), and told my father that I had a disbelief in ultimate success that I communicated to others – though this, I think, reflected Parr's own disbelief in my success. But after reading Spanoghe's letter, he gave a far more amiable interpretation of these qualities. 'He has been exceptionally mild, but not thereby ineffective,' Parr wrote. 'He has been respected and liked by all classes . . . I could have wished that he had, in his Eton life, ventured further outside the house.

But he kept to his own ploy and was in consequence little known. From those who have known him he has always earned golden opinions . . .'

My mildness, and the ripples of popularity it briefly spread, can be accounted for by a decision I made to discontinue house beatings. I did not announce this as a new policy (not being a rebel), but simply beat no one. This was unusual in the early nineteen-fifties, but I got away with it because it became the practice almost before anyone noticed.

In his last letter to my father about me, Purple Parr described himself as 'a friend who has now known and liked him a long time'. But over five long years he had been unable to communicate this friendliness. His shyness, detachment and egocentricity (qualities I saw in him curiously similar to those he saw in me) put him beyond my reach, and beyond the reach of other boys.

A year after I left Eton, in the autumn of 1954, I wrote to Purple Parr asking him for information that the Law Society needed relating to my registration as an articled clerk. In the course of my letter I mentioned that I was writing a book. 'I imagine [it's] a novel,' he sighed. '. . . I should think at least one leaver every half writes (or at least begins) a novel in his first year away. You wd certainly be surprised at the number who have from my house.'

This characteristic, slightly discouraging comment was to gain unexpected irony a few years later when David Benedictus published his *succès de scandal*, *The Fourth of June*. Benedictus, who had also been at Purple Parr's, was three years younger than myself. Like me, he became Captain of the House and abolished beating. But by then Parr's was once more becoming a brilliant athletic house. The dining-room glittered again with silver cups and shields, and the dull brown and mauve quarters of his house colours excited admiration on the playing fields. One consequence of this new climate was that David Benedictus had a more awkward time than I did, and was not permitted the same 'mildness'. His novel, written partly in reaction to these difficulties, is a satire that shows up Eton as a totalitarian city state of snobbery and sadism. 'It is inevitable in a book of this kind that some lonely person somewhere will imagine himself portrayed,' he wrote in a careful preparatory note. '. . . care has been taken to avoid such portrayals.' In the novel itself the word 'lonely' is applied to the calculating pusillanimous housemaster, Manningham, and, despite the care taken to convert him into an imaginary character, no one who reads the book and knew Parr can fail to recognise some borrowings. Parr himself read the book in 1962 and was obviously affected. It was adapted for the theatre and, around the time we all saw it in London's West End, he suddenly died, leaving us with very ambiguous feelings of regret.

# 15

## Legal and Military

My first half-dozen years after leaving Eton were strikingly indecisive. They began with two minor operations. The first – to correct some complications in my right knee caused by squash-playing – was counted a success (though it actually masked an injury that led to more serious damage years later). I was given a general anaesthetic and stayed several days in hospital. It was the first time I had been in hospital since having my tonsils and adenoids out as a child, and I was taken aback by how much the experience disturbed me. In the ward men lay groaning, men lay dying. Between the rows of beds marched a starched army of nurses with glinting thermometers and watches, and among them moved a clattering rabble of cleaners and kitchen staff wheeling their trolleys. They looked exceedingly happy, often stopping and laughing among themselves, overcome with hilarity, as if unaware of the sounds of pain and fear all round them, as if they were somehow inhabiting a parallel world where these ranks of sick people were invisible. I could not believe what I was witnessing. I felt I was in hell. After my operation I told the ward sister that I wanted to discharge myself and complete my convalescence at home. But during those early years of the National Health Service, patients were not moved along like a fast-moving queue of 'customers' or treated as expensive 'consumers' to be 'targeted' with medicine; and the practice was to keep them in hospital until the doctors were confident they had fully recovered. The ward sister told me not to be so stupid and, as a precaution, hid my clothes. But I found them, dressed myself, hopped out into the night and took a taxi back to my bedroom at Wetherby Gardens where I felt much better.

It was in this bedroom that I went through my other operation – a succession of primitive and painful clearings of the nasal sinuses by an ear, nose and throat specialist called Miss Wadge. She would stick a thin metal instrument right up my nose, above my eye, and pump sterilised water through it for an hour. After half-a-dozen visits, I was cured of sinusitis. Not long afterwards I suffered the first of a long, though not frequent series of migraines in the very place where Miss Wadge had been needling me. Perhaps unfairly, I have always associated my migraine attacks with her operations.

Around this time, and in the same bedroom one night, I had a frightening experience that enables me now to tell a miniature non-fiction ghost story.

It is a wild night, reader, and a storm has blown up slashing the sky with rents of lightning, with tremendous bangs and rumbles of thunder. I am at the top of the house and my attic window suddenly opens. The wind frantically agitates the glass panes, the curtains streaming in, and the commotion of the storm outside wakes me. I hear the window shivering, see the curtains flapping, the rain driving in, and feel a strange coldness in the room. Perhaps I have woken from a nightmare. Certainly I feel odd and cannot tell for a few moments whether I am really awake or asleep. I take my arm out of the bed and stretch over to turn on the bedside light so that I can get up and close the window. The thunder roars and crashes. Then, as my hand reaches the light switch I feel another hand fixed upon it, a damp, cold, unattached, inexplicable, horrifying hand. My heart gives a thump, I force the terrible thing away and switch on the light, dreading what I will see. What I see is my other hand which has completely 'gone to sleep' and through which I can feel nothing. I am my own ghost.

In later years I have had three or four similar experiences. An animal, perhaps a snake, maybe a rat, lands dramatically on my chest in the middle of the night a second after I have woken. I start up and fling the brute away, but it immediately lands back on me and I cannot get rid of the monster, whatever it is. What it is, of course, is my own absolutely senseless arm I am wrestling with in the dark. For some moments, without the circulation of life, it is a terrifying experience.

Eton had gradually become the most secure of all my living places, and I missed the friends I had made there, Griffy Philipps, Michael MacLeod and a few others. I continued shuttling between Maidenhead and London, Sweden and France. I was travelling to France not with my father now, but my mother. We used to speak of L'Oiseau Bleu as our villa in the South of France, though it was little more than a stone shack with a glorious view of Monte Carlo from above the Grande Corniche. I hated it. I could do nothing with the view or anything else. In my opinion there *was* nothing else – nothing that interested me. I was scared of the frogs, lizards and scorpions that leapt and scuttled about my bedroom, and I disliked the wearisome business of carrying water each day from the village of La Turbie, a mile away. While my mother lay in the sun, I wandered around doing silly things like falling down a mountain, climbing a tree and making myself ill on unripe figs, or simply getting severe sunburn. I was an awful nuisance.

Eventually my mother suggested that I invite my friend Griffy Philipps to join us. We met him at Ventimiglia railway station just over the Italian border, and he stayed three weeks. 'Apart from some alarm about scorpions,' he writes to me, 'nothing very controversial happened.' But it was much better doing nothing together than alone.

On another occasion Kaja came with Biryer Sandström who smoked a wonderfully long cigar and wore dazzling co-respondent's shoes. Edy brought his daughter Gay, and we all stayed in a hotel at Antibes. Gay was a couple of years older than I was, and something of a tomboy. Together, in great excitement, almost hysterics, we put on an excruciating 'entertainment' of music and recitations, through which everyone was politely obliged to sit.

On 16 April 1954 I began a five-year term as an articled clerk. The solicitors to whom I was articled, T.W. Stuchbery & Son, had their offices at the corner of Park Street in Windsor. So I was still very close to Eton, though my new life was a world away.

Messrs T.W. Stuchbery & Son had never entertained an articled clerk before and appeared to have little notion of what to do with me. I was technically articled to one of the senior partners, Ian Hezlett, a Falstaffian character of uncertain temper who had been a drinking companion of my father's (signs of his beer-drinking could be detected after midday on his extravagantly frothing moustache). But I saw little of him in his grand office on the first floor after our initial encounter together with my father. 'We'll start him on tort,' Hezlett announced. 'Donoghue and Stevenson.' My father laughed heartily, and I looked blank. Then I was sent up to a modest office under the attic where a thin, bent, sun-starved, middle-aged solicitor called Mr Owen worked, encircled by papers. An extra desk was moved into his office and I sat at it. I was also equipped with blotting-paper, pen, pencil and rubber. And that was it. All I did in the first weeks was to practise making tea and coffee. But gradually, over the months, my duties were extended. I released Mr Owen from some of his imprisoning papers, filing them in the shadowy attics crammed with documents tied in faded pink string, and covered with dust. Occasionally Mr Owen, who was a well-intentioned if unexciting man, would take me to the County Court in Windsor to sniff the legal atmosphere, and I would sit out the long days there. On one of my first visits, trying to keep awake during the afternoon, I unintentionally released from a large metal radiator a fountain of tepid water over some witnesses. I could not tell afterwards whether Mr Owen was amused or appalled, but I noticed that he began giving me increasingly odd jobs out of the office and would question me quite keenly when I got back as if hungry for some specks of entertainment. I was able to tell him how I had been shot at while attempting to serve a writ (the marksman taking aim through a caravan window as I approached, waving a white handkerchief, across a field), how I had accidentally been locked into a huge fridge among various carcasses which belonged to a litigious butcher who was, I felt, exaggerating the oven-like qualities of his cold storage. Apparently encouraged by my misadventures, Mr Owen saw to it that Stuchbery's craziest clients, those in search of therapy rather than legal opinion, were sent up to me for consultation. I daresay that many country solicitors, before the widespread use of psychiatry, provided such services for those who could afford them. I remember one elderly woman who used to come in fairly regularly complaining of nudity among her neighbours. At twilight, she confided, and at even more revealing times, they would dance in the garden and were, she concluded from the noises she heard at night, tunnelling under her house. I made notes on my pink blotting pad, gave her some of my tea, and eventually prepared an invoice in mock-legal jargon which I think she appreciated.

My worst offence occurred in London during a complicated divorce case. I had made a summary of the husband's and wife's

With my parents                                    Not out at Norhurst

My uncle marries Sheilah Sayers in 1947. I am on the extreme left and next but one in the front row stands Old Nan. My father is behind me and my grandfather is the third man on the right with Adeline on his right. On the extreme right is Bill Stephenson, Chairman of Woolworth, regarding us acutely

Egon Hessel c. 1960

A society wedding, 1955. David and Ulla Nares

My mother, Biryer Sandström, my stepfather Edy Fainstain and Kaja in Nice c. 1950

The boy at Maidenhead

The schoolboy at Eton

The novelist in London –

and his novel

Brocket in the 1920s

Lalique party in the 1930s. My grandfather is at the centre with Adeline on his right next to Yolande and then Ulla. My father in his bow tie stands on the left

Yolande c. 1930

My stepmother, Marlou, Paris, c. 1950

My grandfather, chairman
of the Rajmai Tea
Company, c. 1952

My grandmother outside Norhurst before her husband's funeral, 1961

My mother with Kaja on her last visit to Sweden

My father with his schnauzer puppy

My mother during her cancer treatment

On holiday with my father

At Christmas with my mother

The biographer in Ireland

letters to each other – something of an education for me – and was allowed by Mr Owen to attend the court hearing in London. But the case took an unexpected turn while Mr Owen was in the lavatory, and our Counsel, murmuring to the judge that he needed to take fresh instructions, turned to me. By the time Mr Owen returned, the case had been adjourned and the disgruntled parties found themselves still married.

I did not know what I was doing. What I was meant to be doing was reading law under Ian Hezlett's supervision for some of the time, and working in his legal practice for the rest of the time. In those Dickensian days, articled clerks were not paid salaries, but actually paid the solicitors to whom they were articled. This was not an obvious solution to our financial problems, though my father persuaded himself that it was an astute investment. At the beginning of my second year, acknowledging that I was receiving no training or tuition, but simply doing errands for Mr Owen, Ian Hezlett decided to pay me a modest wage. My father, ever the optimist, interpreted this as a promotion rather than surrender, and for a brief period allowed himself to feel almost happy at the way things were shaping.

The only point of law that was explained to me at Stuchbery's was one that involved a snail in a bottle of ginger beer. 'Do you know Donoghue and Stevenson yet?' Ian Hezlett called out to me one day on his way to the pub. Then it was Mr Owen's turn, 'May I recommend that you peruse the case of Donoghue versus Stevenson?' he said seeing me gazing out morosely at the buses which went one way to Dedworth, the other to Gravesend. 'How are you getting on, young chap?' a visiting solicitor quizzed me. 'Mastered Donoghue and Stevenson have you?' I mastered nothing else, having received the impression that if I got the hang of this famous snail which had gone in its bottle all the way to the House of Lords to establish the manufacturer's duty of care, then I would have cracked the legal code and all would be well.

The most cheerful aspect of my legal career was that it deferred my two years' National Service. But eventually I could endure the pointlessness and boredom no longer. I simply could not credit that people spent their lives shut up in such gloomy buildings, counting themselves lucky as they shuffled through old papers from Monday morning to Saturday lunchtime day after week after year, with only an annual fortnight's holiday, until the long holiday of retirement and the permanent vacation of death. It seemed awful, but then I was intensely lonely, having lost touch with my companions from school and being unable as yet to replace them.

There was at the office a girl who lived on a caravan site which I used to pass in the bus that took me each day from Maidenhead to Windsor and back. She was in her early twenties, slim, dark-haired and with glittering eyes that shone and flashed in my imagination at nights. Was it only in my imagination that she seemed to be making some signal that we might see each other outside the office, in the evenings or at weekends? I will never know. In those days it was difficult for a girl to take the initiative in a relationship, and I was handicapped by poverty and paralysed by shyness.

From these legal experiences I was later able to add to my family's foreboding of bankruptcy my own writer's apprehension of libel. But the only law that genuinely interested me was criminal law, and that is less an interest in law than in human nature. After eighteen months at Windsor, I braced myself for another confrontation with my father. 'I am not angry because you don't like the law,' he wrote to me.

> I am angry because you are apparently prepared to chuck
> it up without an effort. The world is not an easy place &
> I don't want you to miss the boat.
>     I have met hundreds of men of my own age who are
> down & out in life and the story is always the same with

slight variations. They are men of good education who because of indulgent parents never settled down to any job . . . Heaven knows, I don't want you to hate your work, but I don't want to see you a drifter – for I have seen only too often the mess they make of their lives.

My father promised me that I would hate the army even more than the law. A legal qualification, he argued, would be my best insurance policy. 'Your life must be more competitive than mine. If you pass your examinations you still have a big pull over the others because you were at a Public School, but not unless you can back it up with the necessary qualifications.' He stressed the awkwardness of reneging on my articles, but if I was determined to chuck the law then it would be better, he told me, to join the army as a regular soldier rather than a national serviceman. 'At 46 years of age you retire with a lump sum or pension.' Then I could afford to write books. 'You don't know how hellish life can be if you get on the rocks,' he warned me. My father was then, I calculated, forty-six. 'Had I had a firm hand to guide me when I was young I would have been in a damn sight better position in life to-day.' But, he concluded, if I would not continue with the law, not join the regular army, I must simply go my own way.

Things might have been a little easier if I'd known that my grandfather had left Gray's Inn in 1900 without taking any examinations. But though I was still living at Maidenhead, he said nothing to me. In any case my father would have seen this precedent as being out of date. Nevertheless I would not have felt unique in my record of failure as I terminated my articles and, going my own way, prepared for two years' National Service.

Conscription had been introduced after the Second World War partly as a reaction against Britain's military unpreparedness during the nineteen-thirties. Both the Conservative and Labour parties supported it, and it was popular among the majority of older civilians and ex-servicemen. By the end of 1955, when I joined up, two years' military service (followed by three-and-a-half years in the reserves) seemed a natural part of growing up though, since women were exempt, it prolonged the unnatural segregation of the sexes.

'Some of you,' Captain Carlton-Smith announced to our group of raw recruits, 'will be lucky enough to see active service!' There was a titter of disbelief and general air of incredulity. Few young men objected to military service on conscientious grounds because few of them thought they would actually be called on to fight. Ten years after the end of the war, we were still in a state of stunned reaction. Over the eighteen years of its existence, though 395 national servicemen were to be killed in action, parents did not regard National Service as dangerous until the Suez Campaign of 1956. It was generally spoken of, rather vaguely but quite sincerely, as a training for life – something that developed the character, allowed many young chaps to see a bit of the world, made them physically fit, and gave them an opportunity of finding out where their talents lay. It conferred none of these benefits on me.

I joined the Greenjackets because my Uncle Kenneth had been in the Greenjackets. That was how the army worked in those days, at least among its officers. The Greenjackets were barely tolerated by the battalions of Guards, but looked down their noses at the line regiments which in turn were contemptuous of the Royal Pioneers and the Education Corps, which hated the whole lot of us. And the regular soldiers despised the national servicemen who thought the regulars slightly mad. Such was our comradeship. It was, I now see, very much like Britain's education system and operated as a means of keeping separate the various classes and categories in the country. I applied for a Russian course in Cornwall as an alternative to serving in the army, but after the mid-nineteen-fifties this was discontinued. So when I was summoned to Winchester for my basic training, I went like a lamb.

But the Greenjackets at Winchester were not expecting me. There had been a mistake and I was that mistake. The adjutant studied my papers critically and asked me why I had not arrived with the regular intake. I did not know. He was not best pleased, and being uncertain what to do with me, eventually ordered me to 'clear off back home' for a fortnight.

Something similar was to happen at the end of my ten weeks' basic training. The Ministry of Defence suddenly noticed that my mother was Swedish, and decided that this called for an investigation. So while everyone else went on to their next posting I was held in limbo at Winchester with one other national serviceman (who was suspected of having tuberculosis). The barracks were suddenly empty and for two or three weeks there was positively nothing for us to do. We went once or twice to films, stared pennilessly at girls in the street, lay in the sun on St Catherine's Hill overlooking the town. We even managed to commandeer a Land Rover and, with my new friend at the wheel, patrolled the summer countryside. These days, being timeless, have remained with me. But suddenly one day I was ordered to proceed *soonest* to Chester. I never discovered whether my friend had TB.

I was to spend sixteen weeks under the improbable shadow of the Officer Cadet School near Chester. Eaton Hall was a 'Wagnerian palace', as Nikolaus Pevsner described it, with intricate Gothic pinnacles and grandiose battlements, that had once belonged to the Dukes of Westminster. The lodges, chapels and stables, the lakes and neglected rose gardens descending to the River Dee, had been dramatically transformed to cater for the peacetime goings-on of our amateur infantry with its bustling captains and bristling sergeants. Jeremy Isaacs, who was there at the same time as myself, recalls that one of our sergeant-majors was called Blood and another Leach; and that the Regimental Sergeant-Major was Lynch. 'Much gallows humour resulted.'

Eaton Hall was the sort of fantastical place where my late Great-Uncle Pat, the innocent Major of the Militia, might have enjoyed performing manoeuvres and parades. But I did not enjoy the platoon marches and marathons, the kit inspections and fatigues. 'Training consisted of drill with spit and polish,' Jeremy Isaacs writes, 'firmly, but not ferociously insisted on; giving lecturettes; planning and leading field exercises.' Jeremy himself made a brilliant night attack on a group of boulders that he believed were the enemy. I landed in a swamp, sinking with my bren gun up to my shoulders. On Sundays we headed for the comforts of Blossom's Hotel in Chester to forget our humiliations of the week.

Because of my deferment as an articled clerk I was older than most of my fellow officer cadets. Griffy Philipps and even Christopher Capron and John Mein from my Scaitcliffe days whom I might have seen again, had all finished their National Service. I found some boys who had been junior to me at Eton were now my seniors at Eaton Hall. My smiles of recognition often went unanswered. I had become an anachronism. But I did not fall seriously out-of-step until I finished my officer training, was given the rank of Second Lieutenant, and had the good luck to miss active service.

It must seem odd that I became an officer. At the War Office Selection Board near Andover I had not performed well. I used the wrong method of getting a log over a stream and, using arguments of unassailable ingenuity, reached an incorrect conclusion in the written examination. But I had achieved all this error and misjudgement with the aid of proper grammar and the right accent. So, between ends and means, I was an awkward case. Everything depended on my lecture. I spoke on 'Sense of Humour' without a single joke. It was an intimidating perform-ance (extensively cribbed from George Meredith's lecture 'On the Idea of Comedy and the Uses of the Comic Spirit', and also from Harold Nicolson's little book *The English Sense of Humour*): and it worked. For what I was really being tested on was not, fortunately, my military skills, but my acting abilities. Could I convince other ranks that there was no danger in the trenches, that we personally hated the enemy, that our cause was glorious and everyone else's vile? On the strength of my 'Sense of Humour', the War Office Selection Board decided that I could. But I had not passed with distinction and was to be transferred from the Greenjackets to the Royal Fusiliers, at the request of the Greenjackets.

Before I joined my new regiment I was granted three weeks' leave. It was the autumn of 1956. I remember going to John Osborne's *Look Back in Anger* at the Royal Court Theatre and watching many of the red-faced audience leave in the interval. I also went to Ingmar Bergman's sombre film *The Seventh Seal*, and during the Pathé News was surprised to see several of my colleagues from Eaton Hall gesticulating blindly from the screen. Their trapped expressions, like zoo-animals', stared vacantly down at me, while the commentator described the embarkation of the Royal Fusiliers to Egypt. National servicemen, as well as the regular army, were being 'given the privilege of serving their sovereign' by recapturing the Suez Canal from Colonel Nasser.

There spread through me a sense that something was wrong. Surely I should have been up there on the screen instead of in the stalls? That evening I telephoned Griffy Philipps and tried to make a joke of it. 'Will they shoot me?' I laughed. He considered the question far too long. 'I should think, Hagga, that they would grant you a court martial,' he replied, 'first.' Fifteen years later I wrote an account of what happened for B.S. Johnson's National Service anthology *All Bull*.

Next day I telephoned my adjutant ostensibly on a small matter connected with dress . . . Cutting across a detailed query on buttons, he demanded to know 'where the hell' I was. Did I realise I had missed the war? I was to put myself under close arrest and escort myself to the Tower of London . . .

I arrived at the Tower of London later that morning and, standing to attention, was cross-examined by two senior officers. Why, they asked, had I not responded to the urgent telegram summoning me to active service?

I spent the night in 'Napoleon's Room' at the Tower. The following day, unexpectedly, came a reprieve . . . It appeared that the adjutant, in the heat of war, had addressed the telegram to himself. In the circumstances there was little they could do, except have me up on the minor charge of being improperly dressed.

'You are wearing the wrong buttons, Mr Holroyd. Kindly take a week's Orderly Officer.'

However I was not yet out of trouble. The *News Chronicle* that week reported that the Union Jack on the Tower of London was flying upside down. This was certainly news to me since I did not know that the Union Jack possessed an upside down. Yet as Orderly Officer, I was responsible. I think they were happy at the Tower to see me leave at the end of that week. I can still hear the voice of one major who had the job of deciding what to do with me. 'Take a walk, Mr Holroyd,' was his solution. The tone of the sergeant who presented himself in my bedroom one night after I had failed to turn out the guard was more alarming. Snapping on the light, he took three paces forward, came to a crashing halt and after sharply saluting me as I lay in bed, shouted out: 'Permission to speak, sir?'

I had been posted to Connaught Barracks on the heights of Dover cliffs which the Royal Fusiliers had left when setting off for the Suez Canal, and which was now filled with refugees from the abortive Hungarian uprising against Soviet occupation. After my recent misadventures, I was morbidly anxious to get things right. But it was not easy. For example, I had been told on the Saturday night to report on Monday morning in Dover wearing 'mufti'. This featured a bowler hat. I did not have a bowler hat. In desperation I called at Norhurst on the Sunday and retrieved from the garage a very old bowler which my Aunt Yolande had once sported. 'Crowned with this, like a small black pimple at the top of my head, I descended properly dressed upon Dover,' I wrote in my essay for B.S. Johnson.

My instruction had been to make the refugees 'feel at home' on the cliffs. This was not only vague, I discovered, but a euphemism. For my job actually consisted of juggling with inadequate supplies of light bulbs and contraceptives so as to ensure that those Hungarians occupying unlit barrack rooms were protected with French letters, while those left unprotected were bathed, like battery hens, in a permanent glare. The supplies were to be alternated each night. After a few weeks the Hungarians went forth and multiplied.

So ended my first year in the army.

During my second year I perfected the art of being over-looked. Previously I had unwittingly drawn attention to myself by being in various ways out-of-step. Now I used my wits to camouflage myself. At first I had been nonplussed by military terminology – the practice, for example, of indicating a tree by calling it a 'bushy-topped object at four o'clock', which seemed to me a complicated method of attaining soldierly simplicity. I was bemused, too, by the exaggerated way of walking called marching, by the barking out of curious sounds called orders, by the loss of privacy in the general hubbub and frenzy. I decided not to try and analyse all this commotion but to copy, even car-icature it. I watched what the others did and then did it myself, starting a fraction late perhaps but doing it slightly quicker. I positioned myself in the middle rank, towards the middle, and was gratified to see that people were finding it increasingly difficult to pick me out. I always answered with a shout to a number, not a name. I was losing my identity, fading from notice, and feeling all the better for it. When alone, I equipped myself with a board to which I attached some sheets of paper. Carrying this, and a short swagger stick, I hurried round Connaught Barracks after the regiment had returned from Suez, looking urgently at my watch and studying the blank sheets of paper with an expression of severity. It was obvious I was up to something pretty important. I would strut, ostensibly from one significant place to another, though actually from my bedroom back to my bedroom, occasionally calling out the words 'Carry on!' to groups of soldiers slightly beyond earshot. One day, while I was standing alone in the Officers' Mess, someone opened the door, looked round the room where I was standing, and shouted out to some people behind him 'No one here!' And I knew I had achieved my ambition of becoming invisible.

In the army I trained hard as a non-volunteer, shooting up my hand barely too late for everything except the job of Orderly Officer during Christmas and other regimental holidays when the barracks would empty and there was again positively nothing to do. The guard had to be inspected of course, but these were the years of IRA quietude, and there wasn't anything to guard against. All was quiet. The adjutant at Connaught Barracks was a man in his thirties called Dick Jones. He was something of an intellectual but, in the manner of T.E. Lawrence, wanted to change himself into a man of action – and was to die tragically young, climbing a mountain in Wales. He lent me his collection of gramophone records and, while the regiment went on leave and I was alone, the Officers' Mess on top of Dover cliffs was filled with the sound of Sibelius and Nielson symphonies – to which I later added the Swedish composer Franz Berwald to make up my Scandinavian trio. These musical intervals are what I remember most at Dover.

The problem I gave the army was not so different from the one I had presented my grandparents. What were they to do with me? I found myself appointed Motor Transport Officer despite being unable to drive and could, I believe, have awarded myself a driving licence instead of waiting till my mid-thirties. I also became 'Mess Officer', a phrase that quite accurately describes my catering skills (the Royal Fusilier curries were indistinguishable from the innocent fruit salads that usually followed them). Also, for a season on Salisbury Plain, I was appointed ADC to our Brigade Commander, the formidable-looking Brigadier Bernard Fergusson (who had himself been ADC to the legendary General Wavell and written a biography of him).

Despite his ferocious appearance – a flashing monocle and rampant yellow moustache – Bernard Fergusson was a civilised, literate man. Discovering that I was a reader of books and dreamed one day of being some sort of writer, he engaged me in conversation about James Elroy Flecker and Siegfried Sassoon, and then invited some writers he knew – Peter Fleming the travel writer, and the novelist L.P. Hartley – to dinner so that I could meet them. I was very nervous on these occasions and once poured the Brigadier a sherry and soda instead of his whisky. But L.P. Hartley gallantly rushed to my rescue, claiming that he had distinctly heard Fergusson demand sherry and soda. I read his novels with additional admiration over the following weeks.

When Peter Fleming came to dinner, Fergusson invited me to bring along my friend Anthony Howard who became spectacularly drunk by the end of the evening. On leaving the house, he accidentally put on the Brigadier's hat instead of his own. Spotting his sudden promotion when we got back to camp, we then spent the rest of the night employing all the military tactics we had been taught (short of bayonet drill) smuggling the Brigadier's hat back and retrieving his own. Anthony Howard

was the only other national serviceman in the battalion addicted
to the reading of books, and his company and conversation were
a great support to me. There was between us an unintentional
rivalry as to who was more ill-adapted to this peculiar way of
life – a contest, I believe, usually settled in my favour.

It was my job to get Bernard Fergusson to the place of military action each day on Salisbury Plain. But such were my
map-reading skills that we never witnessed a single hostility.
Fergusson was marvellously patient, but sometimes his exasperation broke through and once, approaching midnight, miles
from where we should have been and still no warfare in sight, he
insisted that I come to a halt and give him some salutes.

The last months of my army career were unorthodox. While
the Royal Fusiliers retreated to Sutton Coldfield, I was dispatched to a department of the War Office in Colindale, on the
northern perimeter of London. Here, with one other national
serviceman called Smout, I tackled the vital task of redundancy.
These were early days in the amalgamation of regiments and the
rundown of the army – 'streamlining' it was bravely called.
National Service itself was soon to end. Smout and I divided the
country in half and went through the applications from all field
officers. Some had applied to continue their military careers,
others wanted to accept the money that was on offer for early
retirement and enter the priesthood, run a toy shop in Slough,
start an egg farm in the Hebrides. We would read through these
applications and, knowing what percentage of these officers
would have to go, make our recommendations. One of the
names that came before me was that of the Colonel-in-Chief of
the Royal Fusiliers. He was not a popular man, partly because
he owned a brightly-coloured cat called Cooper which, many
officers thought, made the regiment look ridiculous on parade.
At night the Colonel would emerge from the Officers' Mess
and call: 'Coopah! Coopah!' And various subalterns concealed
in the bushes would miaow back. Our Colonel was one of the

officers who left the army and I later heard he had got a job as television critic on a new fascist weekly.

My knockabout career through the army was crowned with the honorary rank while in charge of redundancy of temporary, acting, unpaid Captain. It all seems more entertaining to me now than it did at the time, and has left me with a weakness for Gothic fiction and barrack-room farce. Then suddenly, after what had felt like a life sentence, it was over. But during the next couple of years, one of my Royal Fusilier colleagues with a genius for practical jokes (he once removed my entire bedroom and reassembled it with the bedside lights shining prominently on Dover cliffs) would telephone me in the early morning and, in stentorian tones, announce that, because of the crisis in Algeria, Cuba, the Middle East, or even Notting Hill, all National Service reserves were being called up: and for a few blurred moments the horror would return.

In *All Bull* B.S. Johnson was to conclude that 'the Army itself did very well out of National Service'. When the book was published in 1973 I sent a copy to Bernard Fergusson who, as Lord Ballantrae, had recently retired as Governor-General of New Zealand and been appointed Chairman of the British Council. He replied: 'National Service may or may not have been a good thing for the nation; it was a bloody awful thing for the army . . . [it] dried up regular recruiting almost entirely; men didn't want to join something voluntarily when it was compulsory for others.' He also deplored the amalgamations of the English line regiments and the formation of 'Big Regiments' without territorial identity, in the initial stages of which Smout and I had been employed. Then he apologised for this 'out-pouring' and thanked me for his 'honourable mention in dispatches', adding: 'You could have had much fun from making me look a real Charlie, instead of just a benevolent old blimp.'

In 1980 I saw him at one of the Literary Society's dinners at the Garrick Club. He was then in his seventieth year and his wife

had recently died. He looked pale and fragile, a ghost of the terrific brigadier I had known. We laughed over our exploits as a
British Don Quixote and Sancho Panza twenty years before on
Salisbury Plain. Then he went out into the night, and I read his
obituary not long afterwards. I remember him with gratitude as
the first person after Peter Spanoghe at Eton to give me genuine
encouragement.

# 16

# The Third Mrs Nares

Although the nineteen-fifties was an indecisive decade for me, my mother was making plenty of decisions. One morning while I was still working as an articled clerk in Windsor, she telephoned me to say that she had discovered her husband Edy had been having an affair with Mrs Hanbury, a tenant on the first floor of Wetherby Gardens. I was surprised by this news and felt curiously disappointed. Frances Hanbury's husband Ronnie was a writer of radio scripts for a famous comedy team, Ben and Bebe Lyons. I enjoyed these programmes but could never believe that Ronnie Hanbury, a peculiarly unfunny man, had written them. 'His wife was a voluptuous blonde by daylight,' Griffy Philipps reminds me. 'With the benefit of hindsight and having read one or two books by Iris Murdoch, I suspect that Mrs Hanbury was much taken by you . . . As an Etonian of that era you were alarmed, and took great pains to enter the front door so quietly that Mrs Hanbury would not delay you.'

It was suddenly clear to me that Griffy's assiduous reading of contemporary novels, though alerting us to a real drama, had seriously misdirected us as to its plot. It was not for me that Frances Hanbury was waiting, her ears alert for the telltale click and muffled crash of the front door, but for my stepfather Edy Fainstain. I had been tiptoeing round the house quite pointlessly. And though I had felt a tremor of alarm at what Griffy insisted were Frances Hanbury's advances, I now felt deprived by the knowledge that she had no romantic interest in me at all. I could have done with some of her delay.

'What shall I do?' my mother suddenly asked. She seldom took any action during the nineteen-fifties, however ruinous, without first asking my advice. But it was awkward giving advice over Mr Owen's telephone in Windsor, with Mr Owen himself standing humbly by me, though his office was packed to the ceiling with valuable precedents. The quality of my advice, its timbre and sheer slowness of delivery, had gained me an odd reputation for maturity. I would pause a good deal and produce a series of noises in my throat that conveyed gravity and experience. My silences, hedged around with an air of pondering wisdom, sounded powerfully deep. When I did speak I used 'whereas' and 'nevertheless' and 'on the other hand' pretty freely. While I was putting on this performance, the other person would usually make it clear what he or she wanted to do – and I would then triumphantly chime in with that conclusion.

What my mother wanted to do, rather to my surprise, was to divorce Edy and start another chapter in her life. Perhaps it was the presence in Wetherby Gardens of Mrs Lupu Fainstain, clothed in black, that had unsettled her, since Edy felt it right to give his mother priority over his wife in most things. But I suspect that Ulla already had her next chapter sketched in and was eager to get on with it. The decree nisi was granted on 25 January 1955 and made absolute in the second week of March.

They had been married almost exactly six years. My mother was now aged thirty-eight.

While these legal matters were proceeding she took off for Stockholm, arriving back with enough kronor in her handbag to pay for several weeks at the Royal Garden Hotel in Kensington. This became her habit: vanishing into Sweden during emergencies and then reappearing with these handbags of kronor – until eventually Kaja was to die a poor woman.

A dozen years after the war people in Britain were just beginning to recover themselves financially in preparation for the good days to come in the nineteen-sixties. But we had gone down too far to recover. Even the richest of us, my Uncle Kenneth who had 'married money', left only £45,000 at the end of the nineteen-sixties. The rest of us had become a species of distressed, not-so-gentle folk, downwardly mobile, indeed charging downhill, led nobly by my grandfather. He was to leave £6,000 in the early nineteen-sixties, having been given more than this amount by Kenneth. My mother, it is true, left £40,000 in the mid-nineteen-eighties, but this included Kaja's estate and the flat in Chelsea I had recently completed buying for her. When I sold the contents of my father's rented flat in 1988, they fetched less than £50 altogether.

My mother made two more telephone calls to me at Stuchbery's that year. One was to tell me that Edy had suddenly died of a heart attack (Griffy wanted to know whether Mrs Hanbury had been with him). I could tell she was genuinely distressed, feeling perhaps a little guilty, at least regretful. Edy died in France. There is no mention of my mother in his Will, and I am surprised to see that he left only £28,000. Some years later, when passing through the South of France, I went to see his gleaming white grave in the cemetery at La Turbie. High in the Alpes Maritimes, overlooking the Mediterranean, such a glorious site I thought was appropriate for a good property owner. And if I could have said this to him, I think I might have heard his gurgling laughter again.

My mother's other telephone call was to tell me she was marrying once more. Her third marriage was celebrated at the Chelsea Registry Office on 12 May 1955. She wore 'a Dior dress of pink and black silk organza and black velvet' according to the evening newspapers. The marriage was widely covered by the national press and there were also reports of it in Sweden. This was partly because my mother had recently begun modelling clothes for the dress designer Charles Creed, having shown the spring fashions that year for the Incorporated Society of London Fashion Designers to Queen Soraya of Persia. The marriage was additionally newsworthy because she was marrying the son of a famous actor-manager.

My new stepfather, David Nares, was a forty-one-year-old advertising executive who managed 'the Martini contract' for the Crawford Agency. He was the son of Owen Nares, a celebrated 'matinée idol' between the wars, and star of several silent films – melodramas and romances such as *The Sorrows of Satan*, *Young Lochinvar* and *The Private Life of Don Juan*. In his *Who's Who* entry, he listed only one son, but there was another, David's younger brother Geoffrey. He had been homosexual, and died in Cairo from a tumour in the brain during the war. Looking back it seems clear that David was anxious to suppress a somewhat feminine strain in himself. He liked firing off reverberating letters to the *Daily Mail* and *Sunday Times*, calling for a stronger British 'fighting force' against the red menace of Soviet Russia, or cursing young people in modern society for expecting something for nothing. 'Let us roll up our sleeves,' one of his letters exhorts readers, 'and get down to hard work.' He himself was a hard drinker and would sometimes roll up his sleeves at dinner when explaining how alcohol was a necessary solvent in his line of business. This was his third marriage, as well as my mother's. He had a very pretty daughter, Caroline, who had been distantly educated round Europe and was to be one of the last débutantes presented to the Queen. A picture of my new stepsister at the front of the *Tatler* at the age of seventeen shows her already beginning to dress like the Queen Mother, as many young girls with their matching accessories dressed before the nineteen-sixties. Nevertheless, the few times I saw her she appeared so dazzling that I was simply unable to speak, and when she invited me to her coming-out dance, I did not turn up.

For the first year of their marriage my mother and stepfather lived in Ennismore Gardens, near the Brompton Oratory in Knightsbridge (it was the same street in which Edy Fainstain had kept a secret apartment for his meetings with Frances Hanbury). They then moved to Turners Reach House on the Chelsea Embankment. Their ground-floor flat, with its wonderfully theatrical split-level drawing-room looking out on the Thames, was directly below the apartment where George Weidenfeld gave his famous publishing parties, and was itself bought, my mother later told me, by the filmstar Sean Connery. She was entering, she believed, a world of glamour.

'MODEL TO MARRY. SHE WILL BE THE THIRD MRS NARES' ran a headline the day before my mother's marriage.

Ulla Hall is a statuesque blonde from Stockholm in her early thirties who was visiting England just before the war and stayed here. During the war she drove an ambulance. She took up modelling a few years ago and appears regularly in the collections of the Top Twelve.

According to this Stockholm beauty, who divides her life between the two countries, it is easy for a Swedish girl to model English clothes 'because we Swedes wear suits and tweedy things like the English women'.

This girl with her cool Nordic look would be at home practically anywhere. She speaks French, German, Italian and Swedish, and is now learning Spanish.

Ulla plans to continue modelling after her marriage.

This article, about a woman who has never been quite 'at home' even in her homes, is a good reminder for biographers not to accept newspaper information naïvely, or to rely on sources where the code of ethics forbids the revealing of sources. My mother, who was actually in her thirty-ninth year when she married David Nares, enjoyed a career of three or four years modelling for Charles Creed who had a fashion house behind Harrods, at the opposite end of Basil Street to my grandfather's Lalique showrooms. There are pictures of her showing clothes to the Royal Family in the nineteen-fifties, and as one of the 'Twelve Smart Women' selected to display British *haute couture* at Lancaster House. 'The blonde Mrs Nares has a flair for enhancing elegant, classic clothes,' declared a reporter on the *Daily Telegraph*, 'which is why Creed chose her.' Charles Creed himself claimed that his wife, the fashion editor of *Vogue*, knew more about the 'mysterious business' of women's clothes than he did. He knew nothing. Though his family had been in tailoring for four generations, you could get more sense on the subject, he would boast, from Crinnie, his small corgi dog. He was buoyantly shallow; never read a book (not even his ghosted autobiography); had no interest in politics or the arts; and listed watching golf and snooker on television as his hobbies. He was very popular.

After leaving the army, I would occasionally call at Creed's couture house to collect my mother for lunch at La Vache à la Cave, a few houses along Basil Street, past the beauticians and hairdressers. Creed's settled belief that fashion 'always comes round to meet the couturier who refuses to follow it' was leading him into an unfashionable hinterland from which he never escaped. The waistless, short-skirted line of the nineteen-twenties, which came round again in the nineteen-fifties with its beads and fringes, had little in common with his tailored suits; while the more abandoned styles of the nineteen-sixties were deeply unappealing to him. To my young and partial eye, one reason why my mother modelled so well for him was that she made women in their forties and fifties believe they could look flatteringly young.

Despite the novelty of this modelling, my mother was not happy in the late nineteen-fifties, and nor was my stepfather. Seeing them together, I could not understand how they had ever wanted to marry one another. Each, I imagine, appeared to offer the other some social advantage. As she glided, glassy-eyed, around the cocktail parties, my mother presented from a distance an image of serene drawing-room credibility. My stepfather, who was anxious to burden himself with the equipage of an English gentleman, gave the impression of being considerably richer than he actually was. Both of them were quickly undeceived.

I occasionally stayed a few days at Turners Reach House. 'I don't want you treating the place like a hotel,' my stepfather welcomed me. But it was difficult not to do so if, simply by going in and out of the front door, you were judged to be downgrading the house in this way. On the other hand, my stepfather added, it would be a pleasant relief to 'enjoy some good conversation for a change'. Women, he suspected, were incapable of conversation – certainly my mother was. The sort of newspaper talk that passed for conversation at Chelsea Embankment struck her as intolerably dull. My stepfather liked to ask me, man to man, what I thought of 'the Cyprus situation', or the CND march to Aldermaston protesting against the hydrogen bomb; and I was clearing my throat, tilting my head, when suddenly my mother would spring up, switch on the radio, and start whirling round the room clicking her fingers. My stepfather, abandoning Cyprus and the CND, unavailingly called her to heel. Both of them were already fairly drunk, my stepfather having tanked up at various clubs and bars on his way back from the office, and my mother having fortified herself against his homecoming with several secret whiskies. At this stage, my stepfather usually said something offensive about Swedish neutrality in the war, and then announced that he was going to 'change for dinner'. He would make his way to the bathroom and we heard the splashing of bathwater. Twenty minutes later he would reappear in exactly the same clothes, except for a new white collar above his old striped shirt. Dinner was served by Giacomo, a young Sicilian who later enjoyed an erratic career in the black market. In the belief, apparently, that he was displaying aristocratic manners, my stepfather called my mother 'Mrs Nares' over dinner, though at no other time. This struck her as unfriendly and led to an increase in her drinking. When she was drunk, she became extraordinarily silly and fell down a lot before passing out altogether; when he was drunk, my stepfather became aggressive; when I was drunk, I was sick.

That was how matters usually stood when, at the end of the evening, my stepfather would bang the table with his fist and shout out the word 'Bed!' He would do this even when there were guests; or go off to his bedroom and then come back in his pyjamas and dressing-gown to show those who still had their wits about them that it was time to leave. My mother did soon leave.

It was, I think, sometime in 1957 that she telephoned to ask again for my advice. She had recently been on holiday with Kaja to Baden – or was it Baden-Baden? Anyway, they had been abroad for the sake of the air or water, and my mother had encountered a very polite Viennese gentleman who apparently manufactured everything from ballpoint pens to motorbicycles somewhere in South America. She had often dreamed of travelling to South America and she wanted my advice as to whether she should set off there now. She had a handbag full of Swedish kronor after leaving Kaja which would take care of the fare (her husband, she reminded me, never gave her anything). Egon, her new admirer, had promised to meet her off the plane. He was wealthy, she added, and passed all his summers in Europe, so she would be able to see me each year. Perhaps, when all else failed, I could come over and manufacture motorbicycles myself . . .

I replied with one of my profound pauses, made a few gravelly noises in my throat and uttered a perfectly-balanced sentence with a 'nevertheless' at its centre. Then we got down to planning her journey. Before she went off to the airport, my mother asked me to draft an explanatory note for 'your stepfather'. This she copied down, leaving it for him on his return from the office.

That evening my stepfather telephoned me to say that 'your mother' had gone abroad. His voice sounded wobbly, and I went over to see him. This was a different conversation from the ones we usually struck up, and all gentlemanly airs and pretences were shed. My stepfather was somewhat bald but had a good growth of hair at the sides of his head which he kept tugging until these tufts stood out fantastically over his ears. We drank several tumblers of whisky, man to man, but for once he did not grow aggressive and I was not sick. Eventually he asked me to help him draft a letter to my mother who had left a forwarding address. 'You're a writer,' he said. 'You can put it on paper.' This was the first time he had acknowledged my wish to be a writer. Much gratified, I took out my pen, the very pen with which I had recently drafted my mother's farewell note, and hoping the whisky would inspire me, began writing.

Some three weeks later I heard from my mother in Acapulco. She had received, she wrote, a very curious letter from 'your stepfather' and was wondering how she should reply. Would I help her? I did try to help her. I drafted an answer. So began what, for eighteen months or so, was to be an elaborate international correspondence with myself. I was not really aware of what I was doing, of the irony of what I was doing, as I bent over these letters, acting barrister for, almost being the biographer of both husband and wife. But I did notice that I was beginning to pay myself extravagant compliments – 'your excellent letter' and so on.

While this correspondence was slowly trundling back and forwards (my stepfather did not like wasting money on airmail), and I was still trundling between London and Maidenhead, writing a paragraph or two in one place, crossing them out in the other, I spent two long summer holidays with my mother's new entourage, moving through Denmark, France, Austria, Germany and Italy. These were extraordinary summers of affluence. A shimmer of sun and beach, the glitter of casino and nightclub, buoyed me up, blinded me, as I floated agreeably off the known map. I hardly knew where I was sometimes. I remember arriving in Vienna and being astonished by how amazingly wet the streets were – before realising I was in Venice. Egon Hessel and his ebullient brother Walter would spend their days in luxuriously carpeted hotels and gorgeous restaurants, their nights at gambling tables and bars – and I went along too.

While we were in Austria, Griffy arrived for a couple of weeks and he was able to explain to me that we were at a lakeside resort called Velden which had once been frequented by socialites from the Austro-Hungarian Empire, and was now haunted by émigrés returning from the New World. At the further end of the Wörthersee, in which we were presently bathing, was Klagenfurt, once a prisoner-of-war camp. Griffy told me that he had been shocked to see one lady who had a death camp number tattooed on her arm. Velden, he thought, was one of those places where a large Jewish community lived before the war, many of whom, like the Hessel brothers, now returned each year. Despite this Germanic piece of scholarship, I noticed that whenever Griffy and I went out to lunch beside the lake, the two of us would land up with three portions of food due to Griffy's habit of confusing *zwei* with *drei*.

Egon Hessel was a leathery sort of man, of medium height, with a crumpled figure and creased features – a smiling, paper bag of a face he had. He could easily have disappeared in a crowd. But the crowd around us was very aware of him because of his wealth. He was a generous, level-headed man, a rock in this fermenting sea of social life and a contrasting figure to his brother Walter with his wicked air of scandal and fountain of gossip. My mother, I think, saw Egon as representing an appealing form of security; and he was attracted to her because she brought a transparently innocent sparkle to his life. They seemed to trust each other. That, at any rate, was what Griffy and I decided as we ate our way through our curiously large lunches.

Griffy had taken to calling my mother 'Madam'. At various stages of our holiday, often quite late at night and from the edge of the dance floor, he would cry out in an anguished voice: 'Steady, Madam! Steady!' But my mother had little grasp of steadiness, and perhaps it was we who needed more unsteadiness. It was as if she were younger than we were, as if she were providing us with an education that we lacked. 'This is where Madam excelled,' Griffy writes to me.

> She was always on the lookout for some fun. She was game to try anything and if it involved a party she would do her best to see that things went with a swing. This ability to enjoy herself was infectious and a wonderful tonic for others. I think she had an uncomplicated and almost childlike approach to life and was not much given to great thoughts about herself or her future. Although she had left Sweden long ago, it never left her. I have learnt never to be surprised at anything which a Swede may suddenly do.

Griffy surprised himself later by marrying a Swedish girl (a friend of one of my cousins) and becoming something of an expert, he believes, in Swedish ways. But at the various stopping-places used by the Hessels as they moved like a travelling circus through Europe, Sweden was represented in its purest form by my grandmother Kaja. She had always dressed up and gone out to my mother's parties, and continued doing so. Though she was not quite at ease in these exotic caravanserai, she wanted to see Ulla safely settled at last. She often looked, I thought, like redoubling Griffy's cries for caution, and made something of a confidant of the remarkable head waiter at the hotel restaurant at Velden. He was a man of terrible dignity and momentous tact with the appearance of an archduke and the spirit of Bernard Shaw's wise waiter in *You Never Can Tell*. I think he impressed my grandmother as the one obvious aristocrat among this miscellaneous throng of middle Europeans.

The following summer, when Egon and Ulla reached Munich, my mother summoned me urgently. She had gone into hospital for an operation to remove one of her ovaries and her womb. Though the operation, for which Egon was paying, was successful, it had a lowering effect on her. It was as if she were at last heeding Griffy's appeals to steady herself. She told me that she did not want to go on with this life of perpetual travelling. She wanted to return home. Home was now London rather than Stockholm. Home was Chelsea. She missed the King's Road. Over the last eighteen months or more, she reminded me, she had been receiving a number of nice letters from David Nares. He had promised to be more friendly to her in future and not call her 'Mrs Nares' when summoning the salt and pepper. He also promised to be more generous and let Kaja come to stay. He had written repeatedly that he wanted her back at Chelsea Embankment, and she had decided that she wanted to go back. But how could she tell Egon? He had been so kind to her. Lying in her hospital bed, rather tearful, she told me that she was not up to telling him. Would I do it for her before I left Munich? Why didn't I explain everything to him that evening over dinner? It would be an immense relief to her.

I was then twenty-two, but an inexperienced twenty-two. This was one of the penalties I was paying for all my mannerisms of maturity and that patina of sophistication I had acquired as a protective carapace. I dreaded the prospect of speaking to Egon, but I did so that evening in a half-empty restaurant, explaining away my mother's decision as a post-operative condition, but one that would persist. I could see he was surprised and I believe he was hurt. As a rich man, he could never be certain that people really liked him and not his money. Though my mother enjoyed much of the brightness that money switched on, she was never commercially-minded, and Egon liked that. He hardly said anything that evening.

Before the end of the year, and after a short spell in Stockholm, my mother was back in London with David Nares. Then, early in 1959, she left him again and, employing me as her travel agent, returned to Egon Hessel in Mexico. Both return flights were disastrous. At Turners Reach House, everything soon reverted to pomposity and drink. Despite what I had drafted in my letters trying to negotiate some common ground, they remained completely incompatible. I had achieved, in a more devastating form, what I had accidentally done while Mr Owen was absent from the divorce court: prolonged an irretrievably unhappy marriage.

What did I feel about this? The answer is that I did not fully recognise at the time the part I had played in it all. Being then in my twenties and quite familiar with the rapid changes in my parents' lives, I was not so worried on my mother's behalf as I later became. I had no moral objections to anything she did. Life, it seemed to me, was a matter of trial and error, and error had legitimacy. I thought of facts and the factual lure of fantasy more than of faults. My own anxieties arose from inaction and experience delayed. Like my grandfather. If I did not really understand my mother's life, it never occurred to me to condemn it.

But what went wrong the second time round with Egon

Hessel? For some time I wondered whether he had deliberately lured my mother back so as to seize the initiative and end the relationship on his own terms. I do not believe he wanted revenge, though his shock and disappointment in Munich could have damaged his feelings. I asked my mother afterwards what happened and she said Egon found out that she had altered the date of her birth in her passport. Looking through so many birth, marriage and death certificates for this book, I am amazed how regularly men raise their status and women lower their age. I have my mother's passport from that time in front of me and can see that she has changed the year of her birth from 1916 to 1918. It seems a harmless vanity, though maybe some customs official noticed it and caused them embarrassment as they crossed from one country to another. But if Egon saw my mother as luminously innocent, perhaps this deception was significant to him, symbolically changing who she was. In any event, his feeling for her altered 'when it alteration found'.

After another short spell in Stockholm with Kaja, my mother returned to London and by the end of 1961 was living in Ebury Street, not far from Sloane Square and the King's Road where she felt at home. In February 1962, David Nares presented a petition for divorce on the grounds of desertion. It was uncontested, and David found himself free to marry for a fourth time on his fiftieth birthday. Two or three years later, when working on my biography of Lytton Strachey, I came across a letter from his father Owen Nares to Strachey and sent him a photocopy of it. 'I'm in good heart,' he replied, 'and now that I've risen to dizzy heights at Crawfords am reasonably affluent, though heaven knows what will happen to us all when Wilson's recent measures begin to bite. Why not come and have a drink before they do?' We met at Turners Reach House and discussed, man to man, Harold Wilson's six months' freeze on wages and dividends. David had already fired off a couple of explosive letters to newspapers and had another, he told me, in the barrel – mercifully they were not the sort of letters he needed any help in writing. This was the last time I saw him. We did not mention my mother and there was no sign of his wife.

Though still only forty-five at the time of her divorce, my mother never remarried. Apparently she had no need to do so – no financial need. Egon had promised to pay her a quarterly allowance. I cannot remember how much this was – something between four and five thousand pounds a year. But unlike my grandfather's arrangement with Agnes May Babb, this was an unwritten agreement and no one knew how long it would last.

# 17

## *Flight into Surrey*

My father (unlike my mother) was very commercially-minded, but unfortunately he had no money. He found the post-war world difficult to understand. Everything appeared topsy-turvy, and he could not manoeuvre round it. After the failure of Editions Begh, he retrenched at Norhurst, still married to Marlou. Then he went west to work as sales manager for a company called Concrete Construction (Wales) Ltd, with its headquarters in Pontlliw. Though it had been my uncle who read architecture at university, it was really my father's interest and, guided by this enthusiasm, he now attempted to make a career in the building trade. Pending success, he lived modestly at a boarding house in Swansea, working at our history of the world at nights so as to save money he might otherwise have spent in pubs or at the cinema. How we actually began this grand enterprise I cannot now remember – perhaps it was after one of the occasions when my father was teaching me the correct way to drink wine. I visited him two or three times and remember reading Joyce's *Ulysses* in the back bedroom there (I was reading Proust in my bedroom at Maidenhead). Then I would go further west to stay with Griffy Philipps at his father's house near Carmarthen. Sir Grismond Philipps, Lord Lieutenant of Carmarthenshire, looked like a Grenadier Guards' version of the Italian film actor Vittorio de Sica whom we had all seen in *Bread, Love and Dreams*. Griffy sometimes referred to his father as 'the Commanding Officer' and, on returning to Swansea, I tried out this formula on my own father as a means of circumventing the difficulties of 'Daddy' or 'Basil'. He took it pretty well and was soon signing his letters to me 'C.O.', while my mother became 'Madam'.

Grismond Philipps followed his son's habit of calling me Hagga. He was an amusing man, with a sophisticated style of humour, who enjoyed teasing me. Initially I found this rather disconcerting until, noticing my discomfort one day, he remarked: 'I only tease you, Hagga, because you're so good-natured' – after which he could tease me as much as he liked. He continued doing so to the end, and even a little beyond by bequeathing me a brace of stuffed parrots (alleged Flaubertian parrots that later turned out to be commonplace pheasants).

My father came once to collect me from Carmarthen and drive me back to Swansea. 'The first impression on seeing him was that he had very blue eyes and was extremely talkative,' Griffy writes to me. 'He was a most unlikely Old Etonian and very hard to categorize. He appeared to possess an optimism and an ability to cope with unpromising circumstances. To me he always seemed a generous person, blessed with enormous energy and probably putting too much trust in the wrong people.'

Before the war the C.O. had been famously able to 'talk anybody into anything'. Now he was obliged to talk himself into anything. It was his way of coping with what Griffy calls 'unpromising circumstances'. I remember him telling me one evening, in his dingy room in Swansea, of the genius of his partner in the construction company, the jewel-like virtues of concrete, and the dawning success awaiting them just over the Welsh horizon. The room itself seemed to glow with early rays of this throbbing success as he strode excitedly up and down, filling it with his splendid vision of the future. A couple of years later the concrete construction had collapsed and the brilliant partner was revealed as a dark villain.

This fall of concrete broke up his marriage to Marlou. She was striving to find a secure place as a publisher in Paris while the C.O. had been driving desperately round Wales, covering 100,000 miles in two years, selling concrete constructions to people who didn't want them. Fighting all the way, he was enormously successful as a salesman – and that had really been the trouble. Concrete Construction (Wales) Ltd simply buckled under the volume of reluctant orders that poured in. The bad debts rose, the company sank, and the geniuses became fools.

At the end of his life the C.O. kept on his mantelpiece a photograph of only one of his wives, fiancées and girlfriends of a lifetime, a picture of Marlou. She is glancing down, her sultry looks partly concealed, her raven hair falling a little forward, her hooded eyelids appearing to guard some secret. That is how I remember her.

The parting between them was wholly amicable. They simply could not find a way of living in the same country. Marlou asked the C.O. for a peculiar acquisition at their divorce: the right to use one-and-a-half of his Christian names as her future surname. She became, at Editions Mondiales and elsewhere, Madame de Courcy, that 'de' adding lustre to her career.

Ten years later I wrote to Marlou asking her for information about various *penseurs* whom Lytton Strachey had met at l'abbaye de Pontigny in 1923. She gave me the facts I needed and offered to introduce me to André Maurois. But Maurois was ill and died before I could meet him. Then, in 1968, after publishing

*Lytton Strachey*, I sent her a copy and she asked me whether she might act as my agent in France. I happily agreed. But when my British publisher raised contractual objections, I was obliged to rescind this agreement. I did not realise how swiftly the wheel of fortune spins. Then in her early sixties, Marlou needed my help, and I could not give it to her. Whatever we did, it did not quite work, and there trailed behind us vague shadows of regret.

Back again at Norhurst for a spell, the C.O. was reduced to selling carbon paper. Even then his optimism did not dim. It seemed obvious to him that, with the advances in typewriter technology and the increasing use of the written word, carbon paper was set to proliferate into the twenty-first century. He was on to a winner. He could even see a way, our verse history having run into the buffers, of writing a bestseller on carbon paper, he jubilantly told me – a prose work that would dramatise an imagined board-room battle between the 'Stable Standby' and the 'Finer Flimsy' as a metaphor for contemporary culture. In short, he was labouring at a novel during the Maidenhead evenings.

By 1957, though still pursuing fiction, he was back in the building trade. Timber, he explained, not concrete, was the stuff of the future. He'd been a fool not to have spotted this earlier. He was now blessed with a business partner who had a genius for all things wooden – a Pinocchio figure he appeared in my imagination. In any event, the future was bright.

Though I still needed my father's help during the nineteen-fifties, I noticed that he was beginning to want my approval. While lying angrily becalmed at Maidenhead, he would some-times take me off in his car to some public house, and later in my bedroom I would make notes of our conversations. These notes then reappeared as chunks of narrative below the printed surface of *A Dog's Life*, in that vast unseen mass of my novel that was never published. The character emerging from this narrative is someone who regularly goes through a transformation scene that, despite its familiarity, always takes me off guard. Alone with me, he is a serious and sensitive person, but as soon as we enter the pub he suddenly changes into a figure of burlesque. 'Now I think I'll have a sherry today,' I record him as calling out to the panic-stricken barman.

> Have you a good amontillado? On holiday in Spain we used to drink the Tio Pepe. But while I was in France I rather lost the habit, I must confess, and now I prefer the medium dry. The French, of course, never were great sherry drinkers. Still, there's no place quite like Paris . . . Oh yes, we'll sample a couple of your amontillados – looks as if you've talked us into it. Ha! Ha! [To me] Here you are, an amontillado sherry. See what you think. Wash it round the roof of your mouth with your tongue – that's the correct way, so the experts tell us. Don't gargle! [To the barman] This is my son and heir. The one that inherits the overdraft. Ha! Ha! Says he wants to be one of those writer-johnnies. I ask you! Still, stranger things have happened I don't deny – though I tell him we all have to ditch some of our fancy ideas in life. He's not got much taste in wine yet, I'm afraid. Said he liked a Sauterne the other day. I told him it's just a woman's wine, though you can taste the grape in it, I grant you. You'd never think he'd had a French stepmother. Of course we're divorced now . . .

This is hardly an exaggeration of our pantomime performances in pubs played out against the struggles of a barman desperate to get free, the rising clamour of the drinkers rhythmically thumping their glasses, and myself, the straight man of the act, staring fixedly into the distance. I daresay that the copying of it down was an act of revenge for my embarrassment.

When I left the army at the beginning of 1958, the C.O. was

temporarily 'cooling his heels' at Norhurst. He took me several times to different pubs to have a serial conversation. It was impossible, he explained, to talk at Norhurst in case someone heard him. Not that anyone ever listened to anything he said, but they were uncannily quick at picking up the wrong end of the stick. Then he came out with the reason for his nervousness. He wished me to meet someone. In fact he rather thought I'd like her. But we would have to be discreet for reasons he would later make clear. Anyway she wanted to invite us both to her flat 'not a stone's throw as the crow flies' from Maidenhead railway station. She was a damn good cook, so it was not an occasion to be missed. She might not be a literary genius, but she'd read a few things in life, and was a good sort. We fixed a date.

Sonia was a well-built woman of thirty-eight who pretended to be petite and rather girlish, it seemed to me, while at other times affecting ladylike airs. She had been obliged to work in a shop at Maidenhead since the dissolution of her marriage, and had a son, to my irritation also called Michael, who had recently gone to what the C.O. described as 'a really rather good minor public school'. It was an impossible evening. The C.O. was dreadfully anxious that we should be immediate friends. He was like an intrusive theatre director, full of gusto and hilarity, putting us right, urging us on, speaking our lines for us until neither of us could behave naturally. The more the C.O. enthused, the more silent I grew, the more wrong notes Sonia seemed to strike. We simply could not hit it off and more than once got into a terrible mix-up over which Michael was being singled out for praise.

In my unpublished novel, I gave an unflattering portrait of Sonia which, because of the guilt I felt for being so disobliging, rises to moments of Dickensian excess. I quote from it, not as an accurate description, but as evidence of my hostility.

She is a large woman. Her head is large and so obviously are her arms and legs. Her hips are very large indeed. The

texture of her face is mottled and spotted like a Spanish
Omelette. But its principal feature is a nose of great
prominence bent upwards at a sharp angle like a bottle
opener. Above it are a pair of wandering eyes of an
indiscriminate pastel, round and wobbly as two lightly-
boiled eggs. Her pallid complexion is offset by deep black
hair which has sprouted into a fuzzy mass.

Why was I so aggressive? Was it because the C.O., then in his
fiftieth year, could apparently attract all sorts of women, and I
could not? Or did I resent the feigned admiration he kept pumping out of me? Or was it simply that Sonia and I did not very
much like each other? As he drove me back from this disastrous
first evening, the C.O. was bubbling with enthusiasm. And I was
so laconic that he had to supply the answers to his own questions.

Good-looking woman, isn't she? Yes, I always believe in
choosing attractive women in life. Pretty good cook, too,
don't you think? That soufflé! You must come over again
when you're not too busy with your masterpiece. She
obviously took a shine to you. Told me so. Can't imagine
why. She's had a pretty rough time of it and coped bloody
well. I'll tell you all about it.

That 'rough time' was an allusion to Sonia's marriage and
divorce. Rather to the C.O.'s chagrin, Sonia often spoke in dramatic style of her ex-husband: how violent he was, what a bully,
how deranged – 'a thoroughly nasty customer', my father concluded. All this seemed to be borne out when he turned up one
evening at Sonia's flat and made a scene. The police were called
and the C.O. described the rumpus to me in his special low
voice. But the police were apparently powerless to do anything
'unless he's committed a few murders recently'. Something
would have to be done.

For several weeks the C.O. had been confiding to me how the family was 'driving him crackers', how he could not spend much more time at Norhurst 'getting ticked off like some infant in swaddling clothes'. But things were looking up since he met this prodigy in timber and been made sales director of Seamless Floors. Now he had a spot of cash in his hands, he was going to change his life. Not that he would jump the gun. But he had decided to take the plunge. In short, get hitched up again. To Sonia. He didn't like to think of her alone at night while this madman roamed the streets. Of course it would be impossible to marry in Maidenhead. They must do it somewhere he wouldn't find them. The C.O. had already alerted estate agents.

They were married on 2 September 1958. It was a strange day. 'We'll lead him a merry dance if he tries to follow us,' the C.O. grimly announced, referring to Sonia's ex-husband. He dreaded telling the family at Norhurst and left it to the last minute on the grounds of not breaching security. 'I only hope she's a bit better than the last lot,' Adeline said by way of congratulations. We set off early from Maidenhead, driving at a furious pace but by a circuitous route out of Berkshire and up to Hendon in Middlesex where the ceremony was to take place. The C.O. and Sonia were in the front of the car, I and my new stepbrother (the other Michael) sat in the back with orders to look out for pursuing vehicles. On the marriage certificate at Hendon Registry Office, the C.O. described himself as 'Sales Manager (Timber Buildings)' and gave as his home his new partner's address in north west London which enabled him to claim residence in Hendon. Sonia put a line through the box marked 'rank or profession', and we two Michaels signed up as witnesses. After a furtive celebratory lunch, we struck southwards, zigzagging into Surrey where the C.O. had rented what looked at first sight like sheltered accommodation next to a cemetery. The day ended with the exhausted couple planning redecorations to their new home.

Over the next few years I used to go down intermittently for Sunday lunch. Sonia, I thought, was soon showing signs of boredom with life in Surrey. In any event the redecorations were never finished. She would attempt to prise exciting news of London from me. But though I did take myself to cheap seats at plays, concerts, films, I had little that was interesting to tell. I felt grateful when she changed her line of questioning from myself to my mother. The C.O. would listen sardonically, giving an occasional chuckle, as I described a few of my mother's goings and comings. Sonia wanted to know whether I had really drafted my mother's farewell note to her husband and, if so, what I had written. I reproduced it to the best of my ability. Soon afterwards she wrote a very similar note herself when taking her leave of the C.O. Though I never knew the details of their separation, I got an impression that after half-a-dozen years both of them were happy to be shot of one another. The divorce petition came to court in 1966, and I see that the C.O. did the gentlemanly thing by allowing his wife to be the petitioner and appearing himself as respondent. But the document makes curious reading. For the co-respondent is Sonia's previous husband, the 'madman' from whom we had made such a dramatic flight, and back to whom, after this interval of marriage, she now escaped from the C.O.'s insolvency in Surrey.

# 18

# Scenes from Provincial and Metropolitan Life

'Is everyone still alive?'

I had forgotten this cry and the collective groan that, mounting in volume as it went from room to room, rose to meet it three mornings a week as our cook opened the front door at Norhurst. It was thanks to my Uncle Kenneth that we still employed a cook. By buying the house he had saved my grandfather £150 a year in rent, besides the heavy repayments on our double mortgage raised to pilot me through school.

Our cook was a morbidly cheerful character who refused to take offence at the family's barrage of insults. 'Go on then, knock me down! String me up!', she would cry in ecstasy. And then, to my grandmother: 'I know you don't really mean it, madam.' She went on joking in the kitchen until she eventually forced a smile from my grandmother. This did not recommend her to Fraser, Basil, Yolande or Old Nan, all of whom were on shouting but not speaking terms with Adeline. If only she would spend less time gossiping with the cook, they sighed, they might get a few meals.

Our gardener still came too, his pale face and wavering smile lighting up as we shouted at him that he was a 'damn fool' and a 'bally idiot' after seeing how he had planted, in a straight line, all the weeds we had dug up the previous week. We were also visited by a daily woman who came weekly. She was a remarkable diplomat. With her understanding smile, the appropriate exclamation, a supporting shake of her head, she managed the all-but-impossible feat of getting along with everyone. We called her a 'treasure' until, after many years of loyal service, we found she had been steadily stealing our cutlery, china and still-unbroken pieces of Lalique (the Narcissus mirror with frosted glass, the lotus cups, the bowl with sirens, the Avalon vase). By the time I got back from the army to live at Norhurst again, almost the only Lalique left were the eagles, fish and sparrows with which Yolande had decorated the dogs' graves in the garden.

Everything was agonisingly familiar to me. The passing of the hours from All Saints Church; the squabbling birds congregating on the lawn for their meals; the leaping red and grey squirrels, the hovering multicoloured dragonflies, all darting here and there; the garage with its music and cider and lurking treasures; the magical tea chests arriving from India with their silver foil under wooden casing, and when they were excavated, like an Egyptian tomb from under the stairs, the bitter-sweet smell of Rajmai tea.

Each morning the family would plunge down Castle Hill into the mêlée of Maidenhead, then lumber slowly up carrying heavy bags of shopping – only to find when all was unloaded in the kitchen that they had bought the same things again and again. The air trembled with recrimination and dismay.

There were changes. Our parrot, the female Mr Potty, had flown out into the trees one day while her cage was being cleaned and though we stood below calling, making bird noises, whistling, swearing, she merely swore back, then flew away.

We were reduced now to one dog, a labrador called Don, whom my Aunt Yolande dragged gasping over the fields and round the Thicket each long day. If she got back in time, we might play tennis together in the late afternoons, rallies rather than games as each of us was frightened of the other one losing. We began playing at the children's playground, occasionally bicycled over to some courts at Cookham (where I once caught sight of Stanley Spencer *en plein air*), and then we played at a private court belonging to Yolande's friend Cathie. This was the Cathie who appeared in family photographs in the South of France during the early nineteen-thirties. But we were nervous of going to the court in her garden too often, not liking to 'trouble' her, though the court was never used. Yolande would telephone, and we pedalled across, darting down the garden from tree to tree, and later darting back again along the line of the bushes so as not to be seen. It was not, I think, Yolande's shame at our poverty that drove her to avoid her friend so assiduously, but dread of Cathie's sympathy.

My grandmother welcomed me back from National Service as if I had been in hand-to-hand combat, thanking God and the Mother of God for the miracle of my survival. She wanted to hear my news, my special news. 'That child tells us nothing of what's going on,' she would complain to the cook and the gardener. 'Just like a bally clam. I don't know where he comes from. He's a proper mystery.'

'Oh do leave the boy alone, Di,' Fraser would interrupt before tumbling out to the garage to find another celebratory bottle of cider.

They all seemed to me significantly older, especially my grandmother. As she meandered from room to room, rattling the door handles, rearranging the cushions, her head full of empty plotting, she looked so small and bent. Yolande, I noticed, could hardly bear to glance at her – the thin grey curls under a dilapidated hairnet, the old powdered and lined face, the bloodshot eyes, her feet in their slippers misshapen with bunions. 'It's high time you went aloft,' she would shout to herself. All her Maidenhead friends were dead, but she lived on. 'Are you decent?' she always cried through my bedroom door. 'Are you visible?' I would hold my breath, knowing I could be invisible but not indecent enough yet. Then, with a sigh, she would wander away, heavy with her uncommunicable love.

An important new feature at Norhurst was our massive television device. It was unlike any other television in the world. My Uncle Kenneth had bought this portmanteau of a set which we stood, a substantial piece of furniture, in the middle of the hall. From a porthole in this object, when the right buttons and knobs were pushed and twisted, a picture could be projected on to a large screen. This screen had to be unpacked and raised up each evening, then folded down at night and put away under the stairs with the tea chests. It was a magnificent contraption – I have never seen anything like it. Our hall, which was the largest space in the house, was converted into a cinema in time for the six o'clock news each evening. It took an hour to prepare the screen which was responsible for new bumps, bruises and cuts ranged across my grandfather's head. But television became his passion, and after a few weeks none of us could remember what we had done before it arrived. He would sit himself behind the machine studying the controls, endeavouring to focus the images, while the rest of us chimed eagerly in with our advice. Old Nan, whose eyesight was failing, sat in a garden chair at the foot of the staircase, crouching forward so as to be almost touching the screen, the outline of her imposing form appearing as a shadow on the corner of all pictures. She watched everything, commented on nothing. Yolande never watched and was audibly contemptuous of the rest of us for sitting hunched up in the dark. It was impossible for any of us to go to any room without passing in front of the screen. My grandmother would actually stand in front of it, achieving an almost total eclipse as she complained to us of the dust created by the contrivance, or simply asked what we would like for lunch next day, switching on the light so as to make sure we heard her. She had found a new way of driving Fraser frantic.

I did not stay long at Norhurst after leaving the army. Smout, my colleague in redundancy, had discovered that we were entitled to special allowances at Colindale, and while we waited for this bonus to come through, I remained there. In my bedroom, still reading Proust, I could hear the whistle of the trains passing along the valley beyond All Saints Church on their way to London and wished I were on one of them. We lived at the respectable end of Maidenhead where nothing happened. But at the other end lay the 'Maidenhead Riviera' with its nightclubs and hotels, expensively lined along the Thames, in particular the notorious Skindles where couples were said to spend illicit weekends, and the smart Guards' Club in whose grounds 260 false wedding rings were later unearthed. The Maidenhead Public Library, near the centre of town, was midway between our respectability and that bohemianism. After a day there, as from a launching pad, I would sometimes take off on my bicycle and look across the Thames with its twin bridges, the red-brick Brunel railway viaduct with its two shallow semi-elliptical arches, and the white-stone eighteenth-century bridge, with its seven small water-arches, that carried traffic to London.

Before I made my way over these bridges, I tried to reconnoitre a literary career from Norhurst, offering my services in the role of book editor or reviewer to our local paper, *The Maidenhead Advertiser*. In fact the paper carried no book reviews, but this did not deter me. Surely, I appealed, they needed for this enterprise, the creation of a book section, someone like myself – young, unencumbered by university degrees, with a bit of legal and military experience to hand, and already deep in Proust.

I am still waiting for an answer.

This reversal spurred me towards London. Maidenhead, it was clear, was a bit off the intellectual map. There was no virtue in the place. But getting a foothold in London was not easy. At first, I could find only intermittent quarters in the Chelsea consulting room of my mother's doctor. On his dark leather couch, the only other occupant a dimly suspended medical skeleton, I passed my nights, rising at dawn to avoid the eager invalids who came beating at the door. Then I stayed with Griffy Philipps at a mews house in Mayfair belonging to his mother. I slept in the attic beside a water-tank, wrapped up on cold nights in brown paper – something between a tramp and an undelivered parcel. In the morning I would descend a ladder to the comfort of the drawing-room where I was transformed into a man of letters in his study.

Griffy at this time was working in the City. I must have murmured something one evening about Rajmai Tea, asked him perhaps whether he could find out anything about it. This obviously took time, but he was at last able to pinpoint it on the map at Boorbarrie and Behora, and, possibly under the impression I was passing on a hot tip, though probably from a feeling of friendliness, or even, I like to think, acting under the spell Rajmai cast on the imagination of all who heard its name, he bought some shares. 'It was better than a seat at the opera,' he writes to me. 'The company staggered from one disaster to the next, but like a lifeboat it always recovered and came back for more. In no particular order I remember floods, strikes by boatmen and porters, rock-bottom tea prices and lastly the Chinese invasion.' At the risk of insider trading, Griffy was receiving unusual dividends.

It was my mother's doctor, Larry Heyman, who at last found

me a more permanent place to live. He was an Irishman with a weakness for the arts who lived with his wife and daughter in Jubilee Place off the King's Road. He was immensely proud of his daughter who was training to be a ballet dancer. She would go in and out of the drawing-room on pointe, showing off her amazing *entrechats* and *fouettés*, performing complicated capers back and forth while her father looked on benevolently. His wife Irene appeared to me a fabulous creature in the high Spanish style. She had been painted by Matthew Smith in Chelsea Cloisters. This portrait, executed in vivid reds and making her appear to be bleeding luxuriantly to death against some flowers above the fireplace, lit up their otherwise gloomy house. When my mother told me at the hospital in Munich that she missed the King's Road, I could tell she had her friend Irene Heyman in mind. They spent much of their time in secret laughter, probably about men. Once they asked me whether I would mind their using my new address for something they wanted to insert in a newspaper. A week later I received a stiff note from *The Times* saying they did not accept personal advertisements of this kind. Irene seemed to have little involvement with humdrum domestic life. On one famous occasion, having bought her daughter a cat, she heard it purring and shouted out in alarm: 'Look out! It's growling.'

Larry Heyman was considerably older than his wife. His hand trembled as he reached for the whisky glass. He enjoyed pontificating in a stage-Irish voice on matters of dance, literature and painting, and passing on titbits about various artistic patients. But he was a kindly man and, having a surgery at Nell Gwynn House, he persuaded the management to let me have a small flat at the back of the building where coincidentally both my mother and my Uncle Kenneth had put up during intervals in their careers.

In my late 'teens I had begun trying to write in collaboration with my father; then in my early twenties I attempted to base my novel partly on my family; finally, when I reached my mid-twenties, I found a subject that had no connection with my parents. It was at Nell Gwynn House that I wrote my biography of Hugh Kingsmill. I had first made contact with the Kingsmill family through his publishers and was invited to meet them for dinner at the flat of one of his daughters, a strapping ex-chorus girl who, after the appearance of my book, became a nun. In my nervousness I arrived too early. Pacing the street I could not fail to notice that the building was in flames, with flashing fire engines outside. However, I was too polite to volunteer help, suspecting that there may have been some culinary disaster about which it would be tactless for an aspiring biographer to inquire. When things had cooled down, I went in. The evening threw up some photographs of Kingsmill's death mask, his smouldering tobacco pouch and other impedimenta, though little of direct literary use. But I refused to be daunted.

Kingsmill's widow Dorothy, once a revue dancer then a dressmaker, nursed literary ambitions which, after Kingsmill mislaid her unpublished novel on the platform of an underground station, found indirect expression in her work as a lay analyst. She was reputed to have freed the novelist Antonia White from a writer's block by liberating her from her husband, the editor of *Picture Post* Tom Hopkinson, and then marrying him herself. When I met her, she had persuaded Tom to take up the editorship of *Drum*, the picture magazine for young Africans, and they were about to sail for Johannesburg. Dorothy acted very flirtatiously that evening and kept calling me an 'angry young man'. Our relationship eventually made me one.

Once I had been given permission to write the book, I went to see Hugh Kingsmill's elder brother, the ski-pioneer and Christian controversialist Sir Arnold Lunn (they were sons of the Methodist travel agent Sir Henry Lunn, Kingsmill writing under his mother's maiden name in order to distance himself from his father and distinguish himself from his brother). 'My wife,' Sir

Arnold warned me, 'doesn't function too well in the evenings.' She was, he added, 'beyond organising sandwiches'. So the two of us went out to dinner, leaving Lady Mabel in bed. She was, I understood, an insomniac. But left to herself for hours on end in the dark, she would sometimes drop off out of sheer boredom. The Lunns were to be away next morning for some eventing in Switzerland, so it was essential that Lady Mabel rest. After dinner we went quietly back to the flat so that Sir Arnold could present me with one of his books essential, he confided, for my biography. Lady Mabel had nodded off. We moved among the half-packed trunks and suitcases like ghosts, Sir Arnold leading with a candle in his hand. He quarried out the book, signed it, and handed it to me with a whisper. I breathed my thanks, then fumbled my way out. On the staircase outside, plunged into total darkness, I felt for the light button and, pressing it, released a fearful peal of bells into the Lunn sleeping quarters. I saw the light flash angrily on under the door and, coward that I was, I fled. Looking through the book when I got back to Nell Gwynn House, I saw it was full of Swiss mountains but without a mention of Kingsmill. My view that he was an unjustly neglected author had been confirmed.

My flat cost £3 a week. The extra money from the army paid for my first few months. My grandparents had also given me some money, attempting to do so secretly but, colliding on the landing at Norhurst, the notes flapping on to the floor followed by their cries of distress and exasperated accusations, the transaction had been well advertised.

It was easy to live cheaply in the early nineteen-sixties; but it was difficult to earn money. From the *Twentieth Century* magazine I eventually received a commission to review an anthology of Oxford and Cambridge writing called *Light Blue, Dark Blue*. I worked on this piece for weeks, revising it intensely – a comma here, a semi-colon there – and at last sent in a review that some months later was published. This was my first writing to be

printed. The following year a cheque arrived for a little under
£1. Here was success. But could I afford success?

I had notions of supplementing this income with some profitable plagiarism. Taking the hint from an episode in one of
Anthony Powell's novels, I went off to the British Museum's
newspaper library at Colindale and looked through a number of
stories in women's magazines which, I had heard, paid their
contributors well. I copied down one that seemed to me very
characteristic, then brought it up to date by changing the names
of the characters, the speed and make of the cars, the brand of
the breakfast cereals and so on before sending it to the magazine
that had originally published it twenty-five years ago. I hoped
they would be grateful for this made-to-measure contribution.
But their letter of rejection, which allowed me genuine promise,
decided that the story (which involved a flirtation between a
husband and his sister-in-law) was a little too risqué for them.

Though I took one or two odd jobs, it was really the C.O.
who made the writing of *Hugh Kingsmill* possible. Early in the
nineteen-sixties, he decided to pay me an allowance of £8 a
month, and persuaded both my mother and Kaja to do the same:
£288 a year (equivalent to some £3,000 in the late nineteen-
nineties). This allowance dwindled as the fortunes of its
contributors went downhill, the C.O. silently withdrawing after
a year, my mother giving up after almost two years, and my
grandmother in Sweden carrying on for some three years. But it
was enough.

The reason my father offered for this generous arrangement
was that I appeared to be 'wasting my time with the right
people'. By this he meant two of Kingsmill's friends, Hesketh
Pearson and William Gerhardie.

I had written to Pearson in 1958, and over the next half-
dozen years received continual encouragement from him. He
would invite me over to supper with his wife Joyce or take me
out to the theatre (it was with him that I saw my first Bernard

Shaw productions). He also wrote to editors on my behalf so that I could get some reviewing and lent me whatever Kingsmill manuscripts and books he possessed. After his death in 1964, Joyce Pearson told me she thought I had replaced to some extent the son of his first marriage who had been killed in the Spanish Civil War. They had quarrelled over politics on their last meeting, and Hesketh was close to suicide for months afterwards. Perhaps, twenty years later, his goodness to me was a means of reconciliation with his son. Certainly he helped me in ways my father was in no position to do and, without alienating my father, became something of a father figure to me. By an act of imaginative generosity, his assistance was to go on after his and Joyce's death, when his library and copyrights came to me.

Literature was a very tangible affair to Pearson, belonging more to the open air than the study, and reflecting what he saw around him, the people and the landscape he loved. He had once been an actor and knew some of Shakespeare's plays by heart. He was also a man of dramatic opinions. One day, when someone suggested to him that Shakespeare was rather overrated, he stopped the taxi they were travelling in and obliged the man to continue his journey on foot. He was some fifty years older than I was, but we spoke easily, without any sense of a difference in age. Books were not something behind which he sheltered: they were part of his life and he helped to make them part of mine. After cheerless days of doubt, I would come away from an evening with him full of the enthusiasm and vitality he communicated.

Hesketh Pearson described himself as 'a hero-worshipper who likes to take his heroes off their pedestals and get to know them as fellow men'. What I picked up from his biographies was not so much his technique, which derived from his career on stage, as what Graham Greene called his 'sense of life going on all the time'. I admired his ability to tell a story; I shared the endless fascination with human nature from which all his Lives sprang; and I benefited from his gusto and geniality. He was a man without qualifications, an amateur in the sense that he wrote his biographies for love rather than a *curriculum vitae*, who showed me what possibilities might lie ahead and gave me the confidence to follow his example by going my own way.

Kingsmill, like many lonely people, compartmentalised his life, so it was not surprising that his two closest friends over twenty-five years should have met each other only once. William Gerhardie was utterly unlike Pearson, and the most eccentric person I have ever met. Both shared a love of literature and landscape, but whereas Pearson in his direct and upright manner would set off on long vigorous walks in the footsteps of Johnson and Boswell and other favourite characters, his head teeming with lines from Shakespeare and his own explosive phrases bursting with alliterations and assertions, Gerhardie would stay immovably indoors dreaming of what might lie beyond the curtained windows. 'It's a lovely day,' a friend remarked one morning. 'Is it?' he replied eagerly, remaining seated with his back to the window.

In the nineteen-twenties his novels *Futility* and *The Polyglots* had made him, in the words of Arnold Bennett, 'the pet of the intelligentsia and the darling of Mayfair'. He was taken up by Katherine Mansfield and Edith Wharton, H.G. Wells and Evelyn Waugh. 'To those of my generation Gerhardie was the most important new novelist to appear in our young life,' wrote Graham Greene. And Olivia Manning concluded: 'He is our Gogol's *Overcoat*. We all come out of him.'

One of the many articles on Gerhardie in the nineteen-thirties was prophetically subtitled: 'Success: and How to Avoid It'. At this avoidance he became adept. By the nineteen-sixties he could boast of being the most celebrated unknown writer in Britain. He wrote every day but had published almost nothing since 1940 beyond a list of teasing titles in *Who's Who* (an ironical tragedy called *English Measles* for example, and a lyrical comedy entitled *The Private Life of a Public Nuisance*). His background was unorthodox. The son of a British cotton manufacturer settled in Russia, he had been brought up in St Petersburg and being identified as the dunce in the family, sent to England in his 'teens to be trained for a commercial career. During the First World War, equipped with a monocle and a huge sword bought second-hand in the Charing Cross Road, he was posted back to Russia on the staff of the British Military Attaché. When the war was over, he turned up at Worcester College, Oxford, where he wrote a brilliant little book on Chekhov. But by the mid-nineteen-thirties, at the age of forty, he had left the world of travel and adventure, the society of Mayfair and, beginning a career of philosophical speculation, set himself up as a hermit in central London.

William was a good portly man whose figure tapered down to a pair of delicate feet. An amused expression and rosebud mouth, together with his bald head and pink skin, gave him the appearance of a decadent cherub. His eyes protruded in the manner of some tropical fish. He sometimes wore, over his pyjamas, a shiny grey suit and colourful bow tie. I would visit him occasionally at his block of flats in Hallam Street. Whatever time of day you arrived, you were required to ring the night bell, then take the lift to the fourth floor and hammer at his door until you heard him begin to fiddle languidly with the bolts and chains. After a loud exchange of passwords, the door opened and you stepped into the dark guided by William's silhouette. 'This is the gold room,' he would announce with a spectacular gesture, flinging wide an inner door to what appeared like the opening of a coal mine. The floor was crammed with shoe boxes, paper bags and the odd mattress, all bulging with his writings. William moved, despite his arthritis, athletically among the debris. Books were everywhere, but there were no bookshelves except by his bed. A pile of brocade cushions supported him at his typewriter which was itself supported by a tower of empty egg cartons.

Hospitality was a risky business. The flat was freezing and the armchairs, resting on empty coffee jars, slumped to the floor as you sat in them. William shopped by telephone from Selfridges and seemed to live mostly on Coca-Cola and meringues, with the odd sausage thrown in at weekends. But for guests he would go out of his way to prepare something special: a drink of tepid water and raspberry jam called 'All's Well' because, he assured you, 'it ends well'. Few of us got that far. Gerhardie connoisseurs took picnics in order to avoid his prize speciality 'Sherryvappa', a subtle combination of sherry and evaporated milk. After drinking this, you had to be a true friend to come again. The fact was, he did not really want callers. He would insist reluctantly on shaking your hand as you arrived, and then ostentatiously and elaborately washing his own hands. He did not want you going to his lavatory, sitting on his furniture, touching things, breathing his air, seeing what he had written and finding yourself unable to resist making off with his ideas. He could not wait for you to go and, when you did go, would hold you at the door squeezing promises from you to come again.

Gerhardie's early novels, written under Chekhov's influence, explored the comedy of time deferred; his later books, written under Proust's influence, investigated the phenomenon of time regained. He had reached a point of looking into the future with a sense of nostalgia, as if impatient to convert it into the past. Time present remained a fleeting problem. As the solution to its banality, its physical awkwardness, he had hit on the telephone. The telephone avoided problems of actual contact, time could be extended almost indefinitely into the future and then to some extent recaptured with another call. Once we spoke for seven hours on the telephone, and I had two meals during our conversation. Another time I played him a Wagnerian opera down the line. Though he was a very funny man, there was often pathos in his stories. He would be telling an amusing story, suddenly interrupt himself with a cry of 'Oh God!', and then continue with the story. You could telephone him if you were in trouble at any time – three or four in the morning – all time was the same to him. But he was not understanding if you happened to be in a hurry. Once, in desperation, I exclaimed: 'William! I must go! The building is in flames!' But he went on speaking about *The Polyglots*. I noticed, too, how much better I felt if I telephoned him when I was ill – and how exhausted I was at the end of our calls some other times.

I suppose I was flattered that someone who had been taken up by Katherine Mansfield and H.G. Wells should now be taking me up. Unlike Hesketh Pearson, Gerhardie also wanted something from me. He wanted me to take my admiration for his novels like a torch into the future, and light up understanding among a new generation of readers. This I tried and failed to do by writing ten prefaces to a collected edition of his work in the early nineteen-seventies and then, a little more successfully perhaps, by editing with my friend Robert Skidelsky his posthumous book, the ingenious *God's Fifth Column*, in the early nineteen-eighties. Finally I wrote my valediction in *The Dictionary of National Biography*, in the 'Missing Persons' volume of which I also wrote tributes to Hesketh Pearson and Hugh Kingsmill.

The world that William Gerhardie opened up for me was a very unEnglish one without straight lines of cause and effect, where moral certainties are ironically undermined, where comedy thrives as part of tragedy, where progress comes unpredictably and secret lines of communication lie between opposing forces.

According to his biographer Dido Davies, Gerhardie dreamed of possessing all the comely women in the world in a 'cumulative consummate kiss'. His preoccupation with hygiene modified, but did not curb, his obsessive seduction of women. He had picked them up working in shops, strolling in the park, walking home in the streets from their offices, anywhere. Dido Davies herself was one of the girls, then in her 'teens and sometimes with her mother, I met at William's flat. He behaved to her as he did to every girl who visited him. 'Isn't it extraordinary how she resembles Goethe's Mignon?' he would ask. 'Do you find her attractive?' Then, turning to her: 'Come out here into the centre of the room. Why not stand on that table so that this young genius can see you better? And now turn round. What calves!' With obvious pleasure, he would run the palms of his hands lightly up her legs. 'And what fine breasts too, don't you think?' he would add with rich appreciation.

Though these performances were outrageous and embarrassing, I noticed that the girls themselves took a benevolent attitude to William. They giggled a lot but did not feel threatened and were never frightened. For all their shyness, they were not displeased. Everything that was objectionable seemed to have been harmlessly dissolved.

If Hesketh Pearson was a father figure to me, William Gerhardie played the part of a wicked uncle. How was my love life? he immediately wanted to know. My stammering replies did not satisfy him, so he introduced me to his great-niece Jackie, a beautiful dancer who led me into the world of ballet at the time of Nureyev's arrival in Britain and introduced me to the music of Prokofiev.

I could afford to take Jackie out to supper once a fortnight. I would count up to a hundred before telephoning her and try to sound casual. But when we met I had almost nothing to say. I always prepared a few amusing things to tell her, hoping to hide behind these anecdotes, but to my dismay they tumbled out in the first few minutes and then I came to a halt. Twenty-six silent suppers a year were more than Jackie could face, so she made arrangements with one or two of the other dancers at her digs in Earls Court to go out with me in rotation. To waiters at the bistros and coffee houses we ate in, I must have appeared a regular ladies' man. Eventually one of these ballet girls, Jennifer it was, listening to some music in Nell Gwynn House after supper, grew impatient with my lack of initiative. So she got into bed, my bed, while I was in the bathroom, and so I followed her in. After ten minutes or so in the dark, she asked: 'Is that all?' 'I don't know,' I answered truthfully.

We began to laugh.

While getting a foothold in London, I kept being pulled back to Norhurst for short spells to see my grandfather. Things had looked up for him briefly after the war. Towards the end of 1947, at the age of seventy-two, he had gone out to visit the Rajmai Estate in India and came back with a report recommending new houses, schools and a hospital for the company employees and their families. The following April he was elected Chairman of Rajmai. It was a peak in his career. But the board meetings were nervous affairs. Though he armed himself with all the regular protective equipment, including a military-looking umbrella, correct gloves, polished shoes and a venerable double-breasted suit, he still could not ward off the terrible outbursts from his cousin 'Mad Ivor', and would sometimes arrive back in Maidenhead looking very miserable. It was a mystery how his brother Pat, the mildest and most innocuous of men, could have produced such an intemperate son. At Norhurst, a rumour soon sprang up that Ivor was having 'an operation to his head'. The minutes of Rajmai Tea Company show that he resigned from the board in 1950 and that there were 'circumstances under which this resignation has become necessary'. Attached to this minute is a note: 'In case there may be repercussions legal or otherwise arising from letters which have passed between Ivor Holroyd's solicitors and the Chairman, the Board desire to protect and indemnify the Secretaries against any such eventuality.' The source of Ivor's anger had probably been Fraser's borrowing of

money from Pat shortly before his death. As an act of reconciliation, Ivor's wife was appointed to the board on his resignation;
and it was from her that Kenneth bought extra Rajmai shares
for himself and his father. When Fraser retired from the chair-
manship in 1952, Kenneth became a director.

Life would have been easier now if my grandfather's health
had not begun to fail. It was his wish to make one more journey
to India and, after various false starts and amid waves of chaos
and commotion at Norhurst – everyone running around in perplexity and the dog wringing its hands – this he achieved in
1955, touring the company's gardens at Assam in his eightieth
year. There is a picture of him there, smiling benignly while various estate workers are doubled up in laughter. Seven years later,
as Chinese troops invaded Assam, we were privileged at
Maidenhead to get our first glimpse of the Rajmai plantations,
edged with Old Nan's silhouette, on our television. But by then
my grandfather was dead.

He had not been well for almost a decade. Indeed for much of
that time he had been stubbornly dying, on bad days in desperation and terror in front of us. He died a little upstairs in his
front bedroom and then a little more downstairs in the morning-
room where the family had made up a bed for him. He died on
a stretcher going down the stairs and in the ambulance going off
to the hospital; and then he went on dying as he was moved in
and out of hospital, back and forth between the wards, again,
again. It took a fearful time his dying, and we all felt we had
died a little with him.

Until I witnessed this, I had thought of death simply as a disappearance, someone walking into another room and shutting
the door; or a trick performed by a conjuror, painless and inexplicable, leaving the sensation that behind the descending curtain
everything was actually all right. I saw the process as we all saw
it in films; a lying down and closing of the eyes on camera.
Nothing more. I had known death only as part of fiction. My

grandfather showed me the fact. I was wholly unprepared for the awfulness of his final years and could not credit what was happening to him. Ours had been the sort of life at Norhurst, blasted with quarrels, saturated with an engulfing misery, that naturally drove us to entreat death – until my grandfather began to die. It was then we realised, all of us, how preferable a living death is to a dead one.

My grandfather died what is called a natural death ('congestive cardiac failure'). He was in his eighty-sixth year by the time the last painful breath had been crushed out of him. So he had had 'a good innings' despite not quite being 'a safe pair of hands'. Surely there could be nothing of which to complain? Yet I was horrified. My father, seeing my distress and suffering distress himself, remarked that through the long horrors of history many people had gone through worse experiences. He began to recite them as if finding comfort from this frightful litany.

In rooms close to where my grandfather was dying, we would gather to discuss his condition, discuss his life. I know more of his life now than I did then. I know that he did not enjoy a successful business career, or a happy marriage, or achieve anything of special distinction. His one romantic adventure had ended in disaster and he had done very little with the fortune he inherited from his father except lose it – indeed he would have ended up a bankrupt had he not been rescued by Kenneth after the war. Yet we spoke of him with reverence, as if he were a truly great man. Not that he ever said anything of greatness. His political opinions, which were expressed as a series of slogans ('Jack's as good as his master') were a hundred years or more out of date and, I believe, copied from his father, the Major-General, who perhaps had more right to them. We thought of him as a Christian Gentleman, though he never went to church and the disgruntled clichés he aimed at socialists were profoundly unChristian. Once he had been a believer, or believed he had been, and he still wanted to believe. But he simply could not. During this last phase of his life, his bible was Gayelord Hauser's *Look Younger, Live Longer*. All his life he had longed to look and feel younger, and now he was striving fearfully to live longer. It was the pathos of his predicament that touched us all so unbearably. Here was a gentle man whose home had resounded with vituperation, nothing if not well-meaning and now coming to nothing, whose long life had been largely unlived and whose fear of hurting others had now turned to a fear of being hurt himself, of being extinguished, buried, burnt.

He had watched his own father die, his infant son Desmond, his brother Pat. And his mother had killed herself. These deaths, I believe, had destroyed his Christian faith. Now it was his turn, and there was to be no miracle. As the realisation spread through him that there was no place for him to go but into oblivion, the change in him became dreadful. His life, for so long incomprehensible and bleak, now appeared wonderfully desirable. He yearned for more of it, for another chance to do better. The remorselessness of his dying made him unrecognisable. All the resilience, good humour, niceness were gradually prised out of him. He did not know how to behave. He was afraid: afraid of more pain, afraid of the nurses, afraid of the medical instruments to which he was attached, afraid of everything. Of what use now were his gentlemanly standards? He had left his card, but the Great Gentleman above was not at home. He was nowhere.

As a source of hope and strength, his vanished faith was replaced by drugs, and these also changed him. They allowed him to sleep, but seemed to give him no rest. His sleep was pitted with nightmares. He shouted out incomprehensible cries, struggled in his bed as if against invisible bonds, and then woke exhausted from hours of wrestling with his unseen opponent. His face sank in, the colour of his skin went to green and purple. The hospital ward was crowded with patients bandaged and strapped like grotesque babies lying in their cots, all alike, all waiting. One day, after a couple of taut hours at the bedside, I was relieved by my aunt who wearily pointed out that I had been sitting next to the wrong bed.

I hated these sessions beside the bed. I seemed to become infected with all my grandfather's fear and sadness. And I could do nothing to help. The wards were like parade grounds where the Last Post was constantly sounding, and marks were awarded for deportment and smartness. By such standards, his own until recently, my grandfather was not making a good death. He was drawing attention to himself, creating trouble, not going quietly, letting himself down, letting us down. This must have been in his mind when he looked across at me and gasped out: 'I'm sorry.'

Those were the last words I heard him speak. On 24 February 1961, the hospital telephoned to say that he had died 'fairly comfortably' early that morning. None of us had wanted him to die and all of us were relieved now he was dead. My grandmother sang out her grief in a frightful dirge that scraped our nerves but gave us a target for our hostility. My Uncle Kenneth began talking, and went on talking, about farming matters to take his mind off it all. 'My God, this is an awful place,' my father unconsciously quoted as we stood together in the undertaker's office. Then my aunt rushed in, looking tired and furious. It was almost as if she were preparing for another washing-up battle over the spoons and saucepans. But then she steadied herself. Her father had been her god. No one could match her sense of loss. We fell back as she advanced upon his corpse, plastered with frozen pink cosmetics. She leant over and lingeringly kissed the gaping face – something I had never seen her do to the living man, or any living man; something I could not do myself.

I do not remember the funeral service, only the burying, so far down in the earth it was, at Braywick cemetery.

A month later a terrific storm broke out at Norhurst as to

whether my grandmother was older than Old Nan. Yolande claimed that Old Nan was now the senior member of the household, and Nan herself forcefully nodded her agreement. But my grandmother, bitterly disputing this, appealed to me to get her birth certificate from Cork. This was not easy. The Corbet family, which had once teemed so prolifically over Ireland in the late nineteenth century, dazzling my grandfather, had left no sign of their existence in the Register Office in Dublin, or the National Library, or National Archives. They had vanished. But eventually I did get the birth certificate and was able to show that for the last quarter of a century my grandmother had been lying over her age, and that she was indeed older than Old Nan. The rage this provoked in Yolande took me aback. She shouted that it was a forgery, that you could never trust Irish records, that I had somehow invented it. She put it under a light and stared at it disbelievingly. She was tempted, I could see, to destroy it and swear it never existed. This was my grandmother's one triumph over her family.

She needed a triumph to compensate a little for the shock of not having been left Norhurst outright by her husband. He had given the house jointly to Yolande and herself, and made Yolande his sole trustee 'of my family's financial interests'. It was this deprivation, this sense of being under her daughter's control, of feeling almost a lodger in her own home, that prompted her to assert her seniority and also, perhaps, to commit some strange acts of demolition. She tore up and threw away a number of innocent objects from her past, mainly photographs of better days. I saw the pieces littered across her bedroom and can see now the rents she made with a knife through some of the family albums, obliterating figures she had known.

My aunt believed, or affected to believe, that she had finally gone mad. She pointed to the scoldings my grandmother would give invisible servants, the way she broke inexplicably into French. But she had done such things for years. I could remem-

ber as a child hearing her cry out the word 'Jamais!' and thinking it was some kind of confectionery. Besides, the mad have
perfectly sane reasons for their madness. Her destruction of
these photographs struck me as an act of revenge for the loveless
disappointment of living.

She had so often called upon God to take her that her quiet
death in hospital, on 21 January 1969 at the age of ninety-two,
seemed an anti-climax, like the opening of a play we had long
been watching in rehearsal. I remember the funeral service in All
Saints Church at the end of our garden: the sudden piercing
beauty of a hymn, then nothing.

We kept the news of her death from Kenneth who was himself
dying (I visited him in a Sussex hospital and he braced himself
on his deathbed to be a perfect host). My grandmother had
made a Will at the beginning of 1968 in which she left Yolande
and Basil £100 each. But her estate was valued at only £217 and
there was nothing left after the payment of debts and funeral
expenses. She had signed her name, Adeline Holroyd, on the
Will, but added 'also known as Adeline Genevive Holroyd'.
None of us knew the name Genevive and it does not appear on
her birth certificate. Perhaps it was a special name Fraser had
called her in Ireland before their marriage, or a name her father
used when she was a child, or possibly an invented name signifying her wish to become someone else.

# 1 9

# *Missing   Persons*

It took longer to publish my Life of Hugh Kingsmill than to write it. I finished the writing when I was twenty-four, but did not see it in print until I was in my thirtieth year. The book was a labour of love but much of the labour was wasted and the love did not shine through. The words seemed strung across the page like dumb notes on a piano, and my judgements relied too much on other people's opinions. It was also rather incompetently put together, an apprentice work, fumbling, defensive, gauche – otherwise fine. Dorothy Hopkinson never sent the unpublished material I expected, writing from South Africa to say that she was composing a book on Kingsmill herself.

But what chiefly deterred publishers was the towering commercial impracticality of a biography about a forgotten author by an unknown writer. I sent the typescript eventually to sixteen publishers who insisted on returning it to me as if it were a tennis ball sent over to them for that purpose. The rally lasted four years, and I noticed with surprise, as the battered package came back and I posted it off again, an obstinacy mounting in me to a point of exhilaration. Perhaps, as Purple Parr predicted, I had some determination in me after all.

William Gerhardie and Hesketh Pearson did whatever they could to help. Gerhardie wrote a long characteristic article in the *Spectator* entitled 'The Uses of Obscurity'. With my two grand-mothers, he told readers, I had already achieved the status of Grand Old Man of Letters. My *Hugh Kingsmill*, he continued, had received such glowing rejection notices from so many publishers that 'it may fairly rank as the best book never published'. On the strength of this piece I wondered whether to produce extra copies of my typescript to meet the demand. Unfortunately the author of 'Success: and How to Avoid It' had slipped in a sentence indicating that I had once been a promising squash player. 'His father,' Gerhardie revealed, 'though encouraging a literary career, regrets that in pursuit of the quite hopelessly neg-lected Kingsmill, Michael should be seriously neglecting his squash.' Others appeared to agree. From publishers, even from poets and historians – James Michie, Robert Skidelsky – I received letters exclusively on squash rackets. Kingsmill again had been neglected.

Hesketh Pearson wrote to several publishers and gave me a generous quote that could be used on the jacket. It was partly through him that Martin Secker at last offered to bring out the book from his Unicorn Press in the Royal Opera Arcade, allow-ing me an advance of £25. Though this, to use a phrase of Kingsmill's, may have 'looked more like a retreat than an advance', it was a generous gesture since the money came from his own pocket. Equally generous was the long Introduction Malcolm Muggeridge contributed free of charge. Early in 1964 Malcolm Muggeridge, Hesketh Pearson, Martin Secker and myself lunched at the Café Royal, and Martin Secker was able to report that, following a favourable review in the *Observer*, sales had topped thirty-nine copies.

I had, as Dickens might have said, 'commenced biographer'.

To the C.O. it was immediately clear that something extra was needed to transform the book into a popular success. His dog knew the dog belonging to a man he believed to be a band leader. From two leads' distance he suggested interviewing this man and, if his answers proved satisfactory, engaging him professionally for a special launch party. We would have to see our bank managers of course, but it should not be impossible to put on something modestly spectacular. In any business, he explained, some form of advertising, some promotion of good will, was essential. I would be a fool to ignore this. In a spasm of fantastical magniloquence he appeared to be peopling Maidenhead Thicket with literary celebrities such as J.B. Priestley and Daphne du Maurier. He saw them sipping their drinks, moving gracefully around as in some ballet, and putting my book on the map. This plan, or some version of it, was frustrated barely in time by the intervention of a libel action from Dorothy Hopkinson.

Unknown before I came to write about him, Kingsmill has stubbornly remained unknown since the publication of my book in 1964 and the selection from his writings entitled *The Best of Kingsmill* that I brought out six years later. But he had started me on my way. In so far as he wrote biographies himself, Kingsmill had been described as a follower of Lytton Strachey, a categorisation I attempted to refute. So began the pattern of my future work where a significant minor character in one biography develops into the subject of the next.

During the nineteen-sixties and nineteen-seventies I became increasingly absorbed in my subjects' lives. 'Writing is a form of disappearance,' the poet Simon Armitage writes. From my parents I certainly began to disappear. I was like a science fiction character, travelling across time, stretching out and trying to make contact with people I had never met. I travelled on a current of energy ignited by their work, concentrated in their loves and spread around widening circles from their deaths. I was attempting, or so I sometimes felt, to retrieve something from death itself, having been so shocked by my grandfather's dying. Kingsmill and Strachey, Augustus John and Bernard Shaw became the maverick teachers I never had at a university. I learnt emotionally as well as intellectually: and then there was the archaeological digging up of facts. With these I plotted patterns and contours showing different aspects of cultural and political history between the mid-nineteenth and mid-twentieth centuries, and endeavoured to give my answer to a contemporary question: how did we get here?

I led a gregarious and solitary life. My research journeys took me eventually all over the world. Then, back in London, I would shut my door against the world and write for days and weeks in bed. There was no one 'at his desk' earlier than I was, I explained to my father, who seemed determined to catch me napping. All this distanced me from my parents, the C.O. and Madam as they now were.

Ignoring the libel action over *Hugh Kingsmill* (which obliged me to utter an apology, pay costs and rewrite some pages on Dorothy Hopkinson), my mother was happy to see me become self-supporting, as a man should be. The sort of career I had chosen was incredible, but then she had never taken any interest in men's business affairs. The *Sunday Times*'s serialisation of *Lytton Strachey* and *Augustus John* in the late nineteen-sixties and early nineteen-seventies was evidence enough for her that I was properly employed. But her relief could not altogether conceal her wonder that such books could find a single reader.

My father's attitude was more complicated. When I handed him my *Hugh Kingsmill*, he placed it carefully on a table and asked in a tone of urgency how *Lytton Strachey* was coming along. When I eventually gave him *Lytton Strachey*, he inquired gravely after my progress on *Augustus John*. The public was notoriously fickle, he reminded me, and if I didn't bring out a book each year, every year, readers would quickly forget about me. 'Your name has not been mentioned,' he volunteered after reading an article on contemporary writing in the *Daily Express*. I never saw him open one of my books and he was disparaging about my subjects (Strachey was a queer fish; John completely out of fashion; Shaw a cynic whose bluff had been called). His concern on my behalf was somewhat lowering to the spirits. So I was later surprised to find that, after I returned to London, he would go round the village boasting of my achievements to bewildered neighbours.

During the late nineteen-sixties my parents marked time. My mother, who was still receiving a quarterly allowance from Egon Hessel, lived in a series of rather smart apartments taken on short leases. Over seven or eight years she moved from a flat near Sloane Square to another above Elizabeth David's shop in Ebury Street overlooking Orange Square, and then to a mansion apartment near Earls Court. The future frightened her and, unlike William Gerhardie, she lived wholly in the present. It was an attractive quality, especially for young people on whom she spent her money – actually Egon Hessel's money and Kaja's. 'I was young, inexperienced, rather gauche,' my ballet student girl-friend Jennifer writes to me. She had come down to London from Lancashire at the age of twenty and 'to be plunged into your world of expensive restaurants and clubs, taxis everywhere, apparently wealthy people, fashionably dressed was pretty heady stuff'.

> When I think of Ulla I think of champagne. Even her hair, her colouring and a lot of her clothes were the colour of champagne. There seemed a champagne-tinted aura around her . . . I remember Ulla for her enthusiasms and exuberance – the way she greeted the French onion man in Orange Square like a long lost friend; her childlike delight at purchasing in the Portobello Road two green

Chinese vases which were to be converted into table
lamps; and an evening at a restaurant called Chez Victor
where, having said farewell to Kaja that day she was
inclined to sob on the proprietor's shoulder and had to be
restored with champagne cocktails.

In Jennifer's eyes I was a young man with parents, but no
cohesive family. She could discover nothing in common between
my father and my mother. Certainly my father had an innate
sense of fair play, but he believed that the rules of the game had
been unfairly changed at half-time. A vast store of good will
seemed locked in some secret chamber within him and no one
could find the key. But he was still on the lookout for some
woman or business partner who might know where it lay. I
would sometimes go for a drink on Sundays and he would whisper over a sherry that he wanted me to meet someone he thought
I'd like. There was a high-flyer from Epsom to whom he had
given 'one of your tomes'; there was a lady temporarily down on
her luck who worked at Bobby's of Bournemouth ('the sort of
place your publishers should try to get rid of your stuff'); and
there was a woman he had met at the village pub who could type
('might be rather valuable to you, Michael'). But it was difficult
for him to sustain a relationship without money. After the collapse of timber and insolvency of Seamless Floors, he became
'not exactly dour, perhaps sombre or withdrawn are better
words to describe him', Jennifer writes to me. The three of us
would occasionally have lunch in the empty kitchen at his mock-
Tudor refuge where he frantically pressed extra helpings on us.
As his fortunes went downhill he would give me increasingly
elevated advice on how to manage my literary career and issue
darker warnings against fecklessness.

The worst of times was beginning for my father, and the best
of times for me. The revolution of the nineteen-sixties reached
me late, but not too late. The sudden freedom between the sexes,

the greater equality too, and the easy atmosphere that allowed us all to resolve many differences into games, came as a wonderful liberation for men as well as women – at least it did for me. A more natural life, with wider emotional horizons, opened up. I moved into it gratefully. To those dead men, my biographical subjects, who had laboured in their fashion for change, and to the living women who transformed my experience of the world, I owe all that I value most. For two or three of the latter I was more than a request stop along their emotional routes. Ideally I had always been 'one for whom the visible world exists'. In these women's eyes I recovered my visibility though some habits could not be changed and I remain invisible to myself. Observation and participation grew so involved that I cannot now separate them. Looking out of the window at the multitude of birds, squirrels and cats in the garden I easily forget myself (I am a cat person unlike my family who were all dog people). If I look out of another window I see the men, women and children walking past in the street, all part of a narrative, each with a story, and I follow them in my imagination. I never tire of watching. I watch, therefore I am; I am what I watch; and what I watch entrances me. This has been my exit from myself.

All these new interests carried me further from my family but when matters began to go seriously wrong I was quickly drawn back. I began my biography of Bernard Shaw where he had begun his life, in Dublin, and was abroad in Ireland and the United States for some two years. The change in my parents after I returned in 1977 was striking.

At the start of the decade Egon Hessel's allowance had suddenly dried up. My mother retreated to a one-room flat in Chelsea Manor Street off the King's Road where I had written most of my *Lytton Strachey* after leaving Nell Gwynn House. Like my father in Surrey, my aunt at Maidenhead, she looked out on a cemetery. 'Moved to Daver Court,' she noted in the account she later wrote for me, 'where I still am – goodness knows for how long – getting too expensive. Bank owns my flat.' She made several visits to Stockholm, but Kaja was not well and needed to borrow money herself. 'Trying to sell my Swedish Pewter this year,' my mother wrote to me. She also sold pictures and furniture that had belonged to Kaja.

She still had a regular 'boyfriend'. Jimmy was not sophisticated or wealthy or romantic. But he was kind and had a whacky sense of humour that agreeably bewildered my mother. He protected her from loneliness. But when she met a rather dashing gentleman with a title (who by a coincidence lived on the edge of Maidenhead Thicket) she could not resist one more escapade. It would be fun to escape again and forget her age, her financial worries. It was a short affaire and the only one, I believe, she truly regretted. 'Wish I had not met him,' she wrote, 'as I lost Jimmy then.'

In her late fifties she was obliged to start work. She took a job as a 'floating supervisor' at Bourne and Hollingsworth, but left it after one week. Then she started working as an occasional interpreter at business conferences and exhibitions. Her letters to me mention events at the Goldsmiths Hall, Earls Court, Olympia, Grosvenor House, the Hilton Hotel in London and the Metropole Hotel in Brighton. For short spells she was working 'like billy-ho'. There are photos of her at gift fairs, electrical exhibitions, brewery conferences ('no free samples') holding a microphone and wearing the glazed expression I know so well (and struggle myself to conceal at committee meetings) as she translates what is unintelligible in one language into what is accurately unintelligible in another.

Now that she was responsible for herself, my mother's life grew bureaucratically more complex. I would receive letters from building societies, banks, insurance companies asking me how long Mrs Ulla Nares had been in my service, whether she was on my permanent staff, what the nature of her duties were and the amount of her monthly salary. 'God help me with the

dole!!!' she exclaimed in one letter. She spent many indecipher-
able hours at the Inland Revenue headquarters being
encumbered with the correct assistance. 'Am shaking at the
knees,' she wrote to me, 'but say to myself they are trying to help
me. Waterford House seems like my second home by now!'

In the autumn of 1976 she was sixty. I was then abroad and
did not particularly notice her birthday. Not that she ever forgot
mine. She would write apologising for having no expensive presents or exciting news. 'I am thinking of you all the time & wish
you all the best in the world in every respect. Love Madam.'

Her moods varied. 'Sometimes I'm glad to be alone & not
having to cope with difficult men and their tantrums & whims.'
These men, businessmen from conferences, would still telephone
on the off-chance, but she could not pretend to enjoy their company anymore and now avoided them. Nevertheless it was not
impossible that an incredible someone might ride up and rescue
her. 'No social life at all,' she noted. 'Too old & getting very
tired of everything. Waiting for the next exciting thing to
happen, but I think time is running out and age has taken its
toll – but who knows?'

While I was out of the country I asked my parents to telephone each other. 'I spoke to your mother a few evenings ago,'
my father reported. 'She seemed very depressed. It's understandable as everything is going from bad to worse. She is
complaining bitterly that with your departure she has no one to
advise her & I have a nasty suspicion that I've been selected for
the post.' In fact he had been selected for another post: that of
storing her clothes in the spare room of his flat. 'She arrived
down here to collect her winter clothes,' he notified me later.
These exchanges of winter and summer clothes marked their
first meetings for almost thirty years.

My father's letters over this period are as despondent as my
mother's, but written in an aggrieved tone. Shortly before I
went abroad he had started a new company called Indus that

specialised in brick buildings. Nothing, he remarked, would ever replace bricks and mortar. He wanted to get this business off to a brisk start, but one morning careered his car into a bollard and landed up in the cottage hospital with his leg in plaster. His dog Jonathan was really at fault. My father had bought what appeared to be a miniature schnauzer to keep him company after his wife left him, and this puppy got into the habit of sitting on his lap as he drove around the country looking for work. Unfortunately it soon grew to an enormous size and insisted on its right to occupy the driving seat of the car, squeezing my father to the side, his head and much of his body hanging out of the window in summer and, in the winter months, being displaced largely on to the passenger seat, from which position he did his best to continue driving. He had to chauffeur Jonathan each week between Ewell, the Surrey village where he lived, and Maidenhead because he shared the dog with Yolande (who took sole command while my father was in hospital).

It was a worrying time for my father. He worried, at the age of seventy, that he might be pressed into 'the Great Army of the Unemployed', and become bankrupt as his father had almost done. 'I'll probably end up in quod,' he wrote to me. 'Not a bad way to save money.' He worried too about his dog Jonathan because the Maidenhead vet never agreed with the Ewell vet and both were wickedly expensive. He worried, of course, about me: 'I imagine you may have to do something as well as write about Shaw if you're going to make two ends meet. By the time Shaw comes on the market there'll be no one to buy the book.' But 'I am most worried about Yolande,' he confided.

By the mid-nineteen-seventies Yolande had lived and worked in the house for forty years, looking after her parents, looking after Old Nan. At last, in her early seventies, she owned the house. She felt that she had earned it. She knew she had. She enjoyed having half a dog to exercise, but she dreaded her brother's visits to Norhurst.

What he was writing to me, he was saying to her. To live in a five-bedroom house by herself was utter madness. She had almost no money and 'was trying to live on less and less'. She hardly dared switch on an electric light in case it cost too much, and she never used the heating. She would kill herself and drown the rest of us in guilt. The rooms were so cluttered with rubbish that 'it's hard to find room to put down a plate'. Nevertheless she 'is so set in her ways (like the rest of us) that it's impossible to alter things at all'. He longed to alter things for the better. But how could he when she refused his offers of help? 'I go down weekly and do what I can,' he wrote morosely. He would buy and cook some food for her – a brace of partridges, say, at which she nibbled with distaste. Otherwise she never ate anything cooked at all: only biscuits, bread, cake and fruit washed down with lavish cups of tea. The situation was so bad that 'it really needs me to be there for a month or more', my father concluded. But this was impossible because he was starting up a new company, Framed Building Installations, that made special use of steel.

My father could never understand why anyone should quail before his offers of help. Unfortunately, to help people, he had to make sure that they were worse off than he was. This was increasingly difficult. He was so impoverished now that being the target of his help became a peculiarly depressing experience for the beneficiary. He tormented Yolande with his generosity and advice. Everything he said was factual. But he did not see her fundamental need to keep Norhurst, a need that, though she could not explain it, was stronger than his battalion of facts. 'Yolande won't of course think of leaving as long as Nan is alive,' he reasoned.

Old Nan had stayed on at Norhurst until 1975 and was then moved to the St Mark's Hospice in Maidenhead where Yolande would take the dog to visit her each day. She was to die on 17 May 1976, four months short of her hundredth birthday. My father naturally concluded that 'Yolande is more inclined to think of selling up & getting out, but the trouble is where to get out to.'

But he was wrong. He need not have worried where Yolande was going because she was absolutely determined to go nowhere. Why should she? Why didn't other people mind their own business? The thought that some of the contents of the house belonged to her brother and that their sale would come as a great relief to him, did not occur to her. I argued that since Norhurst was gaining in value it should be sold later. But my father thought differently. He saw the future as so bleak that Norhurst might soon be unsaleable. Its condition was deteriorating rapidly. Besides, everyone knew that property prices would soon take a dive. 'It's on the cards,' he wrote to me, 'that a five bedroom house occupied by one person could be taken over by the State to solve the housing problem. One might get paid some small compensation in a worthless currency.'

We had reached this point in the debate when, one day in 1980, everything changed. Even when my aunt was not looking after her brother's dog Jonathan, she would still charge up to the fields and into Maidenhead Thicket as if leading a phantom pack of all those dogs she had aired and exercised for half a century. She moved amazingly fast for someone now in her late seventies, urging herself on, looking utterly absorbed, fighting old battles. Then, coming into All Saints Avenue from the children's playground, she suddenly staggered, fell, picked herself up, lurched sideways, and began calling incoherently for help. A few people in the street stared and hurried past, probably thinking she was drunk. She tried to stop a car, but it swerved onwards. Eventually she was assisted on to a milk-float and driven slowly back with the rattling bottles to Norhurst. The milkman helped her in, but she refused all other help.

My father, telephoning that evening to make arrangements for Jonathan's next visit, got no reply. After a couple of hours, he spoke to the police. They went round, saw my aunt through the window lying on the floor, and broke in. She was then rushed to hospital.

After her stroke she was severely paralysed. There was no question now of her returning to Norhurst. How could she? But this was what she wanted. She would have preferred to die there, I think, than live anywhere else. The house was full of painful memories. There was no room that had not absorbed years of reverberating anger and the awful atmosphere of our unhappiness. But these echoes from the past now seemed to bring her a ghastly satisfaction. The place was in a terrible state, barely inhabitable, yet she took a grim pleasure living there, a bitter comfort. After all, she had come through. Norhurst was her home. She belonged there: and it belonged to her. There was justice in that, and she did not want to be deprived of justice. To abandon the house, whatever the circumstances, would be a betrayal of her father who had left it to her. She would not abandon it. No one could make her.

Yet she could not go back. She was in a wheelchair, able to move one arm and one leg, but unable to dress or undress, unable to wash, eat or do anything else without help. Years ago the question had been: 'What shall we do with the boy?' Now it was: 'What shall we do with my aunt?'

Until her stroke, I had used whatever male arguments I could summon to support my aunt's need to continue living at Norhurst. But once her course of physiotherapy showed that she was unlikely to regain much movement in her body, I changed my mind. If we sold the house, I told her, we could buy her a flat on the ground floor of the building at Ewell where my father lived. We would have enough money to adapt it for a disabled person, to make it comfortable, and to employ someone to look after her. My soft words sounded so pleasant – almost as if it were worth becoming paralysed to qualify for such luxury. But my aunt would have none of it. From her hospital bed, unable properly to form her words, she fought us all the way. But she could not win because she had granted power of attorney to my father. We were taking away the shell of her life, she believed, wherein her powers of speech and movement might marvellously be restored. She attacked the estate agents even when they brought flowers; she told the auctioneers who sold the contents of the house that they were crooks; and she accused my father and myself of acting as her enemies as we struggled with landlords, bank managers, doctors, the social services and local authorities on her behalf. One day, when she had been particularly dreadful, it seemed to me, about my father/her brother, I stood over her hospital bed as she lay there, still and fearful, shouting at her that she should have had the nerve to leave the house years ago, shouting that her brother had at least tried, and tried again, to make something of his life and been given nothing for his pains, shouting that he was trying now to salvage something of her life as best he could. It was a wretched confrontation.

Norhurst was finally sold for £65,000 and with that money we moved Yolande into a flat close to my father. We had brought over some bits and pieces from Maidenhead to make her feel at home – a couple of Lalique animals, a drawing by Lewis Baumer and one by Anna Zinkheisen, her hairbrushes, a mirror, handbags, familiar china plates and cups – and she moved into her new world.

The contrast with her previous life was extreme. She, who had been so independent, now depended for almost everything on a team of nurses and helpers who came and went from morning until evening. Instead of disappearing across the fields, she sat all day in her wheelchair; instead of eating alone she was fed meals-on-wheels. I did not think she could endure this imprisoned life; I did not think she would consent to continue living. But she adapted to the restrictions miraculously. A peculiar sweetness grew up in her. She was anxious not to cause anyone trouble and, once reassured about this, she became extraordinarily cheerful. Jean and Rita, her two special helpers, wheeled her round the village and up to the library for tea. They wrapped her up and took her into the garden so that she could watch the birds. They brought her clothes, washed her, dressed her, arranged her hair, told her about their families, restored her self-esteem. I was touched by how fond they were of her, and she of them. As an embodiment of her class and time, my aunt would have been regarded as something of a snob in the nineteen-eighties. Snobbishness was her form of self-protection, her superior reason for not doing things that frightened her. She had overcome it in the war; she overcame it again now in her adversity with the help of Jean and Rita and others who looked after her. When she said in her indistinct yet still decisive voice that socialists, foreigners and anyone who criticised the Queen Mother should be shot, Jean and Rita would dance round in laughter – and my aunt happily joined in. All this merriment delighted her. In their game these foreigners and socialists were cartoon characters who could be shot again and again with no harm done. She came to feel quite protective of them.

One advantage of this new chapter in her life was that my father could keep an eye on her. Framed Building Installations had buckled almost before it was set up, leaving him at a loss. But Yolande's illness gave him something to do, and the sale of Norhurst and its contents gave him the money with which to do it. Her affairs occupied him a full year, but when she was finally settled into the same building as himself, things started to go wrong.

It began with his teeth. 'Had to have them all out with a general anaesthetic and a plate made,' he informed me. 'I reckon to finish paying for it around the year 2000.' Then it was his eyes. I took him for a couple of cataract operations: one worked well; the other didn't. Suddenly his handwriting, which had marched so straight and clear through all the ups and downs of his adult life, wobbled and veered crazily off the page. His hearing had also begun to fail. I attempted to get him a new hearing aid in London, but he became irritated with it, being unable to see the tiny batteries or adjust the volume.

My aunt's slithering speech and my father's foggy deafness made communication between them an unhappy business. He would find his way to her flat, his dog Jonathan waddling before him, but within minutes the two of them had grown furious with each other, as if their impairments were being purposely exploited. 'She does it deliberately,' my father complained to me after my aunt had failed again to 'speak up'.

He had forgotten her stroke. Soon he was forgetting more: where he was, what he had gone out for, whether it was morning or afternoon. Though I did not realise it, he was more seriously ill than his sister. I would go down to Ewell, take him out to lunch, then have tea with her. I would telephone beforehand to confirm the arrangements, but when I arrived my father had disappeared. When I did find him in the street, he was surprised to see me: 'Oh hello, Michael. What brings you here?' Once I let my impatience show. Then, in a passionate riposte, he came back at me: 'Wait till you're my age and you'll find out what it's like!' I hear his voice more clearly every year.

His lonely figure had become a well-known sight moving through the village streets, standing at a kerb. He did not drive any longer, but would sometimes stop at the traffic lights as if he were a car, his dog Jonathan looking up at him. Occasionally he went to the pub and also for a time to church, hoping to meet someone. But his deafness, poor sight and other ailments isolated him. People occasionally spoke to his dog Jonathan which pleased him, and there is a picture of them together in the local paper under the caption: 'One Man And His Dog'. My father is not quite in focus, but Jonathan spreads himself amply across the page and appears to be drinking my father's half-pint of beer.

One day my father was unable to find his way back to his flat. Someone got hold of his doctor, and his doctor got hold of me. He sounded indignant. 'I cannot have one of my patients wandering round the village like this,' he protested. On his advice, I took my father to be examined by a specialist who told me his heart was beating very slowly and that he needed a pacemaker to restore his circulation. Later I drove him to the hospital for the operation, after which he seemed more his old self, though still far from his young self. My anxieties receded. But by then my mother was ill.

She had telephoned me one morning after her bath to say there was a lump on her breast. What did I think? I heard my voice, confident, clear, categorical, telling her I thought this the most normal thing in the world, and certainly nothing to lose sleep over. These lumps and bumps were, on the whole, quite harmless and perfectly natural. Indeed, it would be curious, almost worrying in itself, if she'd *not* had one or two lumps by her early sixties – though of course, as a precaution, it must be examined. But the tests showed it to be malignant. Again I spoke with authority. Thank God, I exclaimed, she had not suffered such a thing earlier when they could do little about it. Now, I assured her, everything had advanced, everything was different. It was a well-known fact that most women with this trouble came out of hospital in a few days and went on to live the rest of their lives in excellent health. Modern medicine, I reminded her, was amazing. Of course she would have to endure regular checkups and that was a bore. But it was no worse than that.

Before her operation, my mother made one more quick journey to Stockholm. Kaja had become almost blind and my mother was trying to persuade her to live in a Swedish convalescent home in London where, because it was technically on Swedish territory, her pension would still be paid to her. But like Yolande at Norhurst, Kaja wanted to spend her last years at her apartment in Artillerigatan, even if this meant never seeing her daughter again. She could barely see anything as it was and would be lost in unfamiliar surroundings. These few days were to be their last together.

My mother went into the Royal Marsden Hospital as soon as she returned from Sweden. This was only a few hundred yards from her flat at Daver Court. Seeing her in the ward, I told her what a good nurse she would have been. She made friends with all the patients, and seemed naturally popular with everyone. Her operation to remove one of her breasts was a success and when she went for a check-up a few months later there was no cancer in her body. But she had great difficulty with an infected sinus in the pit of her arm. She could never again get comfortable whether standing, sitting or lying down. The arm was fastened with bandages and they treated it in various ways. But it got worse and she was soon having to take pain killers.

Nevertheless, for some months, there was an interval in the descent of both my parents' health, as if they had landed on a ledge. I was at that time giving a platform performance at the Lyttleton Theatre before a production of Shaw's play, *The Philanderer*, and I decided to invite them both. This took considerable planning, but I got them there and, as I walked on to the stage, I saw them sitting together in the audience. My mother had her arm fixed at an acute angle like a child in a classroom asking to be excused. My father battled furiously with his hearing aid from which high-pitched bleats were being signalled. After my talk, we saw the play; and after the play I took them to the National Theatre Restaurant. My father frowned a little at the architecture, but not excessively; my mother looked round the tables and inquired if they played music there. It was difficult sustaining a conversation. Over the coffee my father braced himself, clearing his throat, moving uncomfortably in his chair, looking miserable. I knew the signs. He was searching for something pleasant to say about my lecture. I had reassured them both that I could not speak for long as I would be engulfed by the play itself, like a Stoppardian or Pirandello character. 'Yes,' my father said eventually taking his cue from this remark, 'coming to an end must have been tricky. I thought your ending very timely.'

This was the last time the three of us were together – indeed the only time I can remember us together since my childhood.

Not long afterwards my mother's cancer reappeared. So began a long sequence of treatments and operations that are a blur in my memory now, as if everything happened together and went on happening all the time. This dark period began with the suicide of her closest friend, Irene Heyman, and, a year or so later, the death of her ballet-dancing daughter who, with a final *entrechat*, threw herself in front of an underground train at Sloane Square. Poor Larry Heyman, his hand trembling violently round his whisky glass, moved to the top of a tower block in Fulham, and my mother never saw him again.

But other friends came back. Shirley Morton, from the 'Wilmslow Wheelers', reappeared and insisted on getting a second opinion from her own doctor. And Gay, Edy Fainstain's daughter and my one-time stepsister, returned, bringing flowers, bringing comfort, hugging my mother in a way I had never learnt to do. There were women, too, with whom my mother had worked as an interpreter at business fairs and conferences; and, from further back, women with whom she had modelled in Basil Street; as well as a good drinking friend in Daver Court. Arriving at her bedside in the hospital, or at her flat, I would sometimes find a gang of these friends who had gathered to raise her morale. Griffy, too, suddenly turned up from Wales with his Swedish wife Ingrid, filling the place with children and talking of the old days beside the lake at Velden and above the sea near La Turbie. Outside in the street, as he was leaving, he asked: 'Why are we so gloomy when our mothers are so jolly?' Then, after a moment, he raised his voice in answer: 'Stand up, Purple Parr, and be recognised!'

My father would sometimes telephone with obscure messages. 'Your mother is being very brave,' he said gruffly. Then, in a voice from the past: 'Poor Sue.' Kaja also called regularly from Sweden. She was blind now and many of these talks with her daughter ended tearfully.

My mother was a naturally good patient, but as her condition worsened she found it more difficult to cope with visitors, feeling anxious over entertaining them and guilty at the possibility of letting them go away empty-handed. She would make ashtrays from shells, napkin rings from odd pieces of fabric, cards and trinkets from all sorts of scraps and oddments to give them. Sometimes I would feel irritated by all this trivial and unnecessary work she gave herself. But perhaps it was not trivial or unnecessary. I was exasperated too by some of the things she asked me to do, such as negotiating the renewal of her insurance cover on a fur coat we both knew she would never wear again, and arranging for her to be excused the wearing of a seat belt in a car, though she did not own a car and was unlikely to be travelling in one. I was learning how little we can do to help the terminally ill: and how important that little sometimes is.

There were a few practical things I could do, such as buying her flat at Daver Court from the bank to save her financial on top of medical anxieties. Some days I would telephone the hospital on her behalf because 'they take more notice of a man'. And I would occasionally accompany her to the Royal Marsden Hospital, always anxious over my own loss of working time. She might have an appointment at ten in the morning and actually see the doctor at four in the afternoon. She became exhausted by these hours of waiting and dispirited at times by the impersonal quality of the treatment. 'So what seems to be the matter?' asked one doctor resting his elbow on a huge file of my mother's medical records. Each time, it seemed, there was a new doctor in charge of her; each time we started from the beginning; and every time, in case of legal repercussions, a matron or ward sister stood sentinel over us. 'Whichever way I turn,' my mother complained in her idiomatic English, 'my bottom is still behind me.' Occasionally the ambulance failed to arrive; most days it came at unexpected hours; one day, despite her protests, it took her to the Royal Marsden Hospital in Surrey and had to race back, its siren clanging and lights flashing, to the Fulham Road.

One evening when I was visiting her, I went by mistake into an adjacent ward and saw a surreal sight. I was apparently not in a hospital at all, but in a restaurant. A line of smart waiters stood at one end, and the first guests in their dinner jackets and long dresses stood drinking and chatting round a long table set for dinner, its wine glasses gleaming in the candle-light. I stared in disbelief and then, back in the corridor of the hospital, asked a nurse whether I had been dreaming. She laughed at my surprise. For this was one of the Royal Marsden Hospital's fund-raising events, the success of which was marked by a giant financial barometer on the front of the building. As I sat next to my mother's bed that evening, seeing her suffering, conscious of people close to death in other beds, I could not blot out the picture of that formal scene on the other side of the wall, the grotesque juxtaposition of those diners-out and these in-patients – or 'clients', 'customers' and 'consumers of health' as they were soon to be called in the new political circumlocution. I fantasised over wheeling this army of the old and ill next door and overwhelming that table of money-changers from the so-called 'real world' with actual reality and misrule. But of course I could do nothing, and whatever I can do I do now.

One day a nurse brought my mother the news that Kaja was dead, and she cried. Not long afterwards she had another operation during the course of which she regained consciousness. It was this shock, after enduring so much for so long, that broke her spirit. I saw the skull beneath the skin. I saw the skeleton of death. What upset me was that so soft a person had to be so mutilated. Still uncertain of the facts, I went to speak to the doctor in charge. It was again another doctor, with the matron in attendance. He told me that my mother had only three or four days to live – he would not have told me had I not asked directly. It was necessary, apparently, that she endure these extra days of torment. Was it possible, I inquired, for my mother to be given the strongest sleeping pills by night and the strongest pain killers by day? The matron seemed surprised by my request, but agreed.

So often over the years these doctors and nurses had given us bad news, and more often they had given us no news at all. My role was to be Dr Pangloss and give out a continual stream of glowing news. This was what my mother wanted to hear. I returned to her bed and looked her straight in the eyes, those sunken eyes. The worst, I told her, was mercifully over. She had come through. The pain would recede and she would sleep better. Then after a few bad days she would begin getting better. I can only hope she believed me.

Gay was often at her bed when I was not there and for longer periods than I was. She could do what I still could not do. She could kiss her, touch her, bring her moments of close physical comfort. I could not touch her in this way. I must write this again. I could not touch her.

Even with the drugs, even in her greatly weakened state, she was appallingly restless. This was her deathbed and she wanted to get off it. She twisted and gasped. Her hands, like spiders, crept around the blankets and explored the edge of the sheets. The nurses fixed iron railings to the sides of the bed as I sat there so that she would not fall out. I was so tense and my head throbbed so painfully that I asked the ward sister for an aspirin. She refused to give me an aspirin. I went out to a chemist down the street. When I came back my mother was draped across the iron bars of the bed. No one had yet noticed she was dead. A place of death awaits us all.

My father was too ill to come to the funeral. In 1982 he had

made his Will appointing me his executor with the duty of looking after Yolande should he die first. But it was his dog Jonathan
that died. He immediately bought a new dog, dog William,
almost identical, and then added a codicil to his Will with details
of dog William's breeding and instructions as to his 'upkeep if I
pass out'.

His health was precariously stable. 'I am finding life very
tricky,' he scribbled to me. 'It's like trying to walk on a tightrope
& I have no doubt I'll come crashing down one day.' I was to
take over power of attorney on behalf of my aunt and have a
third-party mandate for my father, with both of which I tried to
spread a safety net under their lives. After complaints from the
landlord I arranged for my father's flat to be decorated and,
approaching eighty, he seized the opportunity to go into business
with the decorator, leasing him his spare room as an office and,
in the role of 'consultant', putting him in touch with people in
the building trade with whom he had not quarrelled. I remember
some architectural drawings lying on his desk. They looked intricate and palatial and he had obviously derived deep pleasure
from preparing them, though he confessed they were merely
changing rooms and lavatories for a golf club.

There were days when he recovered his embattled self.
Though admitting 'things are very very bad', he drew comfort
from the thought that they 'can't be worse than having to live
day & night with that arrogant old gentleman Bernard Shaw'.
He also enjoyed crossing swords with a writer I knew well who
lived in Ewell, John Stewart Collis ('You told me he's a good
writer. He must indeed be good at something'). But on the whole
he appeared to be growing more vulnerable, shedding a skin,
and the sensitivity he had concealed with such flourishes of
antagonism and joviality all his life, began to declare itself. I
took pains to spare him good news, at least to dilute it. I now
drove and owned a car, but pretended I was merely borrowing it
and pointed out that it was an inferior automatic rather than a

properly-geared machine. With unaccustomed mildness my father remarked that some automatic cars were really quite good these days he had heard – though he himself would not like his gears to be changed in Tokyo or Detroit while travelling round Surrey.

I have written that he found it impossible to give praise or receive money, but that is not quite correct and I stand rebuked by two incidents from this late period of his life. In one of his last notes to me, after I had placed some money in his bank account, he wrote to thank me: 'I never expected the sort of help you have given me and I can't remember ever having received anything so welcome before.' One afternoon I sat in the car with him, having to shout because of his deafness, telling him to spend his money on himself and go off at weekends to hotels with dog William (who was in the car at the time making communication more arduous). I tried to explain that it would be easier for me to help him financially if his capital fell still further, for then the State would assist me in helping him. I shouted that I had ensured in my Will that he would inherit enough money if I suddenly dropped dead. This was not charity, I yelled, but the natural dividend from a fatherly investment through childhood and adolescence, and in the allowance he had arranged for me in the nineteen-fifties. He sat staring out of the window and I could not tell whether he had taken it in. The dog leapt backwards and forwards between us. Then he said: 'Your mother said we could not have had a better son' – and he was fumbling desperately at the car door to get out. It was vicarious praise, of course, and very far from the truth, but it signalled a truce over all our animosities. Later I had a dream in which my father asked me if I'd like a smoke. He passed me a piece of iron piping with concrete knobs attached, bent like the starting handle of a car. It wasn't easy to get going, but we managed eventually and I took a puff or two, remarking that it was surprisingly pleasant: after which he took it from me and began puffing himself. Then I woke, and lay wondering whether this had been the Holroyd pipe of peace.

Gradually my father grew more confused again. His easiest moments now came over tea with Yolande. She had never noticed that there was anything wrong with him, and he no longer recognised that she was paralysed. Whenever they were together, they seemed to shed their injuries and impairments. What he said to her, what she attempted to say to him, had no connection – except an unspoken connection going back years – and neither of them grew irritable with the other any longer. These were occasions of excruciating hilarity over which, with my dual legal powers, I sometimes presided while my aunt's helpers, Jean and Rita, poured the tea.

But soon my father's neighbours were complaining to the landlord. Was he not a fire risk? Did he attract mice? Why should there be so much noise from his flat at night? One night there was a terrible sound of crashing, cries and commotion. Having no close friends, he was not missed next day until dog William's barking attracted people's attention. They found him lying unconscious on the floor surrounded by smashed crockery, blood, excreta, chaos. No one knew exactly what had happened.

But he was still alive and in the Sutton Hospital he began recovering physically, though not mentally. He imagined it was wartime again and he was back in the RAF. Looking round the ward at the patients walking on crutches, suspended in slings, caught in odd shapes by plaster of paris or attached to pulleys and plasma drips, he whispered to me: 'I don't think much of the new recruits.' After some months, I was asked to find him a residential home. He was obviously confused by the move and on arrival in Epsom kept calling the staff 'Mein host', as if on holiday in Bavaria. Forty-eight hours later, they telephoned me to say that he was far too ill to be in such a place, or even in one of the private nursing homes which I had been reconnoitring. He was afflicted by persistent hallucinations, believing himself to be under attack from people crawling across the ceiling to his bed. Fighting back as best he could, he was spreading alarm among the elderly residents. I drove him away, with his suitcase of clothes and bundle of medical records, to Sutton Hospital, but the ward he had been in only a couple of days before was now closed and there was no bed for him. We sat in the car. I did not know what to do. Eventually I had him certified under the Mental Health Act and he was then admitted to West Park Hospital.

Somehow my aunt's helpers conveyed her to this hospital and she sat happily by his bed. He did not recognise her. 'I can't think why they're keeping him there,' she later said to me. 'There's nothing on earth wrong with him.'

The specialists at the hospital thought they could bring my father some way back to normality, but their treatment was unavailing. He went on believing he was being assaulted, especially at night, by figures on the walls and ceiling. When I arrived one afternoon I saw him poised with a stick suspended in his hand, half-dressed, crouching but not moving. I tried reasoning with him. Who were these people? Why should anyone want to hurt him? He did not know. But it was impossible to reason with someone who had lost his reason. Then I entered his world of fantasy, assuring him his enemies had been vanquished and would not come again. This worked for as long as I stayed with him and could repeat it, but I could not calm his fears for long because he had no memory.

He was rescued from these harrowing assaults, this harrowing of hell, by pneumonia, sometimes called 'the old man's friend'. That, and senility, were given as the causes of his death.

My mother had died of 'disseminated carcinoma of breast' on 22 January 1986 at the age of sixty-nine, her occupation being given simply as 'Retired'. From life, as it were. My father, a 'Businessman Retired', was eighty when he died on 27 July 1988. Medical records are now kept for twenty-five years, but in the nineteen-eighties they were destroyed after only six years. No records therefore remain. I wrote to my father's doctor in Ewell where he lived his last thirty years, but his doctor cannot remember him. The Patient Affairs Officer at West Park Hospital cannot help me, since releasing medical case-note data would contravene the codes of confidentiality laid down by the Mental Health Act; and the Record Department at the Royal Marsden Hospital, though several times promising to send me clinical information about my mother, never does so. The waters of oblivion have quickly closed over them both.

This surprises me because for most of the nineteen-eighties I was engulfed by the bureaucracy of illness and death. Over this decade, on behalf of my parents and my aunt, there were hundreds of letters to write, documents to send back, telephone calls to make. I had to ensure I was doing the best for them, to understand the support systems and confirm that they were dying properly. I corresponded with a Citizens' Advice Bureau in London, the Department of Social Security in Newcastle-upon-Tyne, the Review Section of the Disability Benefits Unit in Blackpool, a benefits agency in Surrey; I wrote to Age Concern and Willing Hands, to nursing groups and homecare services and health centres; also general practitioners, consultant geriatricians, nursing homes, hospitals and undertakers; I was in communication with landlords, residents' associations, the taxation department of banks, the Inland Revenue, the Post Office, solicitors, accountants, estate agents. Much of this exchange, ingeniously obfuscated by developing information technology, was hardly interrupted by my parents' deaths. 'I keep writing to say that my father, Basil Holroyd, is dead. British Gas insists he is alive. If you have any information I should know, please give me access to it.'

The files that blossom round my aunt's simple life are the most voluminous and complex of all, partly because she lives on into the late nineties, and her late nineties. The number of forms

I must tick and cross, denying she is pregnant or divorced, the quantity of pages on which I must go on copying the words 'Not Applicable' leave me with the sense that I am giving evidence against her, invalidating her life, with these reiterated denials. No. None. Never. My answers cover the pages. Each time she has an extension of her stroke or an ischaemic attack and goes into hospital, each time she makes a partial recovery and comes back to her flat, a 'change of circumstances' is electronically signalled and the interrogation begins again. No. None. Never. I must refer to her as if she were a conscript in the army, a number, not by name, so that she can become compatible with the Social Services computer. That someone whose life was essentially so straightforward (who has no income beyond a State pension and the drops that still trickle through that old Heath Robinson machinery, the Holroyd Settlement), that she, at her age, should be forced into a world so alien goes beyond a joke, beyond my irony. I long to murder some of the courteous, patient, well-meaning officials from these departments, units, bureaux, centres.

My aunt was shocked by my father's death. It came as a total surprise to her and she misses him dreadfully, frequently calling me by his name. She has only happy memories of him, his kindness, his generosity, his fun. All their past furies have evaporated. She now resembles to a startling degree her mother Adeline whom she hated, but hates no more. Her temperament is perpetually sunny – no falls, no fractures, can cloud it. Her doctor recommends that she be removed to 'correctly structured' sheltered accommodation. He puts the facts as my father had once done, encouraging me to get my aunt to 'gracefully accept' them. Otherwise, he warns me, 'serious illness or death' might one day ensue. My aunt is ninety and does not want to move, and so I follow her wishes rather than her doctor's, employing more people to care for her in the flat she never wanted to go to, and now does not want to leave. To Jean and Rita and the others she owes the happiness of this period and the prolongation of her life. They keep her going, and going well, for over six years following my father's death.

After a fall in the autumn of 1995, she has to be moved from hospital to a nursing home at last. By then it no longer matters where she is because she cannot tell where she is. Sometimes she says that she has just come back from Ascot or Wimbledon, but as she retreats further into the world of her imagination she communicates less, then almost nothing.

But who is this coming to see her on her ninety-sixth birthday, this person in his sixties who, aiming a jovial wave at the doctor, a barking laugh at a nurse over the raucous lullaby of moans and shouts, steps so cheerily through these heaps of the half-dead, balancing a miniature cake marked 'Yolande' in red icing? Surely it must be Basil Holroyd, man of many businesses. Jean is there. She clasps Yolande's brown and bony hand and shouts, 'IT'S MICHAEL COME TO SEE YOU!' My aunt, bent double in her chair, her hair like fine white silk, her bruised skin thin as tissue paper, does not stir. She is far away, beyond recall. 'MICHAEL!' Then suddenly she looks up and gives that dazzling smile I recognise so well from the old albums, as if to say: Yes, after all and in spite of all, surely this is the best of all possible worlds.

# ENVOI

# 20

# *Things Past*

Hugh Kingsmill required of the biographer some account of his or her own life as a passport for travelling into the lives of others. If this, my passport, is stamped with the travels of others more than with my own, it is because their travels determined mine which, by themselves, hold little interest for me. Metaphysical journeys are not undertaken alone, but together *and* alone – at least mine have been.

Here, in vicarious fashion, is my story, my still unsolved mystery. To have a good walk-on part in one's own autobiography, as I have tried to give myself, is as much as any biographer can reasonably expect. For it is not exclusively my life I am telling. The story line I have drawn runs intermittently parallel, I believe, with that of many people who feel the impulse to make some reconnection with their earlier lives. This book, my patchwork, the prequel to my biographies, may seem to present an unusual family saga, but beneath the patina of conventional respectability acquired by many families lie secret episodes and half-suspected dramas, sometimes unacted yet still influential, that grow invisible over time. My purpose has been to pare back a little the cuticle of time and to apply the research methods I have learnt as a biographer to my own life for a while, letting the detective work show through the narrative at some places for those who have a similar curiosity in human nature and its reworkings on a family chronicle. Echoes of what I have forgotten, as well as memories of events I have been unable to forget, linked where possible by discovered facts, have been my signposts.

There are, of course, many unexplored trails: the legend of my Swedish grandmother's purloined diaries and the rumoured disappearance of the sketchbook Picasso gave her with its outlines of *Guernica*; the continuing adventures of Agnes May Babb, my grandfather's *femme fatale*, and other inviting sidetracks. These are different stories, other histories.

I have made journeys to places known and unknown – from the weather-beaten expanses of Barkisland to the fixed industrial archaeology of Borås – where the messages were too faint for me to decipher. But there seems to be no holiday restaurant anywhere that is not still playing one of my mother's favourite tunes. At Braywick cemetery, my grandfather's gravestone, some of its letters and numbers now missing, still possesses a surprising resonance. Scaitcliffe, my school, is agonisingly familiar in its every detail – yet is also crucially changed, having become co-educational. Sheffield Place, The Links, Brocket: all these family houses are now owned by public institutions. And then I come to Norhurst.

Outside, the house does not appear greatly altered. But when I step inside, except for a few details (a banister on the staircase, the panelling in the dining-room) all is unrecognisable, though conveying strange hints of the past, and I feel I am walking in a dream (Maidenhead itself, with its convoluted road system, is my nightmare). Norhurst is still owned by the family which bought it after my aunt's stroke almost twenty years ago, and they remember my father coming down to warn them of the submerged air-raid shelter near the end of the garden. This has become part of their own family lore.

All is changed. But in a recess of the attic, behind an old piece of curtain, stands a pile of lost books. Here is my nursery alphabet and my picture history of the United States. Here is *Mumfie*, given to me by my aunt on my sixth birthday: how could I have forgotten the wanderings on which I accompanied this excellent elephant which come instantly back to me when I see the author Katharine Tozer's pink and blue illustrations? The Mathilda stories my aunt read to me by the kitchen stove have gone. But buried away I spy something I have never seen before, a set of designs for glass light fittings drawn and coloured by my father in the distant days of Lalique. Further back, I find a large photograph of my great-grandfather, the Major-General, looking so much more robust and happy than in the Eastbourne family group taken after the suicide of his wife Anna Eliza Holroyd.

Finally, there is her book, my great-grandmother's, she who ended her life at the age of thirty by swallowing carbolic acid. It is an enormous, sombre-brown calf-bound volume with the gold embossed letters AEH at the front and, on its spine also in gold letters, the word FERNS. Her husband must have given it to her while they were in India in the early eighteen-seventies. Into thirty or more of its spacious pages she has beautifully pressed these unusual fern leaves. Then, like a poisoned chalice, the book passes to her daughter, Norah Palmer Holroyd who, in her twentieth year, has had her name tremulously written in it by her father after his stroke above the date 18 September 1896, the time she became so mysteriously ill at The Links. But she adds nothing herself to the volume which after her death passes eventually to my Aunt Yolande. She pastes into its blank pages, between the pressed ferns from India, illustrations of early nineteen-twenties film actors and actresses, scissored from magazines: Mary Pickford, Lillian Gish, Pearl White, Jackie Coogan, and then, suddenly looking out at me, the handsome features of my mother's ex-father-in-law, the 'matinée idol' Owen Nares. At the end there are some unused pages for the next generation, vacant pages left to me. This ill-omened folio volume, tracking the destinies of three generations of women in the family, would have meant nothing to me before I began my own little book in which it finds a final place, and which I must now let go.

> Go little book, go little tragedy,
> Where God may send thy maker, ere he die,
> The power to make a work of comedy . . .
> And wheresoever thou be read, or sung,
> I beg of God that thou be understood!
> And now to close my story as I should.